D0056104

FAITH ALONE

JAMES C. GALVIN
General Editor

FAITH ALONE

A DAILY DEVOTIONAL

MARTIN LUTHER

ZONDERVAN™

GRAND RAPIDS, MICHIGAN 49530 USA

ZONDERVAN™

Faith Alone
Copyright © 1998, 2005 by James C. Galvin

Requests for information should be addressed to:
Zondervan, *Grand Rapids, Michigan 49530*

Library of Congress Cataloging-in-Publication Data

Luther, Martin, 1483–1546
   [Selections. English. 2005]
     Faith alone : a daily devotional / Martin Luther; James C. Galvin,
general editor.—Updated ed. in today's language.
       p. cm.
   Rev. ed. of: By faith alone. © 1998.
   Includes index.
   ISBN-10: 0-310-26536-3
   ISBN-13: 978-0-310-26536-8
   1. Devotional calendars.   I. Galvin, James C.   II. Title
BR331. E6 2005
242'.2—dc22

2005004702

This edition printed on acid-free paper.

An edition of this work was previously published by World under the title
By Faith Alone © 1998 using *God's Word* translation. This updated edition
is based on the *New International Version*.

All Scripture quotations, unless otherwise indicated, are taken from the *Holy
Bible: New International Version*®. NIV®. Copyright © 1973, 1978, 1984 by
International Bible Society. Used by permission of Zondervan. All rights
reserved.

All rights reserved. No part of this publication may be reproduced, stored in
a retrieval system, or transmitted in any form or by any means—electronic,
mechanical, photocopy, recording, or any other—except for brief quotations
in printed reviews, without the prior permission of the publisher.

Interior design by Michelle Espinoza

Printed in the United States of America

---

05 06 07 08 09 10 11 12 /❖ DCI/ 10 9 8 7 6 5 4 3 2 1

INTRODUCTION

Martin Luther is one of the most important figures in church history because God used him to launch one of the greatest revolutions of all—the Reformation. His writings are nearly five hundred years old yet still meaningful for us to read today.

Born in Germany in 1483, Luther studied law at the University of Erfurt. During a violent thunderstorm, he made a dramatic vow to become a monk and soon after entered the Augustinian order. After rigorous academic study and intense, personal struggle to find God's approval, he rediscovered the gospel. He realized that we are saved by faith alone. After he was ordained, he was sent to the University of Wittenburg to teach theology. While there in 1517, he nailed the Ninety-five Theses on the church door to invite a theological debate. The topics he listed caused such a furor that the debate never took place. As Luther continued to write, preach, and teach, he quickly became the leading figure and focal point of the Reformation.

Luther was a professor, theologian, former monk, scholar, author, Bible translator, and defender of the faith. But he was also a pastor, husband, father, and good friend to many. Luther was prolific. Besides writing commentaries, theological papers, and letters to friends, his students and followers took careful notes of his university lectures, sermons, and later in life, even his dinner conversations. He died in 1546 at the age of sixty-three.

These selections, originally written by Martin Luther between 1513 and 1546, have all been freshly translated into English for this devotional. The goal was to make this edition both accurate and easy to understand. I selected the readings primarily from Luther's sermons, commentaries, and other devotional writings. These selections cover topics both theological and practical. Some of the theological themes you'll find include the centrality of Christ, justification by faith alone, the authority of Scripture, and the importance of putting faith in God above human reason. Practical themes include the struggle against sin and temptation, prayer, humility, the handling of wealth and possessions, the value of everyday work, the importance of marriage and family, and love for neighbor. You may read one selection a day according to the date or explore themes using the subject index located in the back of the book.

The verse at the beginning of each reading is usually the one that Luther was writing about or preaching on. At times I've attached a different verse that better fits the theme of the devotional thought. If you want to read more on the topic or view the selection in context, you can locate it in English or German using the index to other editions located in the back of the book.

Several talented professionals were involved in helping to make this devotional a reality. I wish to thank the three translators who worked diligently to capture the meaning, tone, and imagery of Luther: Ric Gudgeon, Gerhard Meske, and Trudy Krucke Zimmerman. I also wish to thank the English stylists who improved each reading and made Luther speak English: Jonathan Farrar and Kristine A. Luber. In addition, Jonathan Farrar worked closely with me on the final editing and provided encouragement along the way.

Martin Luther loved God and wanted people to believe in Christ and grow in faith. He forcefully preached and defended the doctrine that we are justified through faith alone—plus nothing. *Faith Alone*, then, is a fitting title for a devotional based on Luther's writings. May this book point you to the Scriptures and help you understand the importance of faith, appreciate the mystery of faith, and encourage you to grow in faith.

James C. Galvin, EdD

FAITH COMES FIRST

*For we are God's workmanship, created in Christ Jesus to do good works,
which God prepared in advance for us to do.*
Ephesians 2:10

You have often heard me say that the Christian life has two dimensions: the first is faith, and the second is good works. A believer should live a devout life and always do what is right. But the first dimension of the Christian life—faith—is more essential. The second dimension—good works—is never as valuable as faith. People of the world, however, adore good works. They regard them to be far higher than faith.

Good works have always been valued more highly than faith. Of course, it's true that we should do good works and respect the importance of them. But we should be careful that we don't elevate good works to such an extent that faith and Christ become secondary. If we esteem them too highly, good works can become the greatest idolatry. This has occurred both inside and outside of Christianity. Some people value good works so much that they overlook faith in Christ. They preach about and praise their own works instead of God's works.

Faith should be first. After faith is preached, then we should teach good works. It is faith—*without* good works and *prior to* good works—that takes us to heaven. We come to God through faith alone.

WE LIVE BY FAITH

For in the gospel a righteousness from God is revealed,
a righteousness that is by faith from first to last, just as it is written:
"The righteous will live by faith."
Romans 1:17

When I was a monk, I didn't accomplish anything through fasting and prayer. This is because neither I nor any of the other monks acknowledged our sin and lack of reverence for God. We didn't understand original sin, and we didn't realize that unbelief is also sin. We believed and taught that no matter what people do, they can never be certain of God's kindness and mercy. As a result, the more I ran after and looked for Christ, the more he eluded me.

When I realized that it was only through God's grace that I would be enlightened and receive eternal life, I worked diligently to understand what Paul said in Romans 1:17—a righteousness from God is revealed in the gospel. I searched for a long time and tried to understand it again and again. But the Latin words for "a righteousness from God" were in my way. God's righteousness is usually defined as the characteristic by which he is sinless and condemns the sinner. All the teachers except Augustine interpreted God's *righteousness* as God's *anger*. So every time I read it, I wished that God had never revealed the gospel. Who could love a God who is angry and who judges and condemns us?

Finally, with the help of the Holy Spirit, I took a closer look at what the prophet Habakkuk said: "The righteous will live by his faith" (Habakkuk 2:4). From this I concluded that life must come from faith. I therefore took the abstract to the concrete level, as we say in school. I related the concept of righteousness to a person becoming righteous. In other words, a person becomes righteous by faith. That opened the whole Bible—even heaven itself—to me!

WHAT IT MEANS TO BELIEVE

Then Jesus cried out, "When a man believes in me,
he does not believe in me only, but in the one who sent me."
John 12:44

There are two ways to believe. The first way is to believe *about God*, meaning we believe that what is taught about God is really true. It's similar to believing that what is taught about the devil or hell is true. This type of belief is more a statement of knowledge than an expression of faith.

The second way is to believe *in God*. This not only includes believing that what is taught about God is true, but also includes trusting him and daring to be in relationship with him. It means believing without any doubt that he really is who he says he is, and he will do all he says he will do. I wouldn't believe any person to this same degree, no matter how highly others might praise him. It's easy to believe that someone is godly, but it's another matter to rely completely on him.

Those who believe in God believe everything written about God in Scripture. They dare to believe this in life and in death. This faith makes them true Christians and gives them everything they desire from God. A person with an evil, hypocritical heart can't have this type of faith, for it's a living faith, as described in the first commandment: "I am the LORD your God. . . . You shall have no other gods" (Exodus 20:2–3).

Therefore, the little word *in* is well placed and should be carefully noted. We don't say, "I believe God the Father," or "I believe about God the Father," but "I believe *in* God the Father, *in* Jesus Christ, *in* the Holy Spirit." Only God can give us this type of faith.

FAITH IN CHRIST ALONE

❧

So we, too, have put our faith in Christ Jesus that we may be
justified by faith in Christ and not by observing the law,
because by observing the law no one will be justified.
Galatians 2:16

We are justified through faith in Christ, not through our own efforts. We shouldn't let anyone confuse us by saying that faith justifies people only when love and good works are added to it.

If people hear that they must believe in Christ and that faith alone doesn't justify unless love is added to it, they immediately fall from faith and think, "If faith without love doesn't justify, then faith is empty and useless. Love alone justifies. For if faith is not formed and enhanced by love, then it's nothing." In order to prove their damaging comments, my opponents point to 1 Corinthians 13:1–2: "If I speak in the tongues of men and of angels, but have not love, . . . I am nothing." They think these verses are an impenetrable wall. But they don't understand Paul's teachings. We should avoid these comments as if they were poison from hell.

Instead, we should conclude with Paul that we are justified by faith alone, not through faith formed by love. So we shouldn't attribute the power of justification to something formed in us that makes us pleasing to God. We must attribute it to faith, which takes hold of Christ the Savior and keeps him in our hearts. This faith justifies us apart from love and prior to love. We concede that we must also teach about good works and love. But we only teach these at the proper time and place—when the question deals with how we should live, not how we are justified. The question here is this: How do we become justified and receive eternal life? We answer with Paul that we are pronounced righteous through faith in Christ alone, not by our own efforts.

UNWORTHY TO PRAY

But the tax collector stood at a distance. He would not even
look up to heaven, but beat his breast and said,
"God, have mercy on me, a sinner."
Luke 18:13

Some say, "I would feel better about God hearing my prayer if I were more worthy and lived a better life." I simply answer: If you don't want to pray before you feel that you are worthy or qualified, then you will never pray again. Prayer must not be based on or depend on your personal worthiness or the quality of the prayer itself; rather, it must be based on the unchanging truth of God's promise. If the prayer is based on itself or on anything else besides God's promise, then it's a false prayer that deceives you—even if your heart is breaking with intense devotion and you are weeping drops of blood.

We pray because we are unworthy to pray. Our prayers are heard precisely because we believe that we are unworthy. We become worthy to pray when we risk everything on God's faithfulness alone.

So go ahead and feel unworthy. But know in your heart that it's a thousand times more important to honor God's truthfulness. Yes, everything depends on this alone. Don't turn his faithful promise into a lie by your doubts. For your worthiness doesn't help you, and neither does your unworthiness hinder you. A lack of faith is what condemns you, but confidence in God is what makes you worthy.

ASKING GOD FOR FAITH

※⌒⌒⌒

Immediately the boy's father exclaimed,
"I do believe; help me overcome my unbelief!"
Mark 9:24

If you have difficulty believing, you should ask God for faith. For the ability to believe is in God's hands alone. God sometimes gives faith openly and sometimes secretly.

But you can spur yourself on to believe. To begin, you shouldn't continually focus on the suffering of Christ. This has already done its work and frightened you. Rather, move beyond that and look at Christ's caring heart. See how full of love it is toward you, so that it drives him to lift the heavy load of your sin. Then your heart will be filled with love toward him, and your faith will be strengthened.

After this, move beyond Christ's heart to God's heart. You will see that Christ wouldn't have shown you love unless God in his eternal love had wanted him to. Christ is being obedient to God when he loves you. You will discover the good heart of the Father, and as Christ says, you will be drawn to the Father through Christ. Then you will better understand what Christ says in John 3:16: "For God so loved the world that he gave his one and only Son." We recognize the nature of God best, not by thinking about his power and wisdom, which are terrifying, but by thinking about his goodness and love. Then we are truly born anew in God, and we can grow in faith.

POUR YOUR SINS ON CHRIST

*God made him who had no sin to be sin for us, so that
in him we might become the righteousness of God.*
2 Corinthians 5:21

When you become aware of your sin and frightened by it, you must not allow the sin to remain in your conscience. This would only lead to despair. Rather, just as your awareness of sin flowed to you from Christ, so you must pour your sin back on him to free your conscience.

So be careful you don't become like the misguided people who allow their sin to bite at them and eat at their hearts. They strive to rid themselves of this sin by running around doing good works. But you have a way to get rid of your sins. You throw your sins on Christ when you firmly believe that Christ's wounds and suffering carried and paid for your sins. As Isaiah said, "The LORD has laid on him the iniquity of us all" (Isaiah 53:6). Peter said Christ himself "bore our sins in his body on the tree" (1 Peter 2:24). And Paul said, "God made him who had no sin to be sin for us" (2 Corinthians 5:21).

You must rely on these and similar verses with your whole heart. The more your conscience torments you, the more you must rely on them. For if you don't do this and try to quiet your conscience through your own sorrow and penance, you will never find peace of mind and will finally despair in the end. If you try to deal with sin in your conscience, let it remain there, and continue to look at it in your heart, your sins will become too strong for you. They will seem to live forever. But when you think of your sins as being on Christ and boldly believe that he conquered them through his resurrection, then they are dead and gone. Sin can't remain on Christ. His resurrection swallowed up sin.

UNDER HIS WINGS

❦

*O Jerusalem, Jerusalem, you who kill the prophets and stone those sent
to you, how often I have longed to gather your children together,
as a hen gathers her chicks under her wings, but you were not willing.*
Matthew 23:37

In this passage, Christ gives us a beautiful illustration of faith.
The Lord tenderly says to the Israelites that he gladly would have
been their mother hen if only they had been willing to be his
chicks. Note carefully his words and illustration. Christ pours this
out with his whole heart and with great seriousness. In this picture, we see how we should act toward Christ. It shows us how he
can help us, how we should make use of him and enjoy him. If
we watch how a hen behaves with her chicks, then we will see
Christ and ourselves depicted better than any artist can paint.

Our souls are the chicks, and the devil and evil spirits are the
hawks in the air. Except, we aren't as clever as the chicks who flee
under their mother hen. Also, demons are more skillful in attacking us than are the hawks in grabbing chicks. I previously taught
how it isn't enough to be devout, do good works, and live in
grace. For not even our righteousness, let alone our unrighteous-
ness, will endure before God's eyes and his judgment. I have said
that faith, if it is genuine faith, doesn't rely on its own ability to
believe but holds on to Christ and places itself under his righteousness. Just as chicks don't rely on themselves and their own
quickness but simply flee under the hen's body and wings, so we
must run to Christ and let him be our shield and protection.

TEMPORARY RESIDENTS

Since you call on a Father who judges each man's work impartially,
live your lives as strangers here in reverent fear.
1 Peter 1:17

Peter is saying, "Because you have a Father who doesn't play favorites, live your life during the time of your pilgrimage on earth in fear." In other words, you should fear the Father. You should not fear him because he will punish you, which is the way unbelievers and even the devil fear him. But you should fear that he will leave you and take away his protecting hand, just as a pious child would be afraid of making his father angry and doing something to displease him. God wants you to have that kind of fear so you will guard yourself from sin and serve your neighbor while you live here on earth.

If you are a sincere believer, you have all of God's treasures and are God's child. The rest of your life on earth is merely a pilgrimage. God allows you to live in this body and walk on this earth so that you can help other people and bring them to heaven. Therefore, we must use all things on earth in no other way than as guests who travel across the country and come to an inn. They spend the night there and take only food and lodging from the innkeeper. They don't claim that the innkeeper's property now belongs to them. This is how we must deal with material possessions—as if they do not belong to us. We should enjoy only as much as is necessary for us to maintain our bodies and use the rest to help our neighbors. Similarly, the Christian life is like being an overnight guest. "For here we do not have an enduring city" (Hebrews 13:14), but we must go to our Father in heaven. This is why Peter says we shouldn't behave wildly but live in fear.

THE SPIRIT CRIES OUT

❧

Because you are sons, God sent the Spirit of his Son into our hearts,
the Spirit who calls out, "Abba, Father."
Galatians 4:6

Paul could have said, "God sent the Spirit of his Son into our hearts, the Spirit who *prays*, '*Abba*, Father.'" But he purposely says "calls out," to indicate the anguish of the Christian who is still weak and needs to grow in the faith. In Romans 8:26, he describes this calling out as groans that cannot be expressed in words.

But in the middle of trials and conflicts, it's difficult to call out to God, and it takes a lot of effort to cling to God's Word. At those times, we cannot perceive Christ. We do not see him. Our hearts don't feel his presence and his help during the attack. Christ appears to be angry with us and to have left us. Then during the attack, we feel the power of sin, the weakness of our bodies, and our doubt. We experience the flaming arrows of the devil (Ephesians 6:16) and the terrors of death. We feel the wrath and judgment of God. All this raises very powerful and horrible shouts against us so that there does not appear to be anything left but despair and eternal death. However, in the middle of these terrors of the law, the thundering of sin, the shaking of death, and the roar of the devil, the Holy Spirit in our hearts begins to call out, "Abba! Father!" And his cry is much stronger and drowns out the powerful and horrible shouts of the law, sin, death, and the devil. It penetrates through the clouds and heaven and reaches up to the ears of God.

TENDING THE VINEYARD

I am the true vine, and my Father is the gardener.
John 15:1

This passage presents a very comforting picture. Christ understood all the suffering that he and his followers would experience as nothing else but the work of a diligent gardener. Grapevines can grow and produce much fruit only with careful tending by the gardener. Christ wants to teach us that we should look at trials and suffering very differently from the way they appear and feel to us in this world. Suffering doesn't occur apart from God's will. It's not a sign of his anger; rather, it's a sign of his mercy and his fatherly love. It will serve for the best.

It's an art to believe that what hurts and distresses us doesn't occur to harm us but to make us improve. What if the vine were aware of this, could talk, and could see the gardener cutting around its roots with a hoe? What if it could see the gardener pruning its branches with a pruning knife? After seeing and feeling all of this, it might say, "Oh! What are you doing? Now I will wither and spoil because you are working on me, taking the soil away from me, and scraping me with those iron teeth. You are tearing and pinching me everywhere, leaving me to stand here half-naked. You are crueler to me than you are to other trees and plants."

But the gardener would reply, "You just don't understand. If I cut off a branch, it's because it's a useless branch, which takes strength and sap away from you. The other branches won't be able to produce fruit and will also begin to fail. So off it goes. It's for your own good. I am doing it so you will yield more fruit and be able to produce good wine."

OUR FATHER IN HEAVEN

This, then, is how you should pray:
"Our Father in heaven, hallowed be your name."
Matthew 6:9

How should we address God? How should we honor the one we pray to? And how should we present ourselves so that he will be gracious and willing to listen to us? No name anywhere makes a more favorable impression on God than the name "Father." Calling him Father is a friendly, affectionate, deep, and heartfelt way to address him. It wouldn't comfort us nearly so much if we were to call him Lord, or God, or Judge. For the name Father is instinctive and naturally affectionate. That is why hearing us call him Father pleases God the most and moves him to listen to us. By doing so, we acknowledge ourselves as children of God, which again stirs God's heart. For there is no voice more dear to a father than his own child's voice.

It also helps when we say, "in heaven." These words express distressing need and misery because we are on earth and God is in heaven. Those who pray, "Our Father in heaven," and do so out of the depths of their hearts, acknowledge that they have a Father and that their Father is in heaven. Moreover, they acknowledge that they are abandoned on earth and are in misery. Those who pray this way soon feel a heartfelt yearning, like a child who lives far from his father's land in misery and distress among strangers. It's as if they are saying, "O Father, you are in heaven. I am your poor child far from you on earth, in misery, in peril, in distress, and in need. I am surrounded by devils, great enemies, and many kinds of danger." Those who pray in this way stand with pure, uplifted hearts toward God. They are able to pray and move God to mercy.

COMFORT FOR TROUBLING TIMES

❧

Do not let your hearts be troubled. Trust in God; trust also in me.
John 14:1

Whenever we feel distressed and anxious, let us trust Christ and strengthen ourselves with his words. We should receive the comfort Christ offers in this passage. It's as if Christ is saying to us, "What are you doing? Why are you cringing? Are you scared to death? Be encouraged and take heart. All is not lost, even if the devil, the world, or your conscience plagues and terrifies you. You're not ruined if you don't feel my presence. Don't you remember that I told you about this long ago and left these comforting words to strengthen and preserve you?"

From these and other words of Christ, we should begin to know the Lord Christ in the right way. We should develop a more loving confidence in him. And we should pay more attention to his words than to anything that may come before our eyes, ears, and senses. For if we are Christians and stay close to him, we know that he speaks to us. We learn in this passage and elsewhere that he wants to comfort us with his words. Everything he says or does is nothing but friendly and comforting words and actions.

We can be sure of this: a sorrowful, timid, and frightened heart doesn't come from Christ. Christ doesn't frighten hearts or make them depressed. He came to this earth, fulfilled his mission, and ascended into heaven to take away sorrow and fearfulness from our hearts and replace them with cheerful hearts, consciences, and minds. That's why he promises to send the Holy Spirit to his followers. Through the Spirit, he wants to strengthen and preserve his followers after he has left. Whoever can trust in what Christ says in this passage will be in good shape and will have won more than half the battle.

THE HEART OF AN ANGEL

❧❀☙

Suddenly a great company of the heavenly host appeared with the angel,
praising God and saying, "Glory to God in the highest,
and on earth peace to men on whom his favor rests."
Luke 2:13–14

From this angelic song, we can learn what the angels are really like. Forget what the worldly wise teachers speculate about angels. This passage portrays angels so clearly that we can discern their thoughts and hearts. First of all, by joyfully singing about the honor of God, they show how full of light and fire they are. They recognize that everything belongs to God. They don't take credit for anything. They enthusiastically give honor to God, the one to whom it belongs. If you wonder what a humble, pure, obedient, and happy heart in God is like, then think of the angels praising God. This is their first priority as they live in God's presence.

The second characteristic is that angels love us, just as we are taught to love other people. Here you see what wonderful, great friends they are to us. They love us as much as themselves, and they celebrate our salvation as if it were their own. They give us good reason to regard them as highly as we would our best friends. This is the right way to try to understand angels. It's no use trying to understand them according to their essence as the worldly wise teachers do, whose pursuits are futile anyway. The right way to understand angels is according to their inner hearts, attitudes, and minds. We might not know what they're made of, but we do know what their highest desire is and what they're continually doing. In this way, we see into their hearts.

LIVING IN CHRIST

꧁꧂

And now, dear children, continue in him, so that when he appears
we may be confident and unashamed before him at his coming.
1 John 2:28

What should you do when the thought of death frightens you and your conscience bothers you? Continue to live in Christ. You must believe that you can accomplish nothing by your own works and that the only way is through Christ's righteousness. John 6:29 says that the work of God is believing in the one he has sent. So when Nathan corrected David, and David confessed his sin, Nathan replied, "The LORD has taken away your sin. You are not going to die" (2 Samuel 12:13). David simply lived in grace. He didn't even think about trying to satisfy God with his works. When Nathan said, "The LORD has taken away your sin," he was proclaiming the message of grace. And David believed it.

After Adam sinned, he could do nothing that would bring him into a state of grace. But God said that one of his descendants would crush the serpent's head (Genesis 3:15). It was by this promise Adam was made alive. Because he believed in this word, he was saved and justified without any works. Our nature struggles fiercely against being saved without our works and tries to deceive us with a grand illusion of our own righteousness. So we may find ourselves attracted to a life that merely appears to be righteous. Or because we know we aren't righteous, we may be frightened by death or sin. Therefore, we must learn that we should have nothing to do with any way of becoming righteous except through Christ alone.

TESTED BY FIRE

꽃Ꮣ

Do not be surprised at the painful trial you are suffering,
as though something strange were happening to you. But rejoice
that you participate in the sufferings of Christ, so that you
may be overjoyed when his glory is revealed.
1 Peter 4:12–13

Peter uses unusual imagery to remind us what Scripture says about suffering. Throughout the Bible, suffering is described as a hot, fiery oven. Elsewhere, Peter says that these trials test our faith just as fire refines gold (1 Peter 1:7). In the book of Isaiah, God says, "I have tested you in the furnace of affliction" (Isaiah 48:10). In Psalms, David says of God, "You probe my heart and examine me at night . . . you test me" (Psalm 17:3). And regarding Israel, the psalmist says, "We went through fire and water" (Psalm 66:12). So the Bible speaks of suffering as being engulfed in fire or tested by fire. Peter says we shouldn't become upset or think it's strange when we experience this fire. We are tested by fire just as gold is refined by fire.

When we begin to believe, God doesn't abandon us but lays a holy cross upon our backs to strengthen our faith. The gospel is a powerful word, but it cannot do its work without trials. No one will discover its power unless they experience it. The gospel can show its power only where there is a cross and where there is suffering. Because it's a word of life, it must exercise all its power in death. If dying and death are absent, then it can do nothing. No one would discover that it's stronger than sin and death.

Peter says painful trials come on us to test us. This fire or heat is the cross and suffering that make us burn. God inflicts this fire for no other reason except to test us, to see whether we're depending on his Word. That's why God imposes the cross on all believers. He wants us to experience and demonstrate God's power.

RESURRECTION BODIES

But someone may ask, "How are the dead raised?
With what kind of body will they come?" How foolish!
What you sow does not come to life unless it dies.
1 Corinthians 15:35–36

Paul is a masterful teacher to present this subject so well and with such charm. Here he painted such a beautiful portrait. He took what the world considers dead and created a picture of life. He used such ordinary and small objects—seeds and kernels in a field—to portray it. So when a person dies, we should view the process of dying in no other way than as a seed being planted in the ground. If the seed could see and feel what was happening, it would fear that it was ruined forever. But the farmer, if he could talk to the seed, would paint a much different picture. He would portray the seed as if it were already a growing plant with a beautiful stalk and tiny ears of grain.

So we must picture in our own hearts that when we are buried under the ground, we will come up again and grow into a new existence and everlasting life. We don't have to think of ourselves as dead and decaying but rather as planted. We must learn a new way of speaking about death and the grave. When we die, we are not dead; instead, we are seeds planted for the coming summer. The cemetery is not a mound for the dead but a field full of little seeds, which are called God's seeds. They will one day blossom again and become more beautiful than anyone can imagine.

THE BRONZE SNAKE

*You are all sons of God through faith in Christ Jesus, for all of you who
were baptized into Christ have clothed yourselves with Christ.*
Galatians 3:26–27

Some people imagine that faith is a quality that sticks to the heart
on its own, with or without Christ. This is a dangerous error.
Christ should be placed directly before our eyes so that we see
and hear nothing apart from him and believe that nothing is
closer to us than Christ. For he doesn't sit idly in heaven but is
continually present in us. He is working and living in us, for Paul
says, "I no longer live, but Christ lives in me" (Galatians 2:20).
He also says that you "have clothed yourselves with Christ" (Galatians 3:27). Therefore, faith is an unswerving gaze that looks on
Christ alone. He is the conqueror of sin and death and the one
who gives us righteousness, salvation, and eternal life.

This is beautifully illustrated by the story of the bronze snake,
which points to Christ (John 3:14). Moses commanded the
Israelites, who had been bitten in the desert by poisonous snakes,
to look at this bronze snake with an unswerving gaze. Those who
did so were healed, simply by steadily gazing at the snake alone.
In contrast, others who didn't obey Moses looked at their wounds
instead of the snake and died. So if you want to be comforted
when your conscience plagues you or when you are in dire distress, then you must do nothing but grasp Christ in faith and say,
"I believe in Jesus Christ, God's Son, who suffered, was crucified,
and died for me. In his wounds and death, I see my sin. In his resurrection, I see the victory over sin, death, and the devil. I see righteousness and eternal life as well. I want to see and hear nothing
except him." This is true faith in Christ and the right way to
believe.

NO OTHER WAY

*Jesus answered, "I am the way and the truth and the life.
No one comes to the Father except through me."*
John 14:6

I understand what Jesus is saying here in the simplest manner, so that it all applies to this one person, Christ. Jesus is called "the way" because he is the beginning, "the truth" because he is the one who helps us continue, and also "the life" because he is the end. For he must be everything—the beginning, the middle, and the end of our salvation. That is why we place him as the foundation stone on which the other stones are set and on which the entire roof is built. He is the first, middle, and last rung on the ladder to heaven (Genesis 28:12). For through him we must begin, continue, and finally reach the life beyond. So there is only one Christ, but he assumes different roles in our salvation experience.

In the beginning it's hard to find the way. Then life becomes more difficult as we continue to walk along the way. It becomes extremely tough when we have traveled on the way for a long time and are about to reach our final shelter—heaven.

So if you hold on to Christ in faith, then you have started in the right place. If you remain with him, then you will be walking on the right path. If you persevere until the end, then you will be saved. Christ wants to pry our hearts away from trusting anything else. There is no other way, highway, bridge, or path for us than Christ alone.

DON'T WAIT TO PRAY

Have mercy on me, O God, according to your unfailing love;
according to your great compassion blot out my transgressions.
Psalm 51:1

You must pray when you are in the heat of temptation—when your mind is preoccupied with thoughts of lust or revenge. If someone urges you to pray under these circumstances, your mind often insists that it's too impure—as if your dirty thoughts leave no room for prayer. But you must not wait for temptation to end or the thoughts of lust and other sins to totally disappear from your mind before you pray.

At precisely the moment when you feel the strongest temptation and are least prepared to pray, go to a place where you can be alone. Pray the Lord's Prayer or any other prayer you can think of to defend against the devil and his temptations. Then you will feel the temptation decrease, and Satan will run away. Those who think you should wait until your mind is free from impure thoughts to pray only help Satan, who is already far too strong. Waiting to pray is an unchristian approach to prayer. It's a teaching that comes from the devil.

In order to keep yourself from believing these kinds of wrong ideas, you must follow David's example in this psalm. Even after David admitted his terrible sin with Bathsheba, he didn't run away from God. He didn't say what Peter foolishly said while in the boat: "Go away from me, Lord; I am a sinful man!" (Luke 5:8). Instead, David trusted in God's mercy and began to pray, "Lord, even though I am a sinner, have pity on me." The time when you feel your sins the most is exactly the time when you most need to pray to God.

IMMEASURABLY MORE THAN WE ASK

*The babies jostled each other within her, and she said,
"Why is this happening to me?" So she went to inquire of the LORD.*
Genesis 25:22

Rebekah's prayer was for her own life and that of her babies. Yet her prayer resulted in giving birth to two great leaders and all their descendants. She asked God for only a penny but obtained a mountain of gold—something she hadn't hoped for or dared to believe. She kept her prayer modest and reasonable, and she was willing to be satisfied with small favors.

We too are in the habit of praying for trivial and insignificant things. When we pray, we don't take into account the great majesty of God. If God wanted to give us only petty and superficial things, he wouldn't have given us such a magnificent model for prayer: "Our Father in heaven, hallowed be your name, your kingdom come . . ." God has plenty of resources, and he's not a tightwad. He generously offers us the best gifts available in heaven and on earth. He expects that we will ask him for many things and that we will sincerely believe we will get what we request. When we receive what we ask for in the Lord's Prayer, we are, in effect, receiving heaven and earth and everything they contain. For when we ask for God's name to be kept holy, for his kingdom to come, and for his will to be done, we are overpowering countless devils and engulfing the whole world with one prayer.

Because we are so narrow-minded and have such weak faith, we should carefully note how God answered Rebekah's prayer. God isn't content to provide us with a small amount even if we only ask for a little. He prefers to give us "immeasurably more than all we ask or imagine" (Ephesians 3:20).

RESPOND WITH GENTLENESS

⁓⃛

But in your hearts set apart Christ as Lord. Always be prepared to give
an answer to everyone who asks you to give the reason for the hope
that you have. But do this with gentleness and respect.
1 Peter 3:15

When you're challenged or asked about your faith, you shouldn't respond arrogantly. You shouldn't be defiant or forceful, as if you were tearing trees out of the ground. Rather, you should respond with fear and humility, as if you were standing before God and answering him. If you were summoned before kings and princes and had prepared yourself well in advance with Scripture, you might think, "Just wait; I'll answer correctly." But the devil will grab the sword out of your hands and give you a shove. You will be disgraced and find out you put your armor on in vain. He can even take your best verses from your hands so that you can't use them, even though you have them memorized. God allows this to happen to subdue your arrogance and make you humble.

So if you don't want this to happen, you must stand in fear and not rely on your own power. Rely instead on what Christ promised: "But when they arrest you, do not worry about what to say or how to say it. At that time you will be given what to say, for it will not be you speaking, but the Spirit of your Father speaking through you" (Matthew 10:19–20). When you have to give an answer, you ought to arm yourself with Scripture. But don't pound it home with a proud spirit. Otherwise, God will tear the verse from your mouth and from your memory, even if you were armed with all the verses beforehand. Therefore, caution is needed here. But if you are prepared, you can answer princes, leaders, and even the devil himself. Just make sure you aren't speaking insignificant human words but the Word of God.

WHEN WE SIN

My dear children, I write this to you so that you will not sin.
But if anybody does sin, we have one who speaks to the Father
in our defense—Jesus Christ, the Righteous One.
1 John 2:1

Who doesn't go astray at times? I and everyone else have a need for praise. But when we sin, we shouldn't despair of not finding God's mercy. Whoever imagines that their achievements are worth something mistrusts God's mercy and sins in the same way.

Don't despair after you have sinned, but lift your eyes upward, where Christ intercedes for you. For he is your advocate and intercessor. He pleads for you, saying, "Father, for this person I have suffered. I am looking after this individual." This prayer is never useless, because Christ is our high priest (Hebrews 5:10).

Even though we have Christ, our high priest, advocate, mediator, reconciler, and comforter, we have turned instead to dead saints and considered Christ our judge. That's why we should write this passage from the apostle John in gold letters and inscribe it on our hearts. So reach out to him and say, "Lord Christ, I know of no other advocate, comforter, and mediator than you alone. I do not doubt that you are all this to me. I cling firmly to it, and I believe it." Christ was born for us. He suffered for us. He ascended into heaven for our sake, sits at the right hand of the Father, and prays for us. Satan tries with all his might to blind our hearts so we will not believe what the Holy Spirit says in this passage. A Christian's condition is a source of wonder! For Christians are both sinful and righteous. They are sinful because of the sinful nature they carry with them that is contaminated by sin. They are righteous because the Spirit pulls them back from sin. With our reason, we can never understand the wonder of this condition.

GOD'S MERCY AND GRACE

✦

Wash away all my iniquity and cleanse me from my sin.
Psalm 51:2

After Christians have received God's approval through faith and know that their sins are forgiven, they shouldn't become over-confident and start thinking they are immune from sinning. They will still face a constant struggle with what sin remains in them, just as David did.

Because of God's mercy and grace, David received God's approval and was made holy by a righteousness completely out-side of himself. God's mercy and grace aren't human emotions or attitudes. Rather, they're a divine blessing we receive by believing that our sins have been forgiven in Christ. Because of Christ, we can expect mercy and compassion, as David did in Psalm 51. So the righteousness we receive comes completely outside of us. It's a genuine gift from God, who is compassionate and merciful to us because of Christ.

Suppose a man deserving the death penalty was brought to a prince's court. But the prince released him out of compassion, even though he deserved nothing but death. Wouldn't you say that this man's guilt was forgiven, not because of anything he had done, but because of the kindness of the merciful prince? Yet it's not enough for this man to be forgiven for the crime he committed. He also must be released from jail, must be given clothes to wear, and must find a job so that he can live. The same happens to us when we receive God's approval. After God in his mercy frees us from guilt, we still need the gift of the Holy Spirit to clean away what sin remains in us. We need the Spirit to strengthen us so that we are not overpowered by sin and our corrupt desires.

THE GREAT PHYSICIAN

But now he has reconciled you by Christ's physical body
through death to present you holy in his sight,
without blemish and free from accusation.
Colossians 1:22

A Christian is righteous and a sinner at the same time—both a friend and an enemy of God. The philosophers will not admit this paradox because they don't accept the right way of becoming justified. That's why they demand that people keep on doing good works until they don't feel sin anymore. This teaching has caused many people to become very distraught, because they have strived as much as they could to become completely righteous but could never achieve it. Even among those who spread this godless teaching, countless numbers of them have fallen into despair in their hour of death. This would have happened to me if Christ hadn't mercifully looked upon me and freed me from this error.

In contrast, we teach and comfort troubled sinners this way: Dear brothers and sisters, it's impossible for you to become so righteous in this life that you won't feel sin anymore. It's impossible for your body to become as bright and spotless as the sun. Though you still have wrinkles and spots, in spite of this, you are holy. But you may wonder, "How can I be holy since I sin and feel sinful?" Recognizing and feeling your sin is good. Thank God, and don't despair. It's a step toward health whenever a sick person recognizes his disease. "But how can I be freed from sin?" you wonder. Run to Christ, the Physician who heals the broken-hearted (Psalm 147:3). He makes sinners holy.

PRAY WITHOUT DOUBTING

If you believe, you will receive whatever you ask for in prayer.
Matthew 21:22

Before you pray, check to see whether you believe or doubt that you will be heard. If you are doubting or uncertain, or if you are merely trying a prayer to see what happens, your prayer won't be worth anything. For you aren't keeping your heart steady but letting it wobble back and forth. As a result, God cannot give anything to this kind of heart, just as you cannot give something to a person who doesn't hold her hand still.

Imagine how you would feel if a person had earnestly asked you for something but then said to you, "I don't really believe you will give it to me," even though you had promised that you would beforehand. You would think he was mocking you by his request. You would take back everything you had promised and perhaps even punish him on top of it.

How can it please God when we do the same to him when we pray? God assures us that when we ask him for something, he will give it to us. By doubting him, we call him a liar and contradict our own prayers. By not believing him, we insult God's truthfulness, the same truthfulness we rely on when we pray. This is why we say the little word *Amen* at the end of our prayers. We use it to express our firm, heartfelt faith. It's like saying, "O God, I have no doubt that you will give me what I ask for in prayer."

RESIST THE DEVIL

*Be self-controlled and alert. Your enemy the devil prowls around
like a roaring lion looking for someone to devour.
Resist him, standing firm in the faith.*
1 Peter 5:8–9

You should keep your mind clear and be alert. Then your body
will be prepared. But the devil isn't defeated through this alone. By
keeping your mind clear and alert, you merely give your body less
reason to sin. Your true sword is remaining strong and firm in the
faith. If you grasp hold of God's Word in your heart and cling to
it with faith, the devil cannot win. He has to flee. If you can say,
"My God has said this, and I stand upon it," you will find that
the devil will quickly leave. Then apathy, evil desire, anger, greed,
despair, and doubt will soon go away. But the devil is crafty and
doesn't want to let you get to that point. He tries to snatch the
sword out of your hand. If he makes you lazy so that your body
becomes unfit and out of control, he can tear your sword out of
your hand. This is what he did to Eve. She had God's word. If she
had clung to it, she would not have fallen. But when the devil saw
that she held the word loosely, he tore it from her heart. She let it
go, and the devil won (Genesis 3:4, 13; 2 Corinthians 11:3).

Peter has instructed us on how we should fight against the
devil. It doesn't require a lot of running around or doing special
kinds of works. Rather, it calls for nothing more than clinging to
the Word through faith. If the devil wants to drive you to despair
because of your sin, just grab the Word of God. It promises forgiveness of sins. Rely on God's Word, and the devil will quickly
leave you alone.

WHEN NOTHING MAKES SENSE

꙰

"Here comes that dreamer!" they said to each other.
"Come now, let's kill him and throw him into one of these cisterns
and say that a ferocious animal devoured him."
Genesis 37:19–20

God promised to care for his people. But when Joseph's brothers said a wild animal had killed Joseph, Jacob and Joseph were both put through a severe test. This appeared to go totally against God's promise. You would think that God would pay some attention to them and show some concern. But God didn't send an angel, or even so much as the leaf of a tree, to stop the devil or force him away. Instead, he opened all the doors and windows to let the devil rant and rave, attacking both father and son in horrible ways.

God had given Jacob an important promise. In his twelve sons, Jacob had living proof that the promise would be fulfilled. Still, many problems came his way, as if he had no God and no promise. But despite all these problems, God hadn't deserted him.

We can be certain that God's promises will always remain: "Can a mother forget the baby at her breast and have no compassion on the child she has borne? Though she may forget, I will not forget you! See, I have engraved you on the palms of my hands" (Isaiah 49:15–16).

So why do our own flesh and blood—our children and family members—cause us so many terrible problems? This is a part of God's plan. It's the way God works in the lives of his people in this world. So we desperately need wisdom that is above our natural reason. On the basis of that wisdom, we can say, "God won't lie to me or deceive me, though at times, nothing in life will seem to make sense."

FAITH COMES FROM GOD

Then they asked him, "What must we do to do the works God requires?" Jesus answered, "The work of God is this: to believe in the one he has sent."
John 6:28–29

The entire Bible agrees on what it means to serve God. Scripture firmly establishes that if we want to serve him, we must believe in the one whom the Father has sent. If we want to know how to receive God's grace, how to approach him, how to satisfy the penalty for our sins, how to receive forgiveness of sin and escape death, then we must do what God wants and believe in Christ. Here Christ is plainly telling us what we should do—believe.

Faith is the work we must do. Yet faith is also called God's work. Later, Christ tells us how we are able to believe, for no one can believe on his or her own. "No one can come to me unless the Father who sent me draws him" (John 6:44). He also says, "No one can come to me unless the Father has enabled him" (John 6:65). For faith is a divine work that God asks us to do. But at the same time, God must give us faith, for we can't believe on our own.

What an excellent passage this is! Like a lightning bolt, it strikes down all wisdom and righteousness, every law and commandment, even the law of Moses. It lays before us a different work—a work that is above and beyond us. We cannot grasp Christ with our thoughts or our reason. Therefore, faith cannot be our own work. We are drawn to Christ, even though we can neither feel him nor see him.

ENRICHED WITH SCRIPTURE

Fix these words of mine in your hearts and minds;
tie them as symbols on your hands and bind them on your foreheads.
Teach them to your children.
Deuteronomy 11:18–19

When children are old enough to begin grasping the concepts of faith, they should make a habit of bringing home verses of Scripture from church. They should recite these verses to their parents at mealtime. Then they should write the verses down and put them in little pouches or pockets, just as they put pennies and other coins in a purse. Let the pouch of faith be a golden one. Verses about coming to faith, such as Psalm 51:5; John 1:29; Romans 4:25; and Romans 5:12, are like gold coins for that little pouch. Let the pouch of love be a silver one. The verses about doing good, such as Matthew 5:11; Matthew 25:40; Galatians 5:13; and Hebrews 12:6, are like silver coins for this pouch.

No one should think they are too smart for this game and look down on this kind of child's play. Christ had to become a man in order to train us. If we want to train children, then we must become children with them. I wish this kind of child's play was more widespread. In a short time, we would see an abundance of Christian people rich in Scripture and in the knowledge of God. They would make more of these pouches, and by using them, they would learn all of Scripture.

As it is now, people go to hear a sermon and leave again unchanged. They act like a sermon is only worth the time it takes to hear it. No one thinks about learning anything from it or remembering it. Some people listen to sermons for three or four years and still don't learn enough to respond to a single question about faith. More than enough has been written in books, but not nearly enough has been driven into our hearts.

WHEN WE FEEL FORGOTTEN

※ᑈ

The chief cupbearer, however, did not remember Joseph; he forgot him.
Genesis 40:23

After being forgotten by the cupbearer, Joseph struggled with the temptation of becoming impatient and complaining. When the devil saw this, he attacked Joseph with even more fiery arrows. Christ himself felt these arrows when the devil tempted him: "If you are the Son of God, tell these stones to become bread" (Matthew 4:3). In the same way, the devil might have said to Joseph, "Go ahead and continue your miserable struggle. You know that your prayers are useless. You cry to God and believe in him—but all for nothing. You had hoped that God would free you and restore your honor because you interpreted the chief cupbearer's dream. Well, let God save you if he feels like it!" The devil continued to torment Joseph with his fiery arrows, even though Joseph was already weak and wounded.

When faithful people are happy and when they sing, "The LORD is my strength and my song" (Psalm 118:14), the devil stays far away from them. All complaining and impatience soon end. As long as believers praise and thank God, then temptation, sadness, and unbelief disappear. Heaven is opened wide and hell is shut with words like these: "I will extol the LORD at all times; his praise will always be on my lips" (Psalm 34:1).

But as soon as we stop praising God, miserable, lonely, sad thoughts return. That's what happened to Joseph when he remembered how his brothers had sold him. They were at home having a good time while he was lying in prison, tied up and miserable. This is how the devil works. When the water becomes troubled, he likes to fish. He uses these opportunities to tempt people to abandon their faith and give up in despair.

THE GOLDEN RULE

*So in everything, do to others what you would have them do
to you, for this sums up the Law and the Prophets.*
Matthew 7:12

What could be more clear and concise than the truth stated in this verse? But the world won't let us reflect on these words. Our sinful nature won't let us measure our lives against this standard. We let this verse go in one ear and out the other. If we would continually compare our lives and actions against this standard, we wouldn't live so carelessly. We would have more than enough to do and wouldn't need to pursue other works we consider holy. We would become our own teachers and begin teaching ourselves how we should live. We wouldn't need so many lawyers and law books, for this standard is concise and easy to learn. If only we were diligent and serious enough to live according to it!

Let me give a rough illustration. No one would like to be robbed. If you ask yourself, you would have to admit that you certainly wouldn't enjoy it. So why don't you conclude that everyone else feels the same way? At the market, you see that vendors charge as much as they wish for what they're selling, so that it costs three times what it is worth. If you were to ask a vendor, "Excuse me, would you like this done to you?" he would have difficulty replying. If he were honest and thinking sensibly, he would have to say, "I want to pay the market value, what is just and fair. I don't want to be overcharged." So do you see the point? Your heart tells you how you would like to be treated, and your conscience tells you that you should treat others the same way.

FAITH AND WORKS ARE NECESSARY

*If you obey my commands, you will remain in my love, just as I
have obeyed my Father's commands and remain in his love.*
John 15:10

Jesus is saying, "You are in me and remain in me, so make sure you keep my commandments. For I must give each of you a task as a sign to others that you are my true branches. That task is to love each other. I keep this command myself so that I can be an example and model to you. And I remain in my Father's love because I keep this command. Therefore, if you keep my commandments, you will remain in my love." Earlier in this book, Christ also says, "By this all men will know that you are my disciples, if you love one another" (John 13:35).

So there are two parts of Christian teaching that we must emphasize daily. Neither faith nor works can be ignored. For when faith isn't preached—when no one explains how we are joined to Christ and become branches in him—then everyone resorts to their own works. On the other hand, when we teach only about faith, this lopsidedness leads to false Christians. These people praise faith, are baptized, and even call themselves Christians, but they don't show any fruit or power.

That's why it's so difficult to preach. No matter how I preach, something goes wrong. Someone always goes off on a tangent. If I don't preach about faith, the result will be useless and hypocritical works. If I only emphasize faith, no one does any good works. The result is either useless, faithless do-gooders or believers who don't do any good works. So we must preach the message to those who accept both faith and works. We must preach to those who want to remain in the vine, put their trust in Christ, and put their faith into action in their everyday lives.

RELYING ON OUR OWN STRENGTH

*[Peter] began to draw back and separate himself from
the Gentiles because he was afraid of those who belonged to the
circumcision group. The other Jews joined him in his hypocrisy,
so that by their hypocrisy even Barnabas was led astray.*
Galatians 2:12–13

Paul challenged Peter, not over a minor matter, but over the most important teaching of Christianity, which Peter practically ruined with his hypocrisy. Barnabas and the other Jewish Christians were acting like hypocrites. They all sinned, not out of ignorance or malice, but out of fear of the Jewish leaders. These leaders had blinded their hearts so much they didn't even know they were sinning. It's truly astonishing that great men, such as Peter, Barnabas, and others, were so easily tripped up. That's why Staupitz warned that it is very dangerous to rely on our own strength—no matter how holy and educated we are or how well we have understood a truth. For even in matters that we know well, we can fall into error and end up harming ourselves as well as other people.

If God isn't with us, we are nothing at all, no matter how great our gifts may be. If he removes his hand from us, our wisdom and our knowledge are nothing. If he doesn't constantly uphold us, the greatest amount of knowledge will be useless, even if we are experts in theology. For in the hour of temptation, the devil can tear away all the comforting Bible verses from us and leave us with threatening ones that crush our spirits. So we should learn from this passage that we can easily fall if God were to withdraw his hand from us. Let's not boast in our righteousness and in our gifts. But let's humble ourselves and pray with the apostles, "Increase our faith!" (Luke 17:5).

SPIRITUAL FULLNESS

※◦◦❦◦◦※

For in Christ all the fullness of the Deity lives in bodily form,
and you have been given fullness in Christ, who is the head
over every power and authority.
Colossians 2:9–10

In Paul's letters, such as Romans, Galatians, and Colossians, there are many passages that say God has fulfilled all the requirements of the law in Christ (Romans 10:4). Christ is the fulfillment of the law, of time, and of all things. Christ is all and has all. The person who holds on to Jesus in faith will receive forgiveness of sins. God's laws will be fulfilled, death will be conquered, and the devil will be overcome. That person will receive the gift of eternal life. For in this one man, Jesus, all is settled. He has fulfilled everything. Whoever accepts him has everything. As Paul says here, "You have been given fullness in Christ."

When I feel anxious about sin and hell, I remind myself that when I have Christ, I have all that is necessary. Neither death, sin, nor the devil can hurt me. If I believe in Christ, I have fulfilled the law; it cannot accuse me. I have conquered hell; it cannot hold me. Everything that Christ has is mine. Through him, we obtain all his possessions and eternal life. Even if I am weak in faith, I still have the same treasure and the same Christ that others have. There's no difference: we are all made perfect through faith in him, not by what we do.

For example, imagine that two people each have a hundred dollars. One person carries it in a paper bag. The other keeps it in an iron chest. Both have the same treasure no matter where they put it. Similarly, we all have the same Christ. It doesn't matter if one person has a stronger or weaker faith than another. Both of them still believe in the same Christ and have everything through him.

HOLDING TIGHTLY TO THE PROMISE

꽁

Then God said, "Take your son, your only son, Isaac, whom you love,
and go to the region of Moriah. Sacrifice him there as a burnt
offering on one of the mountains I will tell you about."
Genesis 22:2

Whenever troubles come into our lives, we naturally assume that
we are being punished for something we've done wrong. With the
help of the devil, our consciences remind us of past sins. We scru-
tinize our lives and wonder what offended God. This can even
lead to blaming God for our problems. Eventually we can end up
hating him.

Perhaps Abraham had similar thoughts when God asked him
to sacrifice Isaac: "God kept his promise to me. He gave me a son,
and this made me extremely happy. Perhaps I've become proud
because God gave me a son. Perhaps I wasn't as thankful as I should
have been. Maybe the Lord regrets making his promise to me." It's
difficult to silence anxious thoughts like these when we can't understand what God is doing. People can't comprehend how an
unchanging God can change his mind. Inevitably, we come to one
of two conclusions: either God is a liar, or God has become our
enemy. Thinking of God as a liar is blasphemy. Thinking of God
as our enemy leads to despair.

Often, serious doubts arise, such as "What if God doesn't
want me to be saved?" But when our consciences are troubled in
this way, we have to continue to believe the promise of salvation—
a promise we can trust in and depend on. When we doubt God's
promise, we must pray sincerely and persistently. We must hang
on to God's promise, because if Satan can prevent us from believing it, then we have nowhere else to turn. We must hold tightly to
the promise and be ready for the times when God will test us, as
he did Abraham. God doesn't test us because he enjoys it. He tests
us to find out whether we love him above all things.

DON'T PUT GOD TO THE TEST

Jesus answered him, "It is also written:
'Do not put the Lord your God to the test.'"
Matthew 4:7

If we don't use the resources available to us but instead want other resources we don't have, then we're testing God. This is what Satan wanted Christ to do. Satan told Jesus to throw himself from the temple when there were steps he could have used to climb down. Someone who doesn't wear proper clothing in cold weather but expects God to miraculously keep him from freezing is also testing God. This is like the Jewish leaders who ignored the signs they had been given and waited for a different one from heaven. In the same way, people who sleep when they should be working are testing God. Because God promised to take care of them, they assume that God will find a way. But in Proverbs, God told them to work: "Lazy hands make a man poor, but diligent hands bring wealth" (Proverbs 10:4).

God's work is accomplished when we use the resources given to us. He wants us to use our resources but not put our trust in them. While it's true that hardworking hands bring wealth, it's also true that only the Lord's blessing brings it. As Solomon said, "the blessing of the LORD brings wealth" (Proverbs 10:22). When people use weapons to defend themselves, God is still delivering them. Without God's help, people who attempt to deliver themselves will fail. As David said, "I do not trust in my bow, my sword does not bring me victory; but you give us victory over our enemies" (Psalm 44:6–7). God will use weapons to deliver people if weapons are available, but he can still deliver people even if they aren't available. Therefore, we should make use of what we have but not rely on those things. We must trust in God alone, whether we have the resources we need or not.

GOD LISTENS TO US

❧

This is the confidence we have in approaching God:
that if we ask anything according to his will, he hears us.
And if we know that he hears us—whatever we ask—
we know that we have what we asked of him.
1 John 5:14–15

This passage is an encouragement to Christians who have been instructed on how they should believe and love. They must remember that their godliness comes from the Word that has been proclaimed, and they must not live any other way than in faith and love. John anticipates an objection from these people: "What if my heart is cold and I feel that I lack faith?" "Here is the remedy," says John. "Ask and pray. He will hear you."

James says, "If any of you lacks wisdom, he should ask God, who gives generously to all without finding fault, and it will be given to him" (James 1:5). Your best course of action is to rely on prayer. Paul says, "Do not be anxious about anything, but in everything, by prayer and petition, with thanksgiving, present your requests to God" (Philippians 4:6). Likewise, Augustine says, "Lord, give me what you are commanding." So we also should pray, "Lord, give us faith."

This verse is an encouragement to pray, and John describes how to pray in an excellent way. First, he reminds us that we can have "confidence," which is the soul of prayer. Next, he instructs us what to ask for: "Ask anything according to his will." Finally, we must also believe that "he hears us." James supports this: "He [who doubts] is a double-minded man, unstable in all he does" (James 1:8). "But when he asks, he must believe and not doubt" (v. 6).

GREAT ANSWERS FROM A GREAT GOD

❧ ⟨C⟩ ⟨꒤⟩

But Esau ran to meet Jacob and embraced him;
he threw his arms around his neck and kissed him. And they wept.
Genesis 33:4

Jacob's anguished prayer accomplished more than he dared to ask. He hadn't expected so much comfort from God or from his brother. All he had asked for was that his brother would leave him and his family unharmed. He never thought he would receive so much kindness from his brother. Esau even ran to meet Jacob. With tears streaming from his eyes, he hugged and kissed him.

We should pray with confidence, knowing that God will answer our requests without delay. It's impossible for sincere, persistent prayer to remain unheard. But because we don't believe, we aren't persistent enough and don't experience God's goodness and help. So we must become more enthusiastic about faith and prayer, knowing that God is pleased when we persevere. In fact, God ordered us to be persistent in prayer: "Ask and it will be given to you; seek and you will find; knock and the door will be opened to you" (Matthew 7:7).

Our prayers are answered much differently—actually, more generously—than we could ever ask or imagine (Ephesians 3:20). Paul says, "In the same way, the Spirit helps us in our weakness. We do not know what we ought to pray for, but the Spirit himself intercedes for us with groans that words cannot express. And he who searches our hearts knows the mind of the Spirit" (Romans 8:26–27).

We always ask for less than we should and don't even think God is willing to give us what we ask for. We don't ask the right way. We don't understand that what we pray about is more important than we can comprehend. We think small, but the Lord is great and powerful. He expects us to ask for great things. He wants to give them to us to demonstrate his almighty power.

LOVING YOURSELF

※ ⟨ ⟩ ⟩

The entire law is summed up in a single command:
"Love your neighbor as yourself."
Galatians 5:14

Some of the early church fathers concluded from this passage that love begins with loving yourself. They said this because loving yourself was given as the measure for how much you should love your neighbor. I used to consider this from all sides to try to understand it. I understand this commandment to mean that only love toward your neighbor is being commanded, not love of yourself.

First, self-love is already present in all people. Second, if God had wanted to command you to love yourself, he would have said, "You should love yourself and your neighbor as yourself." But he said instead, "Love your neighbor as yourself." In other words, "as yourself" means the way you already love yourself, without a commandment to do so. When describing love in 1 Corinthians 13:5, Paul teaches that love is not self-seeking. It completely rejects self-love. In Mark 8:34, Christ commands us to deny ourselves. Philippians 2:3–4 clearly says, "In humility consider others better than yourselves. Each of you should look not only to your own interests, but also to the interests of others." This commandment presupposes that people already love themselves, just as when Christ says in Matthew 7:12, "Do to others what you would have them do to you." Clearly he isn't commanding you to love yourself here either.

So it seems to me the part of this commandment that says "as yourself" is referring to the wrong kind of love—the kind where you forget your neighbor and seek only your own interests. But this can become the right kind of love if you forget yourself and think only about serving your neighbor.

FAITH IS MORE IMPORTANT THAN WORKS

For we maintain that a man is justified by faith
apart from observing the law.
Romans 3:28

Our opponents insist that good works are necessary for salvation, and the world enthusiastically agrees with them. Certainly, what the saints did was admirable, and they did many great works. But even if you were to show me the holiest saint of all, would that person have done enough good works to earn God's approval?

We also recognize that love is an essential aspect of the Christian life and that all believers need to restrain their corrupt desires and practice self-denial. "But you don't do that," our opponents protest. Our reply is, "Even if we could do all that, would we have done enough for God's approval?" The only reason we think so highly of what we do is that we don't want God to receive any of the credit. We readily admit that good works are necessary. But they're not more important than what we already have: God's approval, which comes through faith. We must understand the difference between what is priceless and what is cheap, what is important and what is trivial. This distinction is important in all of life, but especially in this doctrine. Even animals understand the difference between good and bad food. A dog knows that meat is better than bread.

Therefore, we should value good works and remember that doing them is still necessary. But we should value God's Word and his promises even more highly. We will live in God's presence because we believe in what he says, not because we do good works that make us holy. We have to make a clear distinction between our good works and our faith in God's Word. Believing in God's Word defeats the devil and makes us holy children of God.

THE BREAD OF LIFE

Then Jesus declared, "I am the bread of life. He who comes to me will never go hungry, and he who believes in me will never be thirsty."
John 6:35

These are unusually direct words: Christ is bread. He is food given by God. Whoever eats this bread will be satisfied, will not hunger or thirst, and will live forever. Furthermore, this bread from heaven was standing right in front of the Israelites.

Jesus began his sermon gently enough: "He who comes to me . . ." The further he proceeded, the more pointed and direct he became. He easily could have said, "he who eats of me," instead of "he who comes to me." But that would have been premature. He wanted the people to understand him, so he used the words "he who comes to me" and then explained that he meant "he who believes in me." This is a profound statement: to come to Christ is to believe in Christ. It means having the bread and eating it. Jesus, however, wasn't talking about eating in a church or at a wedding. He wasn't talking about eating beef or veal, as his listeners might have thought. He was speaking of bread in the sense of people coming to Christ—in other words, believing in Christ. For "eating" and "coming to Christ" and "believing in Christ" all mean the same.

Christ comes to us, and the Father gives us manna from heaven. All that is missing is for us to come to him. This may offend you. You can't come to Christ—even if you are his closest relative—unless you believe in him. Through his Word, Christ is closer to you than a child with his arms wrapped around your neck. When you believe in him, then he is with you and close to you. He is right in front of you, before your eyes and ears, so that you can almost see and hear him. Simply believe in him.

STANDING UP AGAIN

❦

Everyone who sins breaks the law; in fact, sin is lawlessness.
1 John 3:4

We are all sinners, and at times we all fall into sin. But when true Christians fall, they soon come back, turn around, and struggle against the sin so that they won't offend their neighbor. To illustrate, it's difficult to avoid being wounded in times of war. Yet it's an honor if one stands up to fight again. But it's a disgrace if someone retreats. Similarly, even if Christians are completely surrounded by sin, they should still fight against it. Some people think they're Christians because they've been baptized. These people give their desires free rein and don't care about conquering their sins. They merely follow their own cravings.

Committing sin comes from following the enticement and desire to sin. Many give these sinful desires free rein. They don't want to repent or stand up to fight again. Today they commit adultery; tomorrow they want to live purely. It's impossible for these people to avoid offending their neighbor. If they don't offend them by something they do, then they certainly will by neglecting what they ought to do for their neighbor.

An important part of Christianity is love, and love is not self-seeking (1 Corinthians 13:5). Insisting on our own way is not loving our neighbor, but following our own desires. So not showing love is the same as being disobedient. Those who aren't pure, who don't struggle daily against themselves, will give in to sin and do wrong. Those who don't have the fruit on the inside won't show it on the outside toward their neighbor. If we have not died to ourselves so that we can disregard our own desires, how can we seek what's best for others?

WAITING FOR THE LORD

The chief cupbearer, however, did not remember Joseph; he forgot him.
Genesis 40:23

No other model we can think of compares to Joseph. He had so many unbearable tortures heaped on him, and he didn't have any help or hope. In contrast, martyrs for the faith usually suffer for only a short time. But Joseph had to suffer for a long time. You won't find many people who, when abandoned like Joseph, wouldn't complain, become angry, and become impatient. Yes, Joseph had his weak moments too. At times he felt depressed and wanted to complain, cry, and give up.

Joseph's example illustrates the importance of waiting for the Lord. In Psalms we read, "Wait for the LORD; be strong and take heart and wait for the LORD" (Psalm 27:14). Habakkuk says, "For the revelation awaits an appointed time; it speaks of the end and will not prove false. Though it linger, wait for it; it will certainly come and will not delay" (Habakkuk 2:3). Isaiah encourages us, "Then you will know that I am the LORD; those who hope in me will not be disappointed" (Isaiah 49:23).

But our human weakness tells us, "It's been too long. I've been waiting for help for five, ten, or twenty years, and there's no end in sight." But remember that God made these promises to you. He is your friend and father. Because of his grace and mercy, God has promised to take care of you like a father cares for his little child. He is your father, and you are his dear child. Does your sinful nature still tell you that hoping in God is foolish? Don't worry. Continue to wait with all believers. What Christ promises in Matthew 24:13 will come to pass: "He who stands firm to the end will be saved."

CALLED BY GOD

Paul, an apostle—sent not from men nor by man,
but by Jesus Christ and God the Father, who raised him
from the dead—and all the brothers with me.
Galatians 1:1–2

Religious leaders face a very foolish yet strong temptation. Some claim they must teach because they have a talent from the Lord and feel compelled to teach because of the command of the gospel. Confused by a foolish conscience, they think that if they don't teach, they're burying the gold of their Lord and will be condemned for it. The devil causes them to think this way to make them neglect the responsibilities to which they are called.

My dear friend, with one word Christ frees you from this notion. Look at the parable in Matthew: "A man going on a journey . . . called his servants and entrusted his property to them" (Matthew 25:14). He called them. But who has called you? Wait for God to call you. In the meantime, don't be concerned about it. Even if you were wiser than Solomon and Daniel, unless you are called to spread the Word, avoid that calling even more than hell. If God needs you, he will call you. If he doesn't call you, you won't burst from the wisdom inside of you. In fact, it isn't even true wisdom. It only appears that way to you. And it's very foolish for you to imagine that you could produce fruit. The only one who produces fruit by the Word is one who is called to teach without wishing for it. For Jesus Christ is our Teacher (Matthew 23:10). He alone teaches and produces fruit through his servants, whom he calls. But those who teach without being called endanger both themselves and their hearers, for Christ is not with them.

LOVE FROM A PURE HEART

The goal of this command is love, which comes from a pure heart and a good conscience and a sincere faith.
1 Timothy 1:5

Love, as everyone already knows, is simply being kind to someone, showing that person goodness, and offering friendship. Now, there are some who preach and sermonize about love, but they slant it to their own point of view and to their own advantage. They are like the heretics, the godless, and evil scoundrels who also have love—but only for themselves and others like them. Meanwhile, they hate and persecute all good Christians and would murder them if they could. Choosing a couple of people who are pleasing to you, who do what you want, and then being friendly to those people is a long way from love. This is a soiled love that doesn't come from a pure heart. It's nothing more than dirt.

For love that flows "from a pure heart" thinks this way: "God has commanded me to direct my love to my neighbor. My heavenly Father wants me to be favorable to everyone, whether friends or enemies, just as he is. He lets the sun rise and shine on both good and evil people." God shows goodness to those who continually dishonor him and misuse what he has provided through their disobedience, blasphemy, sin, and shameful behavior. In the same way, he lets rain fall on both the thankful and the unthankful. He gives money, property, and all types of things from the earth to the very worst scoundrels. Why does he do this? He does it out of genuine, pure love. His heart is full and overflowing with love. He pours his love over everyone, leaving no one out, whether good or bad, worthy or unworthy. This love is righteous, godly, whole, and complete. It doesn't single out certain people or separate people into groups. He freely gives his love to all.

THE MARRIAGE PARTNERSHIP

❧

The man said, "This is now bone of my bones and flesh of my flesh;
she shall be called 'woman,' for she was taken out of man."
Genesis 2:23

The word *woman* presents an amazing and lovely picture of the institution of marriage. Everything the husband has also belongs to his wife. Not only do they share their assets, but also their children, income, food, drink, bed, and home. Besides that, they are to be one in mind and spirit. The only difference between a husband and wife is in their anatomy. Otherwise, they are the same. Because of this, whatever the husband has or owns also belongs to his wife.

Compared to the very first marriage, our marriages today are only pathetic copies of the original design. If a married woman is honorable, moral, devout, and God-fearing, she and her husband will equally share the cares, duties, and responsibilities of their household. This is why she was created and why she is called "woman."

Even though a wife today doesn't come from her husband's flesh and bone as Eve did, she is still a head of the household the same as her husband because she is the wife. This doesn't invalidate the law, given after the fall into sin, which places the wife under the authority of her husband. This punishment, like the others, clouds the glorious life humans enjoyed in Paradise. This passage reminds us that Moses wasn't describing the miserable life of married people today, but the innocence humans enjoyed in Paradise. Back then, the authority of the husband and wife was equal. Now, men are obligated to work by the sweat of their brows, and wives are commanded to place themselves under their husbands' authority. Nevertheless, we still see a remnant of the original design in marriage because the wife is called "woman" and because she owns property and possessions jointly with her husband.

OBSTACLES TO PRAYER

Until now you have not asked for anything in my name.
Ask and you will receive, and your joy will be complete.
John 16:24

There are two major obstacles to prayer. The first obstacle arises when the devil prompts you to think, "I am not yet prepared to pray. I should wait for another half hour or another day until I have become more prepared or until I have finished taking care of this or that." Meanwhile, the devil distracts you for half an hour so that you no longer think about prayer for the rest of the day. From one day to the next, you are hindered and rushed with other business. This common obstacle shows us how maliciously the devil tries to trick us. He often tries this on me. The devil also has an influence over our bodies, which are so lazy and cold that we can't pray the way we want to. Even if we do begin to pray, we become distracted by useless thoughts and lose our concentration in prayer.

The second obstacle arises when we ask ourselves, "How can you pray to God and say the Lord's Prayer? You are too unworthy and sin every day. Wait until you are more devout. You might be in the mood to pray now, but wait until you have confessed your sin and taken the Lord's Supper so that you can pray more fervently and approach God with confidence. Only then can you really pray the Lord's Prayer from your heart." This serious obstacle crushes us like a heavy stone. Despite our feelings of unworthiness, our hearts must struggle to remove this obstacle so that we can freely approach God and call upon him.

SURRENDERING OUR WILLS

꧁ঞ꧂

Your kingdom come, your will be done on earth as it is in heaven.
Matthew 6:10

God's will is done when our wills are broken. It pleases him when our wills are hindered and defeated. So when someone talks about you as if you were a fool, you shouldn't disagree. Instead, agree and let the criticism appear correct, for it's certainly correct before God. If a person wants to take something from you and harm you, you should allow it to happen as if it were all right with you. For undoubtedly it's right before God. Even if the person were wronging you, it still wouldn't be unjust. For it's God's will either way, whether he uses a wicked person or a good person to take something away from you. Instead of resisting, you should simply say, "Your will be done." This is true in both physical and spiritual matters. For Christ said, "If someone wants to sue you and take your tunic, let him have your cloak as well" (Matthew 5:40).

Someone might ask, "If that's what it means for God's will to be done, who can be saved? Who can keep this difficult command to surrender everything and not have their own will in anything?" My reply is that we should learn how great this prayer is, why we need it, and how earnestly we should pray it. It's crucial that we allow our wills to be totally defeated so that only God's will is done.

Notice that in the garden, Jesus said, "Yet not my will, but yours be done" (Luke 22:42). Undoubtedly, Christ's will was good—in fact, the best one of all time. If Christ had to surrender his will so that God's will could be done, why do we poor little worms want to make such a fuss over our own wills?

CHRIST IN US

On that day you will realize that I am in my Father,
and you are in me, and I am in you.
John 14:20

We are in Christ, and Christ is in us. The first truth points upward; the second points downward. We must first be in him with all our being—with our sin and weakness and even with death. We know that in God's eyes we are freed, redeemed, and saved from these through Christ.

Then we must swing above and beyond ourselves to Christ. Yes, we must be totally one with Christ and his people—those who are baptized in him and receive the Lord's Supper. Consequently, sin, death, the devil, and struggles with a bad conscience disappear. We can then say, "I'm not sure about death or hell. If there is death, let it consume my Lord Christ first. If there is hell, let it devour my Savior. If sin, the law, or my conscience condemns me, let it accuse the Son of God. If that happens, then let me be condemned, consumed, and devoured with my Lord. But because the Father and Christ live, I also will live. Because Christ remains undefeated by sin and death, I also will remain undefeated. For I know that Christ is in the Father; therefore, I also am in Christ." This is how we soar above and beyond ourselves to Christ.

After that, Christ comes down to us from above. If we are in Christ, then Christ is in us. We have received him and crept into him. We have left sin, death, and the devil behind. So Jesus shows himself to us and says, "Go. Preach, comfort, and baptize. Serve your neighbor. Be obedient and patient. I will be in you, and I will do all this through you. Whatever you do will be accomplished by me. Be happy. Be bold and courageous. Remain in me, then I will certainly remain in you."

TRAINING GROUND FOR SPIRITUALITY

*[Sarah] said to Abraham, "Get rid of that slave woman and her son,
for that slave woman's son will never share in the inheritance
with my son Isaac." The matter distressed Abraham greatly
because it concerned his son.*
Genesis 21:10–11

Family life is a training ground for faith, hope, love, patience, and
prayer. Sarah and Abraham were arguing about God's promises, but
they were doing so out of fear and respect for God. Some people
give up their homes and leave their families, thinking they are devoting themselves to God. They dismiss the kind of obedience and
devotion we see in this story as the mere efforts of amateurs—something any married couple could do.

This story should reassure married couples. They shouldn't
assume that they'll never have disagreements and arguments.
Even the godliest and most loving spouses will sometimes disagree. We should remember that these disputes are opportunities
for practicing godliness and love.

Abraham was the natural and legal father of Ishmael. Yet Sarah
asked him to give up both Ishmael and Hagar. Because Abraham
was emotionally attached to both of them, this was a difficult decision. Besides, God commands that a husband should protect his
wife and support his children. But Sarah was insistent that Hagar
and her son should be thrown out. They weren't being thrown out
because they were disrespectful to Abraham. I'm sure they treated
him with the proper respect. They were being thrown out for
mocking Isaac.

These are the kinds of problems our opponents know nothing
about. They regard marriage as a secular institution. Yet we should
recognize marriage for what it is—a training ground for spirituality. The greatest passions, both toward God and one another, are
challenged and expressed within marriage.

FAITH SHOWS ITSELF IN LOVE

This is my command: Love each other.
John 15:17

In this passage, Christ repeats the command to love each other. By love, believers are held together, and love is the mark of true believers. Jesus emphasized this command because he knew how many false Christians would arise—how many would praise faith with elegant words and a great show but wouldn't back up their words. Just as God's holy name is dishonored and used for evil, and just as Christianity, the church, and everything that is holy are misused, so the names of faith, love, and good works will also be used for a false show and mask. For the devil doesn't want to be as dark as he is painted, but he wants to shine in the fine clothes of God's Word, the Christian church, faith, and love.

Christ teaches us that it's not enough to praise faith and Christ, but we also need to produce Christian fruit. For where these fruits aren't evident, or where the opposite appears, Christ is certainly not present. In that case, only a false name exists. That's why we must say to these types of people, "I hear that beautiful and glorious name, which is noble and worthy of honor. But what about you?" Similarly, the evil spirit said to the sons of Sceva, "Jesus I know, and I know about Paul, but who are you?" (Acts 19:15).

But some may object, "Doesn't faith justify and save us without works?" Yes, that's true. But where's your faith? How does it show itself? Faith must never be useless, deaf, dead, or in a state of decay. But it must be a living tree that bursts forth with fruit. That's the difference between genuine faith and false faith. Where there is true faith, it will show itself in a person's life.

STRUGGLING WITH OUR WEAKNESSES

❦

*So Jacob called the place Peniel, saying, "It is because I saw God
face to face, and yet my life was spared."*
Genesis 32:30

Jacob provided the church with a beautiful example of faith
struggling in weakness. This helps us to see that the Hebrew
ancestors and prophets weren't like rocks that showed no signs of
weakness. If that were the case, we would have to despair because
of the weaknesses we feel in ourselves. Our bodies often complain
that we're being treated unfairly. We don't want to suffer and be
mistreated by others. But the example of the Hebrew ancestors
can comfort us because they too were not always firm and strong
in their faith.

Jacob was comforted by showers of blessings from God. He
also received the benefits of the blessings that were given to his
father, Isaac, and grandfather, Abraham. Nevertheless, he struggled with his weaknesses.

You should say to yourself, "I am not alone when I'm afraid of
God's anger, when I wonder if God has chosen me, and when I
worry about losing my faith. I am not alone!" All believers—every
believer past and present who has ever believed in God's Son—
experience the same struggle. God uses these experiences to refine
us. Eventually, like Jacob, you'll be able to stand up and joyfully
proclaim, "I saw God face to face, and yet my life was spared."

SINFUL DESIRES

❧

For the sinful nature desires what is contrary to the Spirit,
and the Spirit what is contrary to the sinful nature. They are
in conflict with each other, so that you do not do what you want.
Galatians 5:17

When I was a monk, I thought that my salvation was immediately lost if I experienced a corrupt desire of the sinful nature—for example, an evil emotion, sexual desire, anger, hatred, or envy toward any brother. I tried many spiritual exercises, such as confessing daily, but I made no headway. The desires of the sinful nature always returned so that I couldn't find rest. I was constantly tormented by thoughts such as these: "You committed this and that sin, and you are guilty of envy, impatience, and more. As a result, you have entered this monastic order in vain, and all your good works are useless." If I had at that time better understood Paul's statements about the sinful nature battling against the Spirit and that "they are in conflict with each other," I would not have tortured myself so much.

I would have thought the way I do today: "Martin, you cannot be completely without sin, because you are still in this body. As a result, you will experience the conflict with the sinful nature. The sinful nature battles against the Spirit, just as Paul teaches. Therefore, don't give up, but fight against it so that you do not gratify these evil desires. Then you will no longer be under the law."

PLACES OF HONOR

*When he noticed how the guests picked the places of honor
at the table, he told them this parable: "When someone invites you to
a wedding feast, do not take the place of honor, for a person
more distinguished than you may have been invited."*
Luke 14:7–8

How can sitting in a place of honor be right and not right? It's not prohibited to sit in a place of honor. In fact, Christ himself says, "When your host comes, he will say to you, 'Friend, move up to a better place.' Then you will be honored in the presence of all your fellow guests" (Luke 14:10). Why does he tell us not to sit in a place of honor but also say that it's appropriate to be seated in an honorable place? The answer is found by noting the word *picked* in the verse: "When he noticed how the guests picked the places of honor . . ."

Some people must sit in higher places and some in lower places. For we cannot set aside a special place, time, or chapel for every person in the congregation. Accordingly, we cannot all be princes, counts, preachers, noblemen, townspeople, men, women, masters, or servants. Each of us has enough to do in our own position. So we should not and cannot all sit at a higher place and at a lower place at the same time. But God has arranged matters so that the person in a higher position should rightly sit higher than the others. A count shouldn't set himself above the prince or a servant set himself over the master. So there must also be distinctions between other positions in life.

It's important that you correctly understand what Christ is saying here. If you are in a higher position or above others in some way, realize that God has given it to you. Don't make the mistake of bragging about it and lording it over others as if you were better than them in God's sight. Rather, God has commanded that you should humble yourself and use your position to serve your neighbor.

AS YOU LOVE YOURSELF

꧁ ❦ ꧂

The entire law is summed up in a single command:
"Love your neighbor as yourself."
Galatians 5:14

This statement is expressed in a beautiful and powerful way: "Love your neighbor as yourself." There is no attitude more outstanding, respected, and virtuous than love. No one can show you a model that is better, more certain, and more real than yourself. There is no better object to whom you can direct your love than your neighbor. So the attitude, model, and object are all superior.

If you want to know how to love your neighbor and want to have a clear example of it, then pay careful attention to how you love yourself. In times of need and danger, you certainly would want to be loved and helped with all of the advice, resources, and power of everyone everywhere. So you don't need a book to teach and admonish you how to love your neighbor. For you have the best and the most lovely book about all laws right in your heart. You don't need a teacher; just consult your own heart. It will thoroughly teach you that your neighbor should be loved the way you love yourself. Further, love is the highest virtue. It's prepared to serve not only with words, hands, money, and possessions, but also with the body and even life itself. It's not motivated by reward or anything else. It's not slowed down by any unworthiness or ungratefulness of a neighbor. We should serve our neighbor out of love, just as a mother cherishes and cares for her child simply out of love.

BITTEN BY SIN

*If we claim we have not sinned, we make him out to be a liar
and his word has no place in our lives.*
1 John 1:10

Not only have we sinned, but we also continue to sin. Because of the weakness of our corrupt, sinful nature, which we will have as long as we have these bodies, there is an ongoing battle between the sinful nature and the Spirit. Paul talks about this: "I know that nothing good lives in me, that is, in my sinful nature. For I have the desire to do what is good, but I cannot carry it out" (Romans 7:18). Certainly it's not just the immoral sexual desire of a man toward a woman or a woman toward a man that is sin. In the legends of the saints, there are also many sins that take on the form and appearance of holiness and are passed off as good conduct. For the church fathers usually looked at outward sins and not at inner ones—such as envy, jealousy, a hostile heart, and slippage from faith and hope.

We still have sin that bites and entices us, but it doesn't rule over us. The sin within us is like a person who is tied up and being led away to his death. The weapons that person might use to harm others have all been taken away. But that person isn't dead yet. Similarly, the sin in our bodies surges up, rages and rants, and doesn't let up. For we always love what is ours and depend on our own strength. We don't put our trust in the Word and don't believe God. Our sinful nature doesn't want it any other way. But the best remedy against the pull of this nature is meditating diligently on God's Word.

UNAFRAID OF DEATH

*For if the dead are not raised, then Christ has not been
raised either. And if Christ has not been raised,
your faith is futile; you are still in your sins.*
1 Corinthians 15:16–17

It has wisely been said, "Those who fear death are fools, for by doing this they lose their own life." This would be a good saying if anyone could do it. Everyone knows that people won't get anywhere by fearing death. They will only ruin their lives and never be happy. We see this with people who are in deep sadness. They wouldn't be comforted or feel joyful even if you wrapped them with golden robes, filled them with the best food and drink, and offered them all kinds of entertainment, even music on stringed instruments. They don't feel alive. They walk around with morbid thoughts of death, and they are practically dead already. So people tell us that the best thing to do is to throw off this fear, force it out of our minds, and say to ourselves, "Why should we worry? When we are dead, we are dead." Just as the Corinthians said, "Let us eat and drink, for tomorrow we die" (1 Corinthians 15:32). However, this is a shortcut because it pretends God's wrath, hell, and damnation don't even exist.

But Christians can't pretend that way. They can't just toss this fear out of a heart that wants to believe. In fact, they only feel this fear even more as their faith struggles to grow. We should comfort them by saying, "Dear friend, if you are continually distressed by living, if you feel poor and miserable, then take care and understand this is happening because you are a Christian. Otherwise, you wouldn't be tormented by this fear of death and hell. But you must guard yourself against this fear and hold firmly to the fact that your Christ has risen from the dead."

THE GREATEST PRAYER

This, then, is how you should pray:
"Our Father in heaven, hallowed be your name."
Matthew 6:9

Because Jesus is the author of the prayer in this passage, it's undoubtedly the greatest and best prayer. For if this good, faithful Teacher had known a better one, he certainly would have taught it to us. This doesn't mean a prayer that doesn't use these exact words is worthless. For prior to Christ's birth, many believers who had never heard these words also prayed. But we should be cautious about other prayers that don't convey the meaning of this prayer. The psalms are good prayers, and they express the same thoughts as the Lord's Prayer but don't express them as clearly.

So it's a mistake to prefer other prayers over this one. Watch out especially for those written out with titles decorated in red ink, in the hope that God will give us health and long life, possessions and honor, indulgences to free us from punishment, and so on. Through these kinds of prayers, we pursue our wills and our honor more than God's will and his honor. Many people have begun regarding these other prayers more highly than the Lord's Prayer. Not that I completely disregard these prayers, but people put too much confidence in them. Subsequently, the true Lord's Prayer, which is inner and spiritual, is despised. All forgiveness, all blessings, all that is useful, and everything else that people need for their bodies and souls on earth and in heaven overflow from this prayer.

It would be better if you prayed one Lord's Prayer—praying it with all your heart, really thinking about the words, and letting it change your life for the better—than for you to recite all other prayers combined.

FORGET ABOUT GOOD WORKS

Listen, O daughter, consider and give ear:
Forget your people and your father's house.
Psalm 45:10

Faith is very fragile and needs to hear the command: "Forget your father's house." Something inside of us strongly compels us to keep trying to earn God's approval. We look for good works, in which we can place our trust and which will bring us praise. We want to show God what we have done and say, "See, I have done this or that. Therefore, you must pronounce me righteous."

None of us should be overconfident when it comes to forgetting our own good works. Each one of us carries in our heart a horrible religious fanatic. We would all like to be able to do something so spectacular that we could brag, "Look what I've done! With all my prayers and good works, I've done enough for God today that I can feel at peace." This happens to me too after I have accomplished something in my ministry. I'm much happier than if I hadn't done it. Being happy isn't wrong in itself. But this joy is impure because it isn't based on faith. It's the kind of happiness that can make your conscience confused. Consciences are delicate. We need to guard them against the sin of arrogance. So we can't be overconfident. We who confess Christ should always walk in fear and grow in faith. We should realize that we all carry in our hearts a horrible religious fanatic, who will destroy our faith with foolish delusions of good works.

The Holy Spirit provides us with a way to counter this godless delusion. We need to hold tightly to what we have received through the grace of God. God's approval doesn't come to us by what we do. Rather, it comes through the holiness of Christ, who suffered for us and rose again from the dead.

BLESSINGS FOLLOW TESTING

*Isaac planted crops in that land and the same year reaped
a hundredfold, because the LORD blessed him. The man became rich,
and his wealth continued to grow until he became very wealthy.*
Genesis 26:12–13

We must learn from Isaac's example to be firm in our faith so that
we don't doubt or waver when hardships come our way. After Isaac
sinned, God lovingly forgave him and even blessed him. We learn
from this that God doesn't remain angry forever. If we rely on his
promises, we can remain faithful when things go wrong and say,
"The Lord who asked me to believe in him will keep his promises.
Meanwhile, I will cling to him and trust him." The Psalms remind
us: "Wait for the LORD; be strong and take heart and wait for the
LORD" (Psalm 27:14). "Be strong and take heart, all you who hope
in the LORD" (Psalm 31:24). Believers can remain confident even
in the worst dangers and hardships because God has promised to
take care of them: "Cast all your anxiety on him because he cares
for you" (1 Peter 5:7).

It's important for believers to be tested by trials. Without
these tests, our faith would grow cold and weak. It could eventually disappear completely. But if we are tested with hardships,
we will discover what faith is and will be strengthened in our
knowledge of Christ. We will become so strong that even when
we have troubles and anxieties, we can be just as happy as we are
in good times. We can look at each hardship as if it were a cloud
or a fog that will soon vanish.

REFUSING GOD'S HELP

This is the verdict: Light has come into the world, but men loved darkness instead of light because their deeds were evil.
John 3:19

To us, God may appear to be angry. He seems to be an unjust, harsh, and stern judge. But God is saying here, "Now then, I will cancel the charges against you. You will no longer have to mourn. To be sure, you have sinned and earned the judgment of God. But your sin will be pardoned. The death penalty will be removed. I will no longer remember the sinfulness of the world—the sin in which people were born and in which they lived. Everything is settled. I will no longer look at your sin. Simply believe in my Son."

What's missing? Why does judgment still hang over us if the Son has removed our sins? This judgment remains because people reject Christ, the Son of God.

Suppose a physician is treating a sick person whom he knows he definitely can help. Suppose he has promised to get rid of his patient's pain. The physician suggests a remedy for his patient's illness or an antidote to counteract the poison his patient has ingested. Suppose further that the sick person knows without a doubt that the physician is capable of helping. In spite of all this, the patient says, "Get out of here. I don't need your advice. You're not a physician. You're a fraud. I'm not sick. I didn't eat any poison. And besides, it probably won't hurt me." Then what if the patient tries to choke and even kill this doctor? Wouldn't you say that person is not only sick but also stark raving mad? The spiritual madness of refusing the help God's Son wants to give us is ten times worse than this.

GOD NEVER SLEEPS

❦

*You know with all your heart and soul that not one of all
the good promises the LORD your God gave you has failed.
Every promise has been fulfilled; not one has failed.*
Joshua 23:14

Christians are wise when they accept what God has planned and
persevere in believing the promises they have from him. His promises are dependable and lasting. The Lord's own pledge is permanent, as we read in the Psalms: "Indeed, he who watches over Israel
will neither slumber nor sleep" (Psalm 121:4).

But human reason responds, "That's all fine and good. It
even sounds nice. But I'm experiencing the exact opposite. God
not only sleeps; he snores! In reality, there isn't a God who takes
care of me or watches over me."

Jacob was certain of God's promises. He knew that God's
pledge was permanent. Yet when Joseph's brothers were angry at
Joseph, God didn't spare either Jacob or his son Joseph. It was as
if they had no protection at all from the holy angels. Nobody
resisted the anger of Joseph's brothers (Genesis 37:12–28). God
and the angels remained dead silent. Even today, they appear to
let the devil wreak havoc on the church and believers. Where is
God in all of this?

Examples like these remind us that we must believe God's
promises and never doubt his words. Because God can't lie, he
won't stop constantly watching over us, especially if we believe his
promise. Because he is faithful, God can't abandon us when we
hang on to what he has promised. God may allow us to be attacked,
led to the edge of hell, or even killed. It's during those times that
we need to remember God has promised to be our guardian—one
who never slumbers or sleeps.

THE SPIRIT OF TRUTH

❧

*I will ask the Father, and he will give you another Counselor
to be with you forever—the Spirit of truth. The world cannot
accept him, because it neither sees him nor knows him. But
you know him, for he lives with you and will be in you.*
John 14:16–17

Christians can depend on nothing except Christ, their Lord and God. For the sake of Christ, they surrender everything and declare, "Before I deny or leave my Christ, I will abandon food and drink, honor and possessions, house and property, spouse and child—everything." A Christian's courage cannot be fake or weak. It must be genuine and certain. For Christians cannot encourage themselves with any temporary thing on this earth. Instead, they cling only to the Lord Jesus Christ, who was crucified and died for us. So Christ will say, as he promises in this passage, "Because you acknowledge me, you have this advantage and this comfort. Your courage won't mislead you, for your Helper is the Spirit of truth." All other courage comes from the spirit of lies—a false spirit that cannot please God. But whatever Christians do, or suffer, for their faith in the Lord Christ is done for the truth. They have done what is proper and right. They can boast truthfully and joyfully that what they have done is pleasing to God and the angels. Christians can feel so confident that they don't have to fear the devil or the world. They don't have to be afraid of any threat or terror.

Let this encourage you, for nothing on earth can comfort you more during times of need than a confident heart. As long as your heart is plagued with uncertainty and doubts, you cannot be courageous. But if you live in truth, you can be sure that any suffering you experience isn't caused by your own sin. You're not suffering because you tried to attain possessions, honor, or praise for yourself. The only charge against you is that you believe in the Lord Christ and trust in his Word.

THE HIDDEN KINGDOM

Then the end will come, when he hands over the kingdom to God the Father after he has destroyed all dominion, authority and power.
1 Corinthians 15:24

Paul says Christ will hand over the kingdom to God the Father. How can that be? Everywhere else the Scripture says he will remain king forever, and his kingdom will never end. But Paul says in this verse that Christ will hand over the kingdom and lay in his Father's lap his crown, scepter, and everything else. How can we resolve this? Here is the answer: in this verse, Paul is speaking about Christ's kingdom on earth. This is a kingdom of faith. Instead of reigning in a visible, public way, he reigns through the Word. To us, it's like looking at the sun through a cloud. We see the light, but we don't see the sun itself. But when the clouds leave, we see both the light and the sun at the same time in the same object. Similarly, Christ now reigns undivided with the Father. It's one and the same kingdom. But to us, it appears dark, hidden, concealed, and covered.

He wants to reign secretly and invisibly in our hearts, by the Word alone. Through the Word, he protects and upholds us in our weakness against the world's might and power. Though the kingdom is now here on earth, it will later be in heaven. It will not be covered and hidden as it appears now. A gold coin remains a gold coin whether I hide it in my pocket or pull it out and hold it in my hand. In the same way, Christ will display before the eyes of the whole world the treasure that is now concealed from us.

WATCH OUT FOR SELFISH AMBITION

Test me, O LORD, and try me, examine my heart and my mind.
Psalm 26:2

In this passage, David is saying, "If the doctrine is pure and nothing is lacking in the Word and preaching, then the heart should also be pure. At the same time, I still feel the evil ways of my sinful nature. I feel a tendency toward pride, lust, hate, and envy. In particular, the subtle poison of selfish ambition is always beneath the surface. Even people who have a good understanding of God's Word often stumble over this sin."

This sin causes all heresies. As the saying goes, "Ambition is the mother of heresies and sects." Some people always want to be special. They're never content being like everyone else. This is how they wander off the path without even realizing it. People must pray every day that God would keep this secret rebel inside of them in check. As Paul says, "Honor one another above yourselves" (Romans 12:10). Here Paul acknowledges that the ego—that old idiot—always wants to be the center of attention. As soon as people learn something and can speak about the Lord Jesus Christ, they want to become special. The ego wants people to tell themselves, "Yes, you can get the job done. You're an educated person. You're a cut above the rest." Like a kitten adorning itself, people like to make themselves look good. But afterward, faith and God's Word are no longer important.

We can't do enough to protect ourselves from this shameful wickedness. Other human vices are so crude that we easily perceive them, but this one sneaks up on us. It disguises itself as honoring God and doing what his Word tells us to do. However, selfish ambition lies hiding like a secret rebel behind it all.

CONTROLLING YOUR THOUGHTS

*In great fear and distress Jacob divided the people who were with him
into two groups, and the flocks and herds and camels as well.*
Genesis 32:7

While Jacob was on his way to be reunited with his brother, Esau,
he was plagued with doubts. He learned that Esau was wealthy
and had a large family. He thought, "What if God has changed
his mind? Maybe God has rejected me in favor of my brother."
These were Jacob's thoughts, but they remained just that—
thoughts. Because of human nature and weak faith, people can't
keep from having these kinds of thoughts any more than they can
avoid other emotions, such as impatience, anger, and lust. You
can't keep thoughts and temptations from coming into your head.
Just don't let these thoughts become fixed in your mind so that
they begin to affect your judgment.

You should follow the advice of a hermit who was approached
by a young man complaining of having lustful thoughts and other
temptations. The old man told him, "You can't stop the birds from
flying over your head. But only let them fly. Don't let them nest
in your hair." It's all right to have these thoughts, but let them
remain just that—thoughts. Don't let them grow to the point
where you have to act on these thoughts.

This was the problem that led to despair in the lives of Cain,
Saul, Judas, and others. They let their thoughts grow and grow
until they were saying, "My punishment is more than I can bear"
(Genesis 4:13), or "I have sinned, . . . for I have betrayed innocent blood" (Matthew 27:4). When they did this, their temptation was turned into a judgment because they rejected the Word
of God, faith, and prayer. But in spite of the many thoughts and
severe temptations that Jacob experienced that night, he didn't
throw his faith away.

SHORT PRAYERS

And when you pray, do not keep on babbling like pagans, for they think
they will be heard because of their many words. Do not be like them,
for your Father knows what you need before you ask him.
Matthew 6:7–8

We should pray with few words but with deep, meaningful
thoughts. The fewer the words, the better the prayer. The more
words, the worse the prayer. Few words and deep meaning are
Christian. Many words and little meaning are pagan. That's why
Christ says, "When you pray, do not keep on babbling like pagans,
for they think they will be heard because of their many words."
Similarly, he says to the Samaritan woman, "His worshipers must
worship in spirit and in truth" (John 4:24). The Father looks for
worshipers who pray this way. To pray in the Spirit, or to pray spiritually, is very different from a prayer that comes from our evil
desires. To pray in truth is very different from a fake prayer.

For the showy prayer that comes from our evil desires is pointless mumbling and babbling. It shows no respect for God. To
those who are watching and listening, it looks like prayer. It may
be spoken with words, but it isn't spoken in truth. The spiritual
and true prayer, however, comes from within. It comes from the
sighing and yearning of the depths of the heart. Unspiritual prayer
produces hypocrites and a false sense of security. Spiritual prayer
produces true believers and reverent children of God.

SAINTS WHO SLIP

[Lot] and his two daughters lived in a cave. One day the older daughter said to the younger, ". . . Let's get our father to drink wine and then lie with him and preserve our family line through our father."
Genesis 19:30–32

Moses recorded this despicable sin in Genesis for a good reason. It was horrible enough for so many people in Sodom and Gomorrah to perish. But for Lot and his daughters to fall into such a sin, after witnessing the destruction of so many people, is even more horrible. This incident was recorded in the Bible to frighten the ungodly and to keep believers from becoming smug.

You might ask, "Why did God permit his people, whom he loved, to sink so low?" We shouldn't question God's motives for what he permits. Still, in this case, we can easily find a probable explanation. God wants us to recognize our helplessness so that we don't lapse into a false sense of security. Lot and his family saw the sins of the people of Sodom and condemned them. But then what happened? Lot's devout daughters disgraced themselves by committing incest. This was so scandalous that it seldom occurred even among the people of Sodom.

So God's intent is clear. He wants us to humble ourselves and to find comfort in his mercy and grace. As far as humans are concerned, no one is better or holier than the next person. Thankfully, God protects us from sinning too seriously. But if he were to withdraw his hand, we might fall into the very same sins. So this story teaches us to humble ourselves in God's presence and continually pray for the Holy Spirit's guidance.

THE GREATEST LOVE

Greater love has no one than this, that he lay down his life for his friends.
You are my friends if you do what I command.
John 15:13–14

Christ uses friendly and kind words in this passage to convince his disciples of the importance of the command he was giving to them. He reminds them of his own example of how he loved them and of all that he had done for them. It would take a great and powerful love for someone to give another person in need one hundred dollars, one thousand dollars, or even to pay off that person's entire debt. But think how amazing it would be for a king to give a poor beggar an entire city—even his own kingdom, land, and people. The entire world would hold this up as an unprecedented act of love. But that would be trivial compared to Christ giving his body and life for you. This is certainly the highest expression of love a person can show to another on this earth. People can love and serve others with their money, their property, and even their lives. But everyone would rather give up their money and property, their land and people, than die for someone else. Even if someone did that, it still would be nothing compared to God sending his Son from heaven. It would be nothing compared to God's Son taking your place, willingly shedding his blood and dying for you, even though you were his enemy and were condemned. This love is greater and higher than heaven and earth and anything else you could name.

What will you do for Christ in return? Even if you gave your life for your neighbor, what is that compared to his life? But Christ doesn't even ask that much of you, except in emergencies, of course, when you should risk your life to save others. Christ simply asks you to show love to your neighbor in a tangible way.

WHY OUR PLANS FAIL

❧

The LORD foils the plans of the nations;
he thwarts the purposes of the peoples.
Psalm 33:10

We must do what God wants and stop thinking and worrying about what God hasn't told us to do. Nothing is safer for us or more pleasing to God than when we trust in God's Word instead of our own ideas. In his Word, we will find enough guidance about what we are to do. God requires us to have faith, to love, and to endure suffering. These three should be enough to keep us delightfully busy. We should deal with everything else as it comes along and let God worry about how it all turns out. If we don't want to listen to what God says in his Word, he punishes us by simply letting us torment ourselves for no good reason.

When wise men and princes ignore God's Word, God doesn't let any of their intentions happen, whether good or bad. This psalm says, "The LORD foils the plans of the nations." God will always thwart the plans of those who work the hardest by using their own wisdom. But even this doesn't convince us to subject our plans to what God wants. So our plans and ideas only distress and torment us, even though these are not bad in themselves. As Jesus said, "Each day has enough trouble of its own" (Matthew 6:34). God doesn't send this trouble to destroy us. Rather, he sends it to us to persuade us to give up our foolish ideas and plans. He wants to show us that our wisdom is worthless. Ultimately, our wisdom isn't what makes things happen; only the will of God does that. So we must learn to pray, "Let your will be done."

FLOATING ON GOD'S PROMISE

Then God blessed Noah and his sons, saying to them,
"Be fruitful and increase in number and fill the earth."
Genesis 9:1

The terror of God's anger had come to an end. The earth itself had been ruined, and all life had been destroyed. Now the blessing God promised to Noah and his sons was about to begin. They were going to restart the human race. No doubt they had fears as they waited for this to be accomplished. Living solely by faith is a difficult way of life. Noah and his family lived this way, with their eyes fixed on heaven. The world was covered with water. There was no dry ground to walk on. God's words were their only support as they floated on top of the water.

When people aren't in physical danger, they consider faith something insignificant. But look at Noah. He was surrounded by water—nearly swallowed by the flood. He was saved, not through his own efforts, but through relying on God's mercy. He had confidence because he trusted what God had said.

The words "God remembered" in Genesis 8:1 indicate just how difficult Noah's situation was. Moses points out that Noah drifted aimlessly on the water for so long that he felt as if God had forgotten him. Some people struggle with similar thoughts, feeling that they are living in darkness and without God's favor. People who feel that God has forgotten them soon find that living by God's Word alone—living by faith—is more difficult than practicing a lifestyle of rigorous spiritual discipline.

PRUNING THE BRANCHES

He cuts off every branch in me that bears no fruit, while every branch that does bear fruit he prunes so that it will be even more fruitful.
John 15:2

Christ says his Father is the gardener, who tends and looks after his vine. God separates the wild branches from the others so that they won't spread and spoil the true vine. God singles them out to protect the true vine. He determines which ones should be cut off and tossed into the fire.

But it all appears very different to us. We see these wild branches growing and spreading. They are much stronger and thicker than the others. They look like the only true ones that will produce fruit. In contrast, we appear small, puny, and unfruitful. Yes, people want to root us out and cut us off as useless and unfit. But the false vines appear as if they will remain forever, and the entire world respects them highly.

We need spiritual understanding and vision. No matter how many scoundrels rise up against Christians, God always cuts them off and preserves a remnant of believers. From the time of the apostles until now, many heresies have challenged the teachings of Christ, of baptism, of the Lord's Supper, of justification by faith, and so on. These heresies are so pervasive that it appears they are correct teachings and the Christian church might pass away. But God has cut off all of these wild branches and preserved his true branches, so that we nevertheless hold on to right teaching, baptism, and the Lord's Supper as the apostles gave them to us. Beginning with Abel, faith has pushed forward throughout the world and will prevail as long as there are believers. Not one of them will be cut off the vine. All will remain there. So we must not look at how large and strong these wild branches are. Instead, we should look for the true branches in Christ.

THE ART OF FAITH

*Before this faith came, we were held prisoners by the law,
locked up until faith should be revealed.*
Galatians 3:23

Grace is present when your heart is restored by the promise of God's free mercy. Then your heart can say with the author of Psalm 42, "O my soul, why are you so troubled and restless? Do you see only the law, sin, terror, sadness, despair, death, hell, and the devil? Aren't grace, forgiveness of sins, righteousness, comfort, joy, peace, life, heaven, Christ, and God also present? Stop being troubled, my soul. What are the law, sin, and everything evil compared to them? Trust God. He didn't spare his own Son but offered him up to death on a cross for your sins."

So when you are frightened by the law, you can say, "Lady Law, you are not the only thing, and you are not everything. Besides you there is something even greater and better, specifically, grace, faith, and blessing. They don't accuse, frighten, or condemn me. They comfort me, tell me to expect the best, and assure me of my certain victory and salvation in Christ. So there's no reason for me to despair."

Whoever truly understands this can be called a theologian. Certain leaders who are always boasting about the Spirit believe that they understand living by faith extremely well. I, however, and others like me know that we scarcely possess the fundamentals. We are diligent students in the school where the art of faith is taught. No matter how well it's taught, as long as we remain in these sinful bodies, we will never finish learning.

DON'T PUT IT OFF

When they got up the next morning, [Eleazar] said, "Send me on my way to my master. . . . Do not detain me, now that the LORD has granted success to my journey. Send me on my way so I may go to my master."
Genesis 24:54–56

This Scripture passage provides a good example for us. Isaac's servant was eager to take his master's future bride to her groom. We are reminded here that when it comes to doing God's work, we shouldn't keep stalling and procrastinating. We should clear away all the obstacles that keep us from completing what we are supposed to do.

Even non-Christian writers say that after adequately thinking over a matter, people should follow through with their intentions quickly and bring it to pass without delay. Sallust, the Roman statesman and historian, gave this advice: "After thinking it over, act quickly!" Bonaventure also made an excellent statement about this subject: "Those who pass up great opportunities will be passed over themselves." But worse than all of this is when people postpone doing what God demands.

Procrastination results in serious harm. Those who don't answer quickly when the Holy Spirit calls will miss their chance. The Holy Spirit seldom asks more than once. I've learned this from personal experience. Whenever it was necessary to pray, read, or take Holy Communion, the longer I put it off, the less I felt the need to do it. The Holy Spirit doesn't give his gifts to those who procrastinate. He prefers those who willingly obey and gladly carry out God's commands without delay. We see this eager attitude in Psalm 119:60: "I will hasten and not delay to obey your commands." The Holy Spirit approved of this same eagerness in Rebekah when she quickly gave Eleazar a drink of water and ran to tell her family about Eleazar's visit. Examples like these from the lives of God's servants should inspire us to resist the foolishness of procrastination.

A NEW AND DIFFERENT PERSON

You should not be surprised at my saying, "You must be born again."
John 3:7

This new birth shows itself most clearly when trials and death draw near. Then it becomes clear whether or not a person has experienced the new birth. At that time, human reason—the old light—twists and wrestles, refusing to let go of its own thinking. It doesn't want to give up and turn to the gospel. Reason simply won't let go of its own light. But those who are born anew, or who are being born anew, surrender and follow God. They give up their old light, life, possessions, honor, and whatever else they have. They trust what John records in his gospel and cling to it. As true children of God, they will receive their eternal inheritance.

If your old, arrogant light of reason grows dark, becomes dead, and is replaced by a new light, then your entire life will be transformed. For when your reason is changed, your will follows soon after. And when your will is changed, what you love and desire changes as well. In order to become new, you must crawl into the gospel with your whole self. You must shed off the old skin, as a snake does. When its skin becomes old, a snake looks for a narrow hole in the rock. It crawls through it and sheds its skin, leaving it outside in front of the hole. Similarly, you also must go into the gospel and God's Word. You must confidently believe its promise that God does not lie. So you shed off your old skin, leaving behind your old light, arrogance, will, love, desires, and what you say and do. You become a new and different person who views everything differently than before.

ONE MIND AND HEART

Finally, all of you, live in harmony with one another; be sympathetic,
love as brothers, be compassionate and humble.
1 Peter 3:8

We should strive to live in harmony with each other. Both Peter and Paul emphasize that we all should be of one heart, one spirit, and one mind. What seems right and good to one person should be regarded with consideration by others also. This is a powerful teaching that we should strive to understand.

All of us cannot do the same work. Each one of us must pursue our own work. It's foolish to teach that we all should do one kind of work, as some preachers have taught. They preach about the legends of saints—that this saint has done one work, another a different one. Then they conclude we also should do these works. Undoubtedly, Abraham did a precious work when he offered his son, because it was specifically commanded by God. But then the pagans wanted to sacrifice their children too. That was an outrage to God. Similarly, King Solomon did well when he built the temple, and God rewarded him for it. Now these blind fools come along and tell us to build churches and temples when God has commanded nothing of the sort. So it's reversed today: they say we all should do one work, but there are various opinions about which one. This teaching is directly against the gospel.

So we must teach that there should be one mind and many works, one heart and many hands. We all shouldn't try to do the same work. Rather, each of us should pay attention to our own responsibilities. Otherwise, we cannot be of one mind and one heart. We must allow the works to be varied so that each of us can remain with what God has entrusted to us. We should simply do the work at hand.

CAREFUL OBEDIENCE

꧁ ꧂

Then he reached out his hand and took the knife to slay his son.
But the angel of the LORD called out to him from heaven,
"Abraham! Abraham!" "Here I am," he replied.
Genesis 22:10–11

An angel from heaven was an eyewitness to what Abraham was doing. Yes, God himself and all the angels were watching. The angel didn't come flying in at the last moment from a distant corner of the world. Instead, he was watching over Abraham and Isaac all along. He observed as Abraham tied up his son and raised the knife. The son willingly obeyed and waited for the deadly thrust. Tears undoubtedly were streaming down Abraham's cheeks, and Isaac was lying on his back looking up toward heaven. All the while, the angel was watching. Right when Abraham was raising the knife, the angel shouted to him and called him by name.

How closely the holy angels gather around those of us who follow God and live faithfully! Obedience like Abraham's gives God immense pleasure. Of all the sacrifices we can make, the one most acceptable to God is this: getting rid of sin, living a holy life, obeying God, and killing our sinful nature. This is very painful and unpleasant for us to do. Still, we must get used to God's "good, pleasing and perfect will" (Romans 12:2).

We merely talk about these matters, but Abraham and Isaac actually lived them out. They did what God wanted. In comparison, we haven't even begun to do this. Careful obedience pleases God, but it's unpleasant and distasteful to us. Nothing is more agonizing than getting rid of sin and killing our sinful nature. Still, we must get used to obeying God and start following Abraham's example. Abraham didn't try to get out of what he had to do. Instead, he looked forward to pleasing God with eager anticipation.

SERVING GOD OR MONEY

·⊱✦⊰·

No one can serve two masters. Either he will hate the one and
love the other, or he will be devoted to the one and despise
the other. You cannot serve both God and Money.
Matthew 6:24

The little word *serve* is key to this verse. It isn't sinful to have
money and property, a spouse and children, and a house or home.
But don't let these possessions control you. Rather, make them
your servants and be their master.

Remember what people say about kind and generous individuals: "They are masters of their money." Money doesn't control them, unlike a greedy miser who ignores God's Word and
everything else God wants. A miser would rather withhold a helping hand than let go of money. This kind of greed is the mark of
tightfisted, childish, and insensitive individuals. That type of person doesn't put resources to good use or even enjoy them. They
ignore eternal treasures for the sake of money. They pursue their
own selfish goals and neglect God's Word, thinking they can get
around to it at a more convenient time. Meanwhile, they scram-
ble to get everything they can, without a penny to spare for the
work of God. If left unchecked, they will sink deeper and deeper
into greed and jealousy, moving further and further away from
God's Word. Eventually their hearts will be filled with cynicism,
and they will become enemies of God.

So Christ spoke sternly when he said, "Either he will hate the
one and love the other, or he will be devoted to the one and despise
the other." This is the same as saying, "The love of money makes
people enemies of God." That's ultimately what happens when we
serve wealth. Christ also said, "For where your treasure is, there
your heart will be also" (Matthew 6:21). We pursue what we love.
We talk about it because that is where our hearts and thoughts are.
Augustine came right to the point when he said: "Whatever I love
is my god."

A ROARING LION

*Be self-controlled and alert. Your enemy the devil prowls around
like a roaring lion looking for someone to devour.*
1 Peter 5:8

Peter gives us a warning and wants us to open our eyes. This is a
verse worth writing in gold letters. Here you see what life is really
like. It's almost enough to make us wish we were dead. We're living here on the devil's turf. Our situation is similar to travelers
who stay at an inn where they find out that everyone in the place
is a robber. If they had to stay there, they would arm themselves
in the best possible way and probably wouldn't get much sleep.
In the same way, we now live on this earth, where the evil spirit
is the prince. He controls the hearts of the people under his
power, and he does whatever he wants through them. This is a
horrible situation if viewed correctly.

So Peter warns us to be alert. He wants us to be like faithful
servants who are aware of what is really happening. Therefore, he
says, "Be self-controlled." For those who eat and drink too much
are like stuffed pigs that are good for nothing. Therefore, we must
keep this treasure with us at all times. "Be alert," he says, not only
spiritually, but physically. For lazy people who like to sleep won't
be able to resist the devil after they have gorged themselves and
drunk their fill. After all, it's hard enough for those who have faith
and the Spirit to resist the devil.

DOWN FROM THE MOUNTAIN

Then Abraham returned to his servants, and they set off together for Beersheba. And Abraham stayed in Beersheba.
Genesis 22:19

Abraham left Mount Moriah. This was the mountain where he had been asked to sacrifice Isaac—where he had heard the voice of the angel and experienced God's presence. This place was a holy mountain—a place unlike any other in the whole world. It was where Abraham had received God's promise and pledge.

This story shows how highly Abraham regarded his duty toward his family and his God-given responsibilities as head of the household. Since God gave him no further commands, he didn't start doing anything differently after this experience. Instead, he returned to his familiar household activities—overseeing his servants and guiding his wife and family. His life didn't appear to be especially religious or spiritual. Abraham left all that on Mount Moriah. He didn't even let the fact that he had seen angels on the mountain hold him there. He went back to the young men watching his donkey.

If certain overly religious people were to comment on this passage, they would question Abraham's piety and condemn him for leaving the mountain. They would think that if Abraham really were such an outstanding example for later generations, then he wouldn't have left that holy place. After all, that is where Abraham had met God and his angels. How could he return to his donkey and go back to his everyday work? What kind of piety is that? It's remarkable how much certain religious people despise honest work and everyday chores.

THE UNFORESEEABLE FUTURE

*In him we were also chosen, having been predestined according to
the plan of him who works out everything in conformity
with the purpose of his will.*
Ephesians 1:11

Beware of the philosophy that leads people to say, "What can I do? What's the use of praying? What good is it to worry? If it's predestined, it must happen." Yes, it's true that what is predestined will happen. However, we aren't commanded to know what is predestined. In fact, we are forbidden to know it. We test God when we delve into unknowable matters. God has given Scripture to us so that we can know what we should and shouldn't do. He expects us to act on this knowledge. What we cannot know, we should leave to God. We should stick to our responsibilities, vocation, and position in life. God and God alone knows what is predestined. You aren't supposed to know.

Take for example the time when Joab was being attacked both in front and from behind by his enemies. He didn't say to his brother Abishai, "Wait, let's see what is predestined, and then we will act accordingly." Rather, he said, "If the Arameans are too strong for me, then you are to come to my rescue; but if the Ammonites are too strong for you, then I will come to rescue you. Be strong and let us fight bravely for our people and the cities of our God. The LORD will do what is good in his sight" (2 Samuel 10:11–12).

So we also should concentrate on our duties, whether or not something is predestined. Because we have no word or light from God on that matter, we don't know anything about it. Therefore, we should put the thought of trying to find out whether or not something is predestined out of our mind and heart. Let the future remain in darkness. Let it stay secret and hidden. In the meantime, we should do what we know we ought to. We should live by God's Word and the light he has given to us.

GOD WORKS IN SECRET

So when the Midianite merchants came by, his brothers pulled Joseph
up out of the cistern and sold him for twenty shekels of silver
to the Ishmaelites, who took him to Egypt.
Genesis 37:28

God humbles his people before he elevates them. He kills them in order to bring them back to life. He devastates them before honoring them. He knocks them down in order to pick them up. God's methods show the highest artistry and wisdom. We cannot understand how events like these are a part of God's plan until we see his plan completed. When these events are happening, they can't be understood, except through faith alone.

In the same way, faith in the Son of God will comfort me when I leave this earth. Even so, my body will be buried in the ground and eaten by worms; it will rot and decay (Job 17:14). I don't see God's plan for me when I look at death. Yet God has promised that I will come back to life. Christ said, "Because I live, you also will live" (John 14:19). But how will I live? I will live in eternal life, in a body that is brighter and more beautiful than the sun. I can't see or feel any of this yet. But I believe it, and I can tolerate the short delay. Eternal life is already prepared. As Paul says, "Now there is in store for me the crown of righteousness, which the Lord, the righteous Judge, will award to me on that day" (2 Timothy 4:8).

But God does everything in secret. We have to be patient while God hides his intentions from us. Jacob and Joseph couldn't see the future prize. But with the sale of Joseph to the Ishmaelites, the future was being prepared. God sees everything as if it has all taken place already. Everything he wants to happen will certainly happen!

THE OPPORTUNITIES AT HAND

Be very careful, then, how you live—not as unwise but as wise,
making the most of every opportunity, because the days are evil.
Therefore do not be foolish, but understand what the Lord's will is.
Ephesians 5:15–17

We aren't supposed to question if God in his unchangeable wisdom is willing to help us and give us what we need. Instead, we should say with conviction, "I believe that God will take care of me, but I don't know his plan. I don't know exactly how he's going to fulfill his promise."

So we must take advantage of the opportunities we have at hand. We have to earn our money through hard work and diligence. In order to stay alive, we have to have milk, food, clothes, and so on. This means we have to cultivate the fields and harvest the crops. Providing for ourselves is a God-given responsibility. We can't use God's promise to take care of us as an excuse for not working diligently. That would be wrong. God doesn't want us to be lazy and idle. He tells us in Genesis, "By the sweat of your brow you will eat your food until you return to the ground, since from it you were taken" (Genesis 3:19). He also says of the ground, "It will produce thorns and thistles for you" (v. 18).

The Lord is saying, "I promise that I will take care of you and give you food. But to the best of your ability, I want you to take advantage of the opportunities I have made available to you. Otherwise, you will be testing me. However, if you are in need and have nothing available to you, at that time I will take care of you and give you food in a miraculous way. But keep this in mind: if any opportunities are available to you, don't forget that I am the one who gave them to you so that you would be able to take care of yourselves."

FIGHTING EVIL DESIRES

But if you are led by the Spirit, you are not under law.
Galatians 5:18

When we are fiercely attacked by anger, hatred, impatience, sexual desire, sorrow, or desires of the sinful nature, we cannot get rid ourselves of these desires no matter how much we would like. What should we do? Should we despair? No. We ought to say, "My sinful nature fights and rages now against the Spirit. Let it rage as long as it wants to. I won't give in to it. But I will live by the Spirit and be led by him so that I won't gratify the desires of the sinful nature. If I do this, I am free from the law. It will accuse and frighten me but does so in vain."

When you are suffering temptation, you should not be upset that the devil can exaggerate sin. At the time, he may make your sins appear so large that you fear you will be immediately and totally overcome, so that you feel nothing but the wrath of God and despair. At that moment, don't follow your feelings, but hold on to the words of Paul: "If you are led by the Spirit"—that is, if you encourage yourself through faith in Christ—"you are not under law." Then you will have the most powerful defense with which to extinguish all the flaming arrows that the devil shoots at you (Ephesians 6:16). All the agitation and raging of the sinful nature cannot hurt or condemn you, because you follow the Spirit and don't give in to the sinful nature or gratify its desires. Therefore, this is the only remedy. When we feel the stirrings of the sinful nature raging in us, we ought to grasp the sword of the Spirit—that is, the word of salvation. Then we will undoubtedly be victors, though we will feel the total opposite as long as the battle lasts.

TRUSTING GOD IN DIFFICULT TIMES

But while Joseph was there in the prison,
the LORD was with him; he showed him kindness and
granted him favor in the eyes of the prison warden.
Genesis 39:20–21

The story of the suffering that Joseph experienced when he was sold into slavery can comfort us. He suffered horribly, but God appeared unable to hear or speak. It didn't look like God knew what was happening. In spite of this, Joseph kept his faith. God encouraged Joseph and spoke to his heart: "Dear Joseph, wait. Be patient. Just believe and don't despair. Hang on to the promise you heard from your father." In this way, God talked to Joseph through the words of his father. But Joseph didn't really see or hear anything. This made God appear to be blind or dead. Yet Joseph believed the promise God gave to Joseph's ancestors. He thought, "God promised to be with Abraham's descendants. I believe in the God of my ancestors." Later God would speak in a wonderful way when he made Joseph a ruler and rescuer in Egypt.

We were given these examples so that we would learn to have patience in suffering. Then we will never complain about God, no matter how horrible the grief, fear, or pain may be. Surely Joseph also experienced deep pain and depression when he was unjustly torn from his father and sold to strangers. He realized he would be a slave forever with no hope of owning anything or ever regaining his freedom.

Because our Lord lets such awful things happen to his children, we must patiently bear the bad things that happen to us. They aren't signs that God has abandoned us or is angry with us. Rather, they prove we have his favor. They show us that he's testing our faith.

FOLLOWING CHRIST'S STEPS

To this you were called, because Christ suffered for you,
leaving you an example, that you should follow in his steps.
1 Peter 2:21

As God's servants, we should impress on our hearts that we should be ready and willing to suffer what comes our way because Christ did so much for us. We should think along these lines: "Though completely innocent, my Lord served me and gave his life for me. Why should I refuse to serve him in return? He was entirely pure and without sin. Yet he humbled himself, shed his blood, and died, wiping out my sin. Shouldn't I also suffer a little bit if this pleases him?" Whoever thinks about Christ's death without feeling moved must be made out of stone. For if a master walks ahead and steps in the mud, it's only reasonable for his servant to follow him through the mud.

So Peter says, "To this you were called." To what? To endure suffering as Christ did. Peter is saying, "If you wish to follow Christ, you must not argue and complain very much when you are wronged. You must endure it and even forgive it." Remember that Christ suffered everything for you, even though he was completely innocent. He didn't appeal to justice when he stood before his judges. In the same way, you should set justice aside and say to yourself, "Thank you, God. I'm called to endure injustice. Why should I complain when my Lord didn't complain?"

ONLY ONE GOSPEL

*There is one body and one Spirit—just as you were called to one hope
when you were called—one Lord, one faith, one baptism; one God
and Father of all, who is over all and through all and in all.*
Ephesians 4:4–6

All of the apostles taught one message. So we must be careful
when we talk about four evangelists and four Gospels. Everything
the apostles wrote is one gospel. The word *gospel* means nothing
other than an announcement about God's grace earned and purchased through Christ by his death. Actually, the gospel is not
what we read in books and what is written with letters. Instead,
it's a living word, a voice that rings throughout the whole world.
It is publicly proclaimed and heard everywhere. The gospel also
is not a law book that contains many good teachings, as has been
thought in the past. It doesn't tell us to do good works to become
virtuous but announces God's grace to us, given freely and without our merit. It tells us how Christ stood as our representative.
He paid for our sins and wiped them out so that we can become
faithful and blessed through his work.

Whoever preaches or writes about this teaches the true gospel
as all apostles have, most notably as Paul and Peter did in their letters. Although preachers teach in different ways and choose different words, they preach only one gospel. It may be a shorter or
longer account. It may be presented briefly or more extensively.
But if the preachers teach us that Christ is our Savior, that we are
justified by faith in him without works, then it's the same word.
There is only one gospel, just as there is only one faith and one
baptism.

GOD'S LAWS POINT THE WAY

For the law was given through Moses;
grace and truth came through Jesus Christ.
John 1:17

The laws given through Moses are God's laws. God's laws and the Ten Commandments point you in the right direction. They show you how to live. They tell you about righteousness and eternal life. God's laws are like sermons that point you to life. You must remember these instructions, but they won't give you life.

God's laws are like a finger that points to the right road. Fingers are a useful part of the body. However, if you don't also have feet to take you there, a wagon to ride in, or even a horse to ride on, you'll never be able to get to the right road. A finger can point you in the right direction, but it can't get you there. In a similar way, God's laws tell you what God wants done and how he wants things to be done. They show you that you are unable to obey them. God's laws show you what human nature is really like— what it can do and what it can't do. God's laws were given to you in order to reveal your sins, but they don't have the power to free you from sin or help you get rid of it. God's laws hold a mirror in front of you. When you look at God's laws, you become aware that you don't have life or God's approval. What you see in the mirror forces you to cry out, "Come, Lord Jesus Christ, help me and give me your grace so that I can do what your laws demand!"

SARAH'S FAITHFUL EXAMPLE

They were submissive to their own husbands, like Sarah,
who obeyed Abraham and called him her master.
1 Peter 3:5–6

Abraham obeyed God, who had called him to leave everything and wander in a new country. Yet he didn't flaunt the fact that he was giving up everything he had. And later when God blessed him, he still had to put up with being attacked and raided by unbelievers all the time. His wife, Sarah, voluntarily followed him into this life of hardship. She managed the household and the servants. Yet she was always helpful to neighbors and obedient to her husband.

Duty, obedience, and helpfulness are the highest virtues. But sadly, not everyone practices them. So treasure God's commands and give them preference over all human rules, no matter how noble these rules appear. These rules water down faith in the same way a greedy bartender might dilute wine with water.

We must pay close attention to the biblical story of Sarah. Sarah is praised for her dedication to duty—diligently taking care of her household. For if a woman desires to serve God and please him, she shouldn't neglect her home, spending all of her time at church, fasting constantly, or praying the same prayers over and over. Rather, she should take care of her home and family, raising and teaching the children, preparing meals, and doing whatever else needs to be done. If she does all of this, believes in the Son of God, and lives in the hope that God approves of her through Jesus Christ, then she is truly blessed.

TRUSTING OR TESTING GOD

❧

When Jacob learned that there was grain in Egypt, he said to his sons,
"Why do you just keep looking at each other?" He continued,
"I have heard that there is grain in Egypt. Go down there
and buy some for us, so that we may live and not die."
Genesis 42:1–2

Why did Jacob tell his sons, "Go down there and buy some for us, so that we may live and not die"? Why didn't he trust God's promise to protect and take care of him? Why was Jacob afraid of dying when, up to now, he had experienced God's help and guidance throughout his life? God had protected him, his entire family, and all his servants in the foreign country of Canaan. Why did he stop trusting God's promise when it was still fresh in his mind? He had always taught his children about God's promise. Where is your faith now, Jacob? Where is the promise?

Here is how I reply to these questions: God orders us to believe and trust in his goodness, but at the same time, we should never test him. We must take advantage of opportunities that God gives us. If we don't, we aren't living according to his plan. But we must continue to maintain our faith and hope in God. That's why Jacob didn't say, "Stay here and wait. The Lord is powerful enough to make food fall right out of the sky. Maybe that's the way he will choose to feed us." No, that's not what God's promise means.

There's no doubt that God can take care of you in a miraculous way. But you must not pass up opportunities that could provide the help you need. If you don't use what is readily available to you, then you are testing God. Jacob was careful not to test God. He didn't sit idly at home, hoping to get food some other way. He sent his sons to Egypt to buy grain, saying, "What are you waiting for? Food isn't going to rain down from the clouds. Go! Believe in God and do what you can."

LOOKING BACK ON LIFE

In his heart a man plans his course, but the LORD determines his steps.
Proverbs 16:9

We see the hand of God working in our lives no more clearly than when we reflect back on the years of our lives. Augustine said that if people had a choice of either dying or reliving their lives over again, they would certainly choose death because of all the danger and evil they so narrowly escaped. In one sense, this statement is certainly true.

Looking back, people can see how much they have accomplished and suffered without trying or thinking about it, even against their wishes and wills. They gave such little thought to what they were doing before it occurred or when it was happening. Now, after everything has been carried out, they are amazed and say, "Why did these things happen to me when I never thought about them or thought something completely different would happen?" So Proverbs 16:9 is true: "In his heart a man plans his course, but the LORD determines his steps," even against his plan and will. So we must agree that our own cleverness and foresight don't guide our lives and actions. Instead, God's wonderful power, wisdom, and goodness guide us. Only as we look back do we fully recognize how often God was with us when we neither saw his hand nor felt his presence at the time it was happening. Accordingly, Peter said, "He cares for you" (1 Peter 5:7).

Even if there were no books or sermons to tell us about God, simply looking back on our own lives would prove that he tenderly carries us in his arms. When we look back on how God has led and brought us through so much evil, adversity, and danger, we can clearly see the ever-present goodness of God, which is far above our thoughts, minds, and perception.

EVERYONE EXPERIENCES SUFFERING

It is better, if it is God's will, to suffer for doing good than for doing evil.
1 Peter 3:17

If you think believers will have only good days on earth, while unbelievers don't get to have any—well, it doesn't work that way. Everyone experiences suffering. God said to Adam, "By the sweat of your brow you will eat your food" (Genesis 3:19), and to Eve, "With pain you will give birth to children" (Genesis 3:16). Since that time, everyone has shared in that tragic condition. This makes it all the more necessary for those seeking eternal life to bear the cross. Peter teaches us, "It is better, if it is God's will, to suffer for doing good." Those who suffer for doing wrong also have guilty consciences. So they have a double punishment. But Christians have only half of this. Though they experience suffering outwardly, they are inwardly comforted.

Notice too that Peter has set a boundary for our suffering when he says, "For a little while you may have had to suffer grief in all kinds of trials" (1 Peter 1:6). In other words, God doesn't want us to look for misfortune and choose it for ourselves. So move ahead in faith and love. If the cross comes your way, accept it. If it doesn't come, don't search for it. We should take care of our bodies in such a way that we neither become self-indulgent nor destroy them (Romans 13:13–14). We should suffer willingly when someone else inflicts suffering on us, but we shouldn't bring it on ourselves. This is what it means when Peter says, "If it is God's will . . ." If God sends suffering to us, it's better than if he didn't. We are happier and better off if we suffer for doing good.

DEEP SIGHS AND FEW WORDS

Then Jacob prayed, ". . . I am unworthy of all the kindness and faithfulness you have shown your servant. . . . Save me, I pray, from the hand of my brother Esau, for I am afraid he will come and attack me, and also the mothers with their children."
Genesis 32:9–11

When we pray, we shouldn't "keep on babbling like pagans, for they think they will be heard because of their many words" (Matthew 6:7). People who blather on when they pray aren't thinking about God's promises and commands regarding prayer or even the help they so desperately need. This isn't true prayer. I used to pray this way when I was a monk. I called out to God in times of need, but I didn't know anything about God's promise to hear me or about his command to pray. I was only mumbling words.

Real prayer, on the other hand, comes from deep down. Like Jacob's prayer in this passage, real prayer comes from a heart full of faith that realizes both the need to pray and God's command to pray. Both of these truths should inspire you to pray and to think carefully about the words being prayed. But some people routinely mumble their prayers while their thoughts are far away. They're not really praying, for they don't even know what they're saying.

A real prayer doesn't require a lot of words. Instead, it often involves long, deep sighs, without any words at all. Jacob's prayer probably wasn't limited to the words recorded by Moses here. Most likely, Jacob sighed all day and all night. Judging from this passage, his prayer must have been very long, with few words.

Though we should use few words in prayer, we shouldn't neglect to be thankful for how God has blessed us in the past. Remembering past examples of God's love and faithfulness kindles our faith and pleases God. Jacob showed his gratitude to God when he prayed, "I am unworthy of all the kindness and faithfulness you have shown your servant."

MADE ALIVE THROUGH CHRIST

For as in Adam all die, so in Christ all will be made alive.
1 Corinthians 15:22

Paul is speaking here only about Christians. He wants to teach and comfort them about being made alive in Christ. Although non-Christians also will rise from the dead, their resurrection will not be a comfort or a joy to them, because they will be raised to judgment, not to life. This is not a comforting or happy message to the world. Godless people don't want to hear about this. This is the way I felt when I wanted to be a holy monk and tried to be pious. I would rather have heard about all the devils in hell than about judgment day. The hair on my head stood on end when I thought about it. The whole world hates to think about leaving this life. They don't want to die, and they are terrified when we speak of death and the afterlife. Aside from that, all of us are stuck in the muck of our own holiness and think that by our lives and works we can pacify God's judgment and earn a place in heaven. All we accomplish by this is that we become even worse and grow more hostile toward judgment day.

I won't say anything about the large group of people who look for all their pleasure and comfort here in this life, despise God's Word, and won't give a penny for God and his kingdom. It's no surprise if such people are aggravated by hearing about the resurrection. But to us, this message is pure comfort and joy, because we hear that our greatest treasure is already in heaven. Only a small part remains on earth, which Christ will resurrect and draw to himself as easily as a person awakening from sleep.

April 5

PRESERVING PURITY

꧁ ◦ ꧂

It is God's will that you should be sanctified: that you should avoid sexual immorality; that each of you should learn to control his own body in a way that is holy and honorable, not in passionate lust like the heathen, who do not know God.
1 Thessalonians 4:3–5

All young people should avoid casual sex and preserve their purity. They should resolve to strengthen themselves against lust and sexual passions by reading and meditating on a psalm or some other portion of God's Word. When the flames of passion plague you and sexual arousal reaches unmanageable proportions, go to a psalm or any other chapter or two in the Bible and read. After the flames of passion die down, devote yourself to serious prayer.

If your sexual appetites continually tempt you, be patient. Resist them as long as necessary, even if it takes more than a year. But above all, keep praying! If you feel that you can't stand it any longer, pray that God will give you a devout spouse with whom you can live in harmony and true love.

I have known many people who, because of their crude and shameful fantasies, indulged their passions with unrestrained lust. Because of their insatiable desires, they abandoned self-control and lapsed into terrible immorality. In the end, they had to endure dreadful punishment. Blinded to the realities of married life, some of them took unsuitable mates and ended up in incompatible relationships. They got what they deserved.

You must pray diligently and strive to resist the desires of your sinful nature. Ask God to give you a Rebekah or Isaac instead of a Delilah or Samson—or someone even worse. Finding a devoted, loyal wife or husband isn't a matter of good luck. It's not the result of good judgment, as unbelievers think. Rather, a devout spouse is a gift from God.

A NEW CREATION

Neither circumcision nor uncircumcision means anything;
what counts is a new creation.
Galatians 6:15

A change in clothing or other externals doesn't make a new creation, as some imagine. It happens through the renewal of the mind by the Holy Spirit. This is subsequently followed by a change in the body, limbs, and senses. For when the heart receives new light, new judgment, and new impulses through the gospel, the external senses also are renewed. Then the ears have the desire to hear God's Word instead of human ideas and dreams. The mouth and the tongue no longer praise their own works, righteousness, and rules but joyfully praise God's mercy, which was revealed in Christ. These are not merely changes in words but real changes. They include a new mind, new will, new senses, and also new ways of behaving. Not only do the eyes, ears, mouth, and tongue see, hear, and speak differently than before, but the mind itself resolves to follow a different way of living.

Formerly, when our hearts were blinded by errors in teachings from Rome, we imagined that God was a salesman who sold his grace in exchange for our works and achievements. Now, however, since the light of the gospel has dawned, we know that we are credited as righteous only by faith in Christ. Our hearts throw out all self-chosen works and perform only the work of their calling and the works of love, which God commands. They praise God and joyfully boast in their trust in God's mercy. When enduring danger or disaster, our hearts suffer with joy and gladness, even though our sinful nature continues to grumble. This is what Paul meant by a new creation.

COURAGE TO TRUST GOD

*But Jacob did not send Benjamin, Joseph's brother, with the others,
because he was afraid that harm might come to him.*
Genesis 42:4

Jacob decided to keep Benjamin close to himself in order to prevent him from being killed, as his brother Joseph was. This was a very human, but foolish, thought—as if Benjamin couldn't die at home! Jacob seemed to be thinking that Benjamin's life and well-being were under his control. If such a great spiritual leader—one who had God's promise of protection—showed such weakness, what will we do when faced with danger and trials?

Examples like this are given to instruct and comfort us so that we may learn to always trust in God. At the same time, we have to take care of our children and the jobs that God has given to us. We shouldn't think, "I'm a deacon, and I know that God takes care of his church. That means I can take it easy. I don't need to worry about my responsibilities."

Just as a father can never be lazy or indifferent, we need to be courageous and work diligently to fulfill our responsibilities. God doesn't forbid work. He doesn't want us to be lazy—even though he's in charge of everything, and everything happens the way he wants. We need to be trained and tested by danger, by terrifying trials, and by the uncertain results of our own efforts. However, we must always remember God's promise and be firm in our faith. We must pray and do our daily work, but everything we do must flow from faith.

CRUCIFY THE SINFUL NATURE

Those who belong to Christ Jesus have crucified the sinful nature
with its passions and desires.
Galatians 5:24

Paul says that all those who belong to Christ crucify the sinful nature, along with its shortcomings and sins. We as believers have not yet completely taken off our sinful nature, and we are still inclined to sin. We don't fear and love God enough. We are driven to anger, envy, impatience, sexual immorality, and other evil impulses. However, we don't act on these impulses, because as Paul says here, we crucify our sinful nature with its passions and desires. Suppressing wickedness, fasting, or exercising other spiritual disciplines isn't enough to crucify the sinful nature. It happens only when we live by the Spirit (Galatians 5:16). God's threats to punish sin also serve as a warning and frighten us from sinning. Armed with God's Word, faith, and prayer, we refuse to give in to the desires of the sinful nature. By resisting the sinful nature in this way, we nail its lusts and cravings to the cross so that the sinful nature—though it's still alive and moves—can't achieve what it wants, for it's fastened to the cross by its hands and feet.

In summary, we must crucify the sinful nature for as long as we live on the earth. This means we are aware of its desires, but we don't obey these desires. With the armor of God and with the spiritual weapons of faith, hope, and the sword of the Spirit, we fight against the sinful nature. With these nails, we fasten it to the cross so it is forced against its will to be subject to the Spirit. When we die, we put off the sinful nature completely. When we are resurrected, we will have a pure nature with no sinful passions or cravings.

THE VALUE OF EVERYDAY WORK

*When Jacob saw Rachel daughter of Laban, his mother's brother,
and Laban's sheep, he went over and rolled the stone away
from the mouth of the well and watered his uncle's sheep.*
Genesis 29:10

As the head of God's people and a light for the world, Jacob was an extremely important person. He had the blessing and the promise and had even heard God speak to him. It's remarkable that he lived as if he had nothing at all. He lived like an ordinary person and did everyday work, actions for which God doesn't give any specific instructions in his Word. God didn't tell Jacob how he would help or direct him, how things would turn out, or whether there would be a good harvest in any given year.

Accordingly, we should never say, "I don't know what's going to happen, so I won't do anything." God tells us to do the best we can and leave the rest to him. He didn't promise that everything we do would be successful. We don't need to know what's going to happen or how everything is going to turn out. We should simply do our assigned work to the best of our abilities.

In the Bible, we hear about the impressive and heroic acts of our ancestors in the faith. Along with these, we also hear about the humble, unpleasant, and distasteful work they had to do. This should comfort us whenever our everyday work bogs us down. Then we won't feel depressed or fall into despair, thinking that God will despise us. Instead, we should realize that all work is made holy through God's Word and our faith. But the world doesn't view work in this way. They think that reading stories about people in the Bible doing common, everyday tasks is a waste of time. Only believers are able to see and understand that God is at work in these ordinary activities. This work is precious, not only in our sight, but also in the sight of God.

DEFYING THE WORLD

❦

If you belonged to the world, it would love you as its own.
As it is, you do not belong to the world, but I have chosen you
out of the world. That is why the world hates you.
John 15:19

Christ warns us here about the world's opposition to Christians. We must learn to despise the world's envy and hatred and whatever else it tries to do to us. It's inevitable that the people of the world will hate God and Christ. And because they hate Christ, they will also hate us. Because of this ongoing opposition, we must know how to overcome it. We overcome it by despising the world's arrogance.

The more we let the world's arrogance bother us, the more the devil and the world like it. If the devil could make us agonize and worry day and night about the world's opposition to the gospel, he would have great fun with it and would have to cover his mouth to keep from laughing. The people of the world would only rant and rave longer and louder. They would think they were succeeding because they were making us wail and cry. But if we defiantly ignore them, they become angry, sad, and irritated that their enemies are mocking them to their face—even when their ranting is at its peak.

The devil is extremely arrogant, and so is his bride, the world. So nothing is worse to him than being despised and mocked. When he experiences this and can't do anything about it, he retreats. Otherwise, he doesn't stop until he makes us discouraged and exhausted. He urges and pushes so long and hard that one could die of sorrow. But when he sees that we're determined to hold out against his hatred and that we continue to be cheerful and even mock him, he'll be the first one to grow tired. He's so haughty that he can't tolerate it when we defy him.

CALLING ON GOD FOR HELP

❧

Call upon me in the day of trouble;
I will deliver you, and you will honor me.
Psalm 50:15

This passage describes the lives of faithful believers. All of the misfortunes we experience are nothing but a joyful game that God plays with us. Sometimes a father will tell his little child to do something even though he knows the child isn't strong enough or the task is too difficult. He may tell his little son to bring him a bucket or to take off his socks or boots. When the child tries hard to accomplish the task even though it's much too hard for him, the father will gladly and quickly lend a hand. He will praise his son for his efforts. This praise will train the child to obey, and the child also will learn to love his father more and more.

These are the kinds of games that God plays with the God-fearing and faithful people who are his children and who call him Father. They don't doubt his fatherly love and good intentions in the least. They experience his tenderness firsthand when he reaches down to them and helps them in a fatherly way. God will be pleased with their efforts and will praise everything they do—even if it's small and weak. This is very similar to the way an earthly father appreciates and praises the efforts of his little children when they try to complete a task that is much too difficult for them.

TRUE CONTEMPLATION

*Remember Jesus Christ, raised from the dead,
descended from David. This is my gospel.*
2 Timothy 2:8

Formerly, many people wrote and taught about the differences between contemplating God and serving him in the world. Some people, who had the best intentions, spent their whole lives searching for visions and revelations. Some of them even recorded all of their dreams. They expected to receive personal messages from God without using the Word of God. What else is this but trying to climb into heaven without using the ladder God has provided? They were being fooled by the devil's tricks.

If you want to contemplate, then contemplate the right way. Think about your baptism. Read the Bible. Listen to sermons on God's Word. Honor your father and mother. Help a needy neighbor. Don't hide in a corner like people who think their personal devotions will give them a place on God's lap. They believe that they can be close to God without Christ, without God's Word, and without the sacraments. These people consider living life and doing everyday work beneath them. I also thought that way until God freed me of my error. The idea of spending life in quiet contemplation is very appealing. Human reason enjoys dabbling in miraculous signs and supernatural matters that it cannot understand.

Don't let Satan trick you. Approach spiritual matters in a different way. The true contemplative life is to listen to God's Word and believe it. Like Paul, decide to deal with only one subject: "Jesus Christ and him crucified" (1 Corinthians 2:2). Jesus, along with his Word, is the only worthwhile object of contemplation. Don't neglect him.

UNWAVERING FAITH

Then Israel said to Joseph, "I am about to die, but God will be with you and take you back to the land of your fathers."
Genesis 48:21

Israel's words give us a beautiful example of true faith. When Israel died, he didn't have any doubts. Rather, because of his strong and unwavering faith, he stated, "God will be with you." His faith shows that even though he is dead, he still lives. He went to his grave trusting God and his promises. This kind of faith swallows up death. Mere knowledge of what God has done would never be enough to stand up against death and hell in times of trial. The devil himself possesses that kind of knowledge. But true faith, which believes God's Word and trusts that his promises will come true, gives glory to God and acknowledges that he is trustworthy. This kind of faith defies and conquers death. As Paul says, "Where, O death, is your victory? Where, O death, is your sting?" (1 Corinthians 15:55). Even though death swallows us up, we will return again to light and life.

When I'm talking about faith, I'm not talking about merely acknowledging that something is true. That kind of faith doesn't place any confidence in what God says. It merely states, "Christ's suffering and death are historical facts." Genuine faith, however, confesses, "I believe that Christ suffered and died *for me*. I have no doubts about this, and I rest in this faith. I can depend on God's Word to help me fight against sin and death."

We need to be reminded of Scripture passages such as these. They show us the examples of believers who, by their unwavering faith, showed us the way. We should learn to follow and imitate their faith so that we too may proclaim, "I am baptized and saved. I will die in this faith. Any further troubles I have won't make me abandon my faith."

TWISTING SCRIPTURE

❦

And I will ask the Father, and he will give you another
Counselor to be with you forever.
John 14:16

When otherwise intelligent people hear these words of Christ, they cleverly reply, "Those aren't God's words, but those of a mere human. If he were God, he would say, 'I myself will send you another Counselor.'" These people want to instruct the Holy Spirit and make fine distinctions with grammar and logic. They insist that anyone who has to ask for something can't be God. Therefore, Christ cannot be God. They argue persuasively and even assert that the Holy Spirit doesn't know how to speak correctly. In their eyes, whatever the Holy Spirit says or does is wrong. They find fault with everything. They aren't godly enough to take the time to compare these verses with others. Instead, they take a verse here and a verse there. They pounce on a couple of words and distort them in order to obscure what the Bible means. If it were valid to tear one or two words from the text and forget about the rest, then I also could twist Scripture any way that I wanted.

But this is the correct way to approach Scripture: look at the entire passage; look at what comes before and after the verse. In this case, you will find that Christ speaks both as God and as man. This is powerful proof that Jesus is both true man and true God, as our teaching and faith hold. How can we explain that Jesus speaks as God and as man at the same time? He can speak either way, because he possesses both divine and human natures. If Jesus spoke everywhere as God, no one could prove that he was a true man. If he spoke as a man all the time, no one would know that he is also true God.

COURAGE TO FACE DEATH

❧❦❧

She died at Kiriath Arba (that is, Hebron) in the land of Canaan, and Abraham went to mourn for Sarah and to weep over her. . . . Afterward Abraham buried his wife Sarah in the cave . . . in the land of Canaan.
Genesis 23:2, 19

The stories of people in the Bible should instruct and inspire us. These examples are better than using the Lord Christ as an example for reaching and comforting people who have weak faith. When such people hear the stories of Abraham, Isaac, Jacob, and Sarah and how they all died, these devout and God-fearing people won't be so afraid of death.

It's not their own fragile condition that bothers people with weak faith as much as the gruesome appearance of dead bodies. They say to themselves, "If my body were like the body Christ had here on earth, and if it couldn't be destroyed by death and eaten by worms, then I would wait for my last day with greater courage." Because Christ came back to life in only three days, his death doesn't seem like a good example of dying to people who are weak in faith. So it's reasonable that they are drawn to the examples of other people in the Bible whose bodies decayed, just as ours will.

In contrast, those who have stronger faith laugh at death. They fearlessly defy it: "What is death? What is hell? Christ, the Son of God, placed himself under God's laws and died. But Christ's death defeated death and gave us life." We need the strength to believe and not doubt that Christ died for our sins and was brought back to life. If we believe that Christ did this so that we could have God's approval, then we don't have to fear death. Christ's death assures us that our own death means nothing. But other examples are helpful for those who are weak in faith. For them, knowing that Sarah died and was buried helps them accept the fact that the same will one day happen to them.

TREASURES IN HEAVEN

❧

Do not store up for yourselves treasures on earth,
where moth and rust destroy, and where thieves break in and steal.
But store up for yourselves treasures in heaven.
Matthew 6:19–20

When Christ says, "Store up for yourselves treasures in heaven," he is saying, "Let the world have the earthly treasures, which deteriorate, rust, and are easily stolen. The pleasures these things provide is the only happiness the world knows. You, however, aren't citizens of this world. You are citizens of heaven bought by my blood. You are destined to receive eternal treasures, which have been prepared and reserved for you. Don't let your heart get caught up in material possessions. If you must work with earthly treasures in your job, then guard against their appeal and don't become a slave to them. Instead, set your sights on the treasures that are waiting for you in heaven. Those are real treasures that moths and rust can't touch. They can't be destroyed or stolen."

Whoever wants to be a Christian should be inspired by the possibility of receiving eternal treasures. Undoubtedly, a greedy miser would be overjoyed to receive riches that can't be destroyed by rust or carried off by thieves. Yet the people of this world don't pay any attention to heavenly treasures, because they can't see or touch them. By nature, people are enthralled with love for gold and silver, even though they know from experience that these aren't safe from corrosion and thieves for even an hour. Preaching to these people is useless. If someone refuses to believe what Christ said, preferring instead to rely on their uncertain riches, then let them go. We won't bring anyone to their senses by dragging them by the hair. Just wait until it's time for them to leave this world. Let them try to find comfort from the earthly treasures they have piled up. Then they will realize how little these treasures can actually help them.

THE SIGNS OF FAITH

Since you call on a Father who judges each man's work impartially,
live your lives as strangers here in reverent fear.
1 Peter 1:17

We teach that God saves us only by faith, apart from our works. Why then does Peter say that God judges each person's work? Here is why: What we have taught—that faith alone justifies us before God—is unquestionably true because it is so clear in Scripture that no one can deny it. What the apostle says here—that God judges according to works—also is true. We should always remember that where there is no faith, there can be no good works, and on the other hand, where there are no good works, there is no faith. Therefore, we must keep faith and good works connected. The entire Christian life is embodied by both. The way we live is important, because God will judge us accordingly. Even though God judges us according to works, it's still true that works are only the fruits of faith. This is how we know whether or not we have faith. So God will judge us on the basis of whether or not we have believed. Likewise, the only way to judge liars is by their words. Yet it's still obvious that they don't become liars through their words but that they were already liars before they ever told a lie. For the lie comes into the mouth from the heart.

Works are the fruits and signs of faith. God judges people according to these fruits. These fruits spring from faith in a way that publicly indicates whether or not we have faith in our hearts. God will not judge us by asking whether we are called Christians or whether we have been baptized. He will ask each one of us, "If you are a Christian, then tell me, where are the fruits that demonstrate your faith?"

A LIFELONG PURSUIT

*For we maintain that a man is justified by faith
apart from observing the law.*
Romans 3:28

People are not justified and do not receive life and salvation because of anything they've done. Rather, the only reason they receive life and salvation is because of God's grace through Christ. There is no other way.

Many Christians are tired of hearing this teaching over and over. They think they learned it all long ago. However, they barely understand how important it really is. If it continues to be taught as truth, the Christian church will remain united and pure—free from decay. This truth alone makes and sustains Christianity. You might hear immature Christians brag about how well they know that we are justified through God's grace and not because of anything we do to earn it. But if they go on to say that this truth is easy to put into practice, then have no doubt they don't know what they're talking about, and they probably never will. We can never learn this truth completely or brag that we understand it fully. Learning this truth is an art. We will always remain students of it, and it will always be our teacher.

The people who truly understand that they are justified by faith and put it into practice don't brag that they have fully mastered it. Rather, they think of it as a pleasant taste or aroma that they are always pursuing. These people are astonished that they can't comprehend it as fully as they would like. They hunger and thirst for it. They yearn for it more and more. They never get tired of hearing about this truth. Similarly, Paul admits in Philippians 3:12 that he has not yet reached this goal. In Matthew 5:6, Christ says that those who hunger and thirst for righteousness are blessed.

THE STRENGTH OF GOD'S WORD

Simon Peter answered him, "Lord, to whom shall we go?
You have the words of eternal life. We believe and know
that you are the Holy One of God."
John 6:68–69

Yes, Peter, you speak the truth! This is written as a comfort and example to us. Though one of the Twelve would fall, which in itself is an important lesson to us all, God upheld Peter. Everything rests on God's grace, power, and Word to such a degree that we can't even trust the apostles. Though one of them claimed he was so strong that he would never fall, he couldn't make it unless God blessed him and said, "I have chosen you." The reason the apostles were able to prevail was because Christ said, "I have chosen you." Though Judas would fall and remain fallen, Peter, in contrast, was held so tightly by God's Word that he wouldn't stay down. When he stumbled and fell, he stood up again.

You must realize that God allows people to stumble so that they will despair of trusting in themselves. God is the one who stamps out inborn arrogance. Moses, Aaron, David, and others fell, yet they found their way again. Scripture says that though people fall, God's Word will remain firm and never fall. Anyone who falls will be able to stand up again on the strength of God's Word.

Judas, the one who betrayed the Lord, was the first to defect. He was the one who brought harm to God's kingdom, even though he ranked above the other apostles as overseer of the finances. If I, or someone greater, should fall—may God protect me from that—it would certainly be scandalous. But we should stand firm and rest on the foundation of the Word. Jesus said, "Have I not chosen you, the Twelve? Yet one of you is a devil!" (John 6:70). This example shows that we can't rely on people, but we must learn to depend on God's Word.

WHEN LIFE DOESN'T WORK OUT

*Then Isaac sent Jacob on his way, and he went to Paddan Aram,
to Laban son of Bethuel the Aramean, the brother of Rebekah,
who was the mother of Jacob and Esau.*
Genesis 28:5

Jacob waited many years for the promised blessing, and after receiving it, he had to go into exile. He was forced to leave his dear parents, and they were separated from their beloved son for a long, long time. On the surface, one might think this wasn't so bad. But it's very difficult for anyone to leave a father and mother, an inheritance, and comfortable surroundings and to run away in misery and poverty.

This is a wonderful example that shows us how God works. He requires us to trust his words and his promises even when the opposite of those promises is happening to us. Jacob had the promised blessing, but he had to hold on to it by faith and not doubt what he couldn't see. Jacob had nothing but a stick in his hand and a piece of bread in his bag. He was poor, lonely, and outcast, but he believed God's promises. Jacob's example teaches us to live by faith. We should believe God when he promises to love and protect us, take care of us, and listen to us, even though we might not see it happening.

This story is written as an example for us. We must learn to depend on the visible Word of our invisible and incredible God. Because God doesn't lie or deceive us, we wait with confidence and patience for him to fulfill his promise. This is difficult for us because we are used to things we can touch, see, or feel. We have to learn to let go of what we can experience only with our senses and live according to what is invisible.

KEEPING LAW AND GOSPEL SEPARATE

❦

Is the law, therefore, opposed to the promises of God?
Absolutely not! For if a law had been given that could impart life,
then righteousness would certainly have come by the law.
Galatians 3:21

Those who know how to tell the difference between the law and the gospel should thank God and consider themselves true theologians. In times of temptation, I certainly don't know how to do this as I should. You can keep these two separate by placing the gospel in heaven and the law on earth. Call the righteousness of the gospel heavenly and divine, and call the righteousness of the law earthly and human. You should distinguish the righteousness of the gospel from the righteousness of the law as carefully as God has separated heaven from earth, light from darkness, and day from night. You should consider one as light and day, the other as darkness and night. If only you could separate them even further.

So when dealing with matters of faith and conscience, you should exclude the law and let it remain on earth. But when dealing with how we are to live in this world, you should light the lamp of the law. So the immeasurable light of the gospel will illuminate the day, and the lamp of the law will illuminate the night. If you have a conscience terrified by a sense of sin, you should think to yourself, "While I am on earth, I must work. Just as a donkey should work, serve, and carry the burdens given to it, so my body should obey the law. But when I ascend to heaven, I leave the donkey with its burden on earth. My conscience doesn't have anything to do with the law, works, or earthly righteousness." So the donkey remains in the valley, while the conscience climbs with Isaac up the mountain. It knows absolutely nothing of the law and its works. Instead, the conscience only keeps its eye on the forgiveness of sins and Christ's righteousness.

JOHN POINTS US TO CHRIST

*[John] came as a witness to testify concerning that light,
so that through him all men might believe.*
John 1:7

John, the writer of this book, doesn't put much emphasis on John
the Baptist. All the writer says about him is that John the Baptist
spoke the truth, preaching to the people about Christ, the light
and life of all humanity. The writer doesn't say that John the Baptist taught the people all about his strict ascetic lifestyle—drinking only water, wearing clothing made of camels' hair, and living
on wild honey and locusts. John the Baptist didn't teach about
these as a way to start a new sect. He didn't want people to follow
his example as a way to be saved. If he had done that, John the
Baptist would have attracted a large group of followers and would
have become the founder of a new sect with a new set of doctrines.

John the Baptist didn't do anything like that! He came to
speak the truth. He had the God-given responsibility of pointing people to Christ and telling them that Christ is the Lamb of
God. His mission was to direct everyone, including his own disciples, away from himself and to the Lord Christ. He was saying,
"I am not Christ. I am not the light. I can't enlighten you. I can't
give you life. However, as his representative, I want you to believe
in Christ and let him guide you. I must only preach about Christ.
I don't want to talk about my camel-skin clothes or any other
aspect of my ascetic lifestyle. My repulsive appearance is meant to
force you to pay closer attention to my message than to me.
Christ is the life and the light of humanity. He is eternal, and he
created heaven and earth. But at this point in time, he has taken
our human nature on himself. He is right here with you."

WAITING FOR MARRIAGE

◆C◇~

Isaac was forty years old when he married Rebekah daughter of Bethuel the Aramean from Paddan Aram and sister of Laban the Aramean.
Genesis 25:20

Isaac was forty years old before he got married. In those forty years, he undoubtedly experienced periods of frustration and fiery passion because of his physical desires. A person's physical desires are at war with the spiritual nature. Yet Isaac was obedient to his father, Abraham, who taught him how to meditate on God's commands and promises in the battle against his sinful nature. Later on, God gave Rebekah to Isaac as his wife, and they lived together in harmony.

There is a lesson buried in this passage: Isaac is a great example to young people of a person who abstains from sex before marriage. This is an important subject, because all young people have to face this battle. Isaac's purity and moral integrity are clear indications of the way he was raised. His father taught him to avoid bad friends. Isaac meditated on God's promises, prayed, and did useful work. Though not specifically stated in the text, it's safe to assume that he diligently dedicated himself to meditation and prayer during the first forty years of his life when he wasn't yet married.

But some might say, "Waiting for marriage is unbearable and aggravating!" They're right. It's very similar to other difficulties requiring patience that believers must face, such as fasting, imprisonment, cold, sickness, and persecution. Lust is a serious burden. You must resist it and fight against it. But after you have overcome it through prayer, lust will have caused you to pray more and grow in faith.

BEWARE OF JUDGING OTHERS

*Do not judge, or you too will be judged. For in the same way
you judge others, you will be judged, and with the measure
you use, it will be measured to you.*
Matthew 7:1–2

Forgiveness of sins and tolerance for others are indispensable to the Christian life. We should bear with each other and forgive one another. As Paul taught, "We who are strong ought to bear with the failings of the weak and not to please ourselves" (Romans 15:1). This is what Christ meant when he said, "Stop judging." Some Christians have greater and better gifts than others. This is necessary, especially for preachers. No one should act superior to others or think of himself or herself as better than those who don't have such gifts. Among believers, no one should try to dominate anyone else. On the surface, there is a difference between people. A prince has a higher position than a farmer. A preacher has more education than an ordinary worker. But in their hearts, Christians should be of one mind despite their different positions in society. They should disregard external differences.

As a Christian, you should accept others by making allowances for your neighbor, even if your neighbor occupies a lower position in society and has fewer gifts than you do. You should respect the work of a servant tending horses as much as you respect your own work, whether it is governing or preaching. Your work may appear to have a greater impact than your neighbor's, but you must not judge by outward appearances. You should always remember that your Christian neighbor has the same faith and the same Christ as you do. Your neighbor receives as much of God's grace as you do. There is one God who creates everyone and gives each one of us our own gifts. God is pleased by the least as well as the greatest.

LOVE COVERS MANY SINS

*Above all, love each other deeply, because love
covers over a multitude of sins.*
1 Peter 4:8

Here Peter builds upon a passage from the book of Proverbs: "Hatred stirs up dissension, but love covers over all wrongs" (Proverbs 10:12). And this is what Peter means: If you don't restrain your sinful nature and desires, you will easily become angry with others. You will be unable to forgive others easily. So make sure you curb your evil desires. Then you will be able to love and forgive others, for love covers sin.

Some interpret this verse as if it goes against faith. They may say, "You claim that faith alone makes a person godly and that no one can get rid of sin through their works. Then why do Solomon and Peter say that love covers sin?" You can answer them this way: "Solomon is saying whoever hates another person doesn't stop quarreling and bickering. But wherever love is, it covers sin by gladly forgiving it. Where there is anger, you will find a defiant person who won't reconcile and remains full of hatred. On the other hand, people full of love don't become angry no matter how much someone tries to offend them. They cover all these sins and pretend not to see them. Though they can overlook their neighbor's sin, they cannot make God overlook it. No one can cover his or her own sin before God. Only faith can do that. But with our love, we can cover our neighbor's sin. And just as God covers our sins with his love if we believe, so we also should cover our neighbor's sin. Peter says that we should love one another so that one person can cover the sin of another. Love doesn't cover just one, two, or three sins, but a whole multitude of sins."

GIVING THANKS TO GOD

Extol the LORD, O Jerusalem; praise your God, O Zion.
Psalm 147:12

We should be ashamed that we're so lazy we need to be prodded into praising God or awakened to do so, as if we were sleeping. We're showered with blessings every day, and we're always using what God gives us. Why do we need to be continually reminded of the wonderful things God does for us? We should be able to remember to thank him without reminders from the Psalms. God's gifts alone should inspire us to praise God. But this doesn't happen. We have to be yelled at before we start praising the Lord. The words have to be written down for us and spoon-fed into our mouths, as this psalm does.

More shocking still is that the one who is giving us all these blessings has to be pointed out to us. Jerusalem must be admonished, "Do extol the Lord," and Zion told, "Go ahead and praise your God." We all use God's blessings every day, but we never think about where they come from—God. He is the one who gives us everything. Instead, we accept his gifts as if they simply appeared out of nowhere or as if we earned them through our own efforts, diligence, or wisdom. We think that God somehow owes us these things, and therefore we don't need to thank him. Even animals don't live that shamefully. Pigs recognize the person who gives them their food. They'll run after her and cry to her. But the world doesn't even recognize God, let alone thank and praise him for these blessings. If God's people must be encouraged to praise him, how can the world be expected to do any better? It's astounding how unwilling people are to acknowledge what God has done for them and to praise him for it.

JUDGING BY APPEARANCES

❦

Stop judging by mere appearances, and make a right judgment.
John 7:24

Jesus warned the Pharisees that they shouldn't judge others by their own foolish thinking or according to their own opinions. Looking through colored glass distorts the color of everything. In the same way, the distorted thinking of the spiritually blind doesn't allow them to perceive the truth accurately, even though they have the truth right before their eyes. Their hearts are bitter, and they burn with hatred. Like colored glass, their hearts color the way they look at others. They see people as enemies whom they resent and find repulsive.

In the world, no one sees anyone else through clear glass except for Christians, because their eyes are bright and pure. Christians see their enemies with the eyes of mercy and compassion. They don't wish evil on those people. If an enemy is bitter and mean toward them, believers think, "This big shot is miserable. He is already eternally condemned. Why would I want to wish more evil on him? If he keeps going this way, he will certainly belong to the devil." Christians have compassion on their enemies and hope for their salvation. Meanwhile, others only view their neighbors with hatred, envy, and pride. So it follows that they also view us as scoundrels. To the Pharisees, Jesus said, "Stop judging by mere appearances, and make a right judgment." In other words, he's saying, "Look at what I do and who I am through clear glass."

Our enemies will always criticize us. They will always look at us through colored glass. We must let it be. No matter what we do, they will still view us through colored glass.

LEAVING THE OUTCOME TO GOD

*Jacob looked up and there was Esau, coming with
his four hundred men; so he divided the children
among Leah, Rachel and the two maidservants.*
Genesis 33:1

This story is a good example of doing what you can and leaving the outcome to God. Jacob doesn't hesitate to do what he is able to do in this situation. He divides the people who are with him into two groups, sends presents to his brother, and travels ahead to take care of every possible thing. Someone in despair would have said, "I'm not going to do anything. If I'm meant to be killed, I can't prevent it anyway."

People will draw the same conclusion regarding their salvation and say, "If I'm meant to be saved, I won't be lost no matter what I do." Beware of those wicked words! Certainly, it's true that what is meant to happen will happen. But you have to remember that you don't know what will happen. You don't even know if you will be dead or alive tomorrow. God doesn't want you to know. That's why it's foolish to search for something that God in his wisdom has intentionally hidden from you.

Similarly, it's foolish to blame everything on what God has predestined. God's plan includes his secret wisdom. We can't understand it. God doesn't want you to know the future. So stick with your calling, remain within the limits of God's Word, and use whatever resources and wisdom God has given you. For instance, I can't foresee what my preaching will produce—who will be converted and who won't. What if I were to say, "Those who are meant to be converted will be converted even without my efforts, and what's the use of trying to convert those who aren't meant to be saved?" Saying that would be foolish and irreverent. Who are we to ask such questions? Take care of your responsibilities and leave the outcome to God.

IMPOSSIBLE TO BELIEVE

*No one has ever gone into heaven except the one
who came from heaven—the Son of Man.*
John 3:13

Only Christ would be able to testify to a truth this remarkable. How can human reason make sense of this strange teaching, or how can it understand how it all fits together? How can Jesus come down from heaven and at the same time live above? How can Jesus ascend back to heaven and yet continuously be in heaven? No one could have conceived of such a thought, whether in the heart or in the mind. Human reason says it's impossible for someone to *descend from* heaven and *be in* heaven at the same time. That is why Christians are considered foolish. We believe something directly contrary to reason.

Whoever has a difficult time believing that Christ can come from heaven and yet be in heaven shouldn't worry about it. It doesn't matter if we can't grasp this truth right away. If we are considered fools because of believing this, our foolishness won't hurt us. For Christians are certainly not foolish. We know perfectly well what we believe. We know where we can find counsel and help in all situations. We know we will live eternally after we have been delivered from this world.

But if some people refuse to believe this truth, then they should leave it alone. Instead, they want to figure it out. These people want to resolve the paradox in their own crazy head—first this way, then that way. All of them think they will find God by figuring it out, but they won't.

However, you must hold tightly to the testimony that was brought down from heaven by Jesus, God's Son. You must believe it, for all Christians dare to believe what Jesus says.

CHRIST IS OUR RANSOM

*I have been crucified with Christ and I no longer live,
but Christ lives in me. The life I live in the body, I live by faith
in the Son of God, who loved me and gave himself for me.
Galatians 2:20*

The phrases "Son of God," "loved me," and "gave himself for me" are lightning and thunder from heaven against the idea that we are saved by good works. Our will and understanding contained such great wickedness, error, darkness, and ignorance that we could be freed only by an exceedingly high-priced ransom. Why do we think that our human reason is naturally inclined to the best and can correctly lead us? Why do we think each person should do as much as they can? Why do we bring our terrible sins, which are mere straw, to an angry God, whom Moses calls "a raging fire"? Why do we want to haggle with God, trying to exchange our stubble for grace and eternal life? Listen to this passage. It says there's so much evil in our nature that the world and all creation can't reconcile us to God. God's Son had to be offered for our sins.

But consider the price of this ransom carefully. Look at Christ, who was captured and offered for you. He is infinitely greater than and superior to anything else in creation. How will you respond when you hear that such a priceless ransom was offered for you? Do you still want to bring God your own good works? What is that compared to Christ's work? He shed his most precious blood for your sins.

THE WORD IS GOD'S SON

The Word became flesh and made his dwelling among us.
We have seen his glory, the glory of the One and Only,
who came from the Father, full of grace and truth.
John 1:14

This is the first time that John called the Word the only Son of the Father. You might have wondered who the Word was when John said, "In the beginning was the Word" (John 1:1), "Through him all things were made" (v. 3), and "In him was life, and that life was the light of men" (v. 4). In this passage you can see that the Word, who existed with the Father from eternity and is the light for humanity, is God's only Son. The Word alone is the Son, and no one else. Now we know what John meant when he used the term *Word*. From verse 14 on, John will speak plainly about Christ's kingdom. Up to this point, he spoke with strange and unusual words. They weren't clear in any language. But now he says, "The Word is the one and only Son."

God also has many other children. However, he has only one Son through whom he created everything. The other children are not the Word through whom everything was created. Rather, these children were created through this only Son, who is coequal Creator of heaven and earth with the Father. All the others became children through the Son. The Word alone is, as Paul states, the only "Son of God" (Romans 1:4). Through him, God makes and rules all things.

We must hold this passage from the book of John in the highest honor. We should comfort ourselves with it in times of sorrow and temptation. We should hold on to it in faith, because it reminds us that we are children of God.

YOUR WILL BE DONE

Father, if you are willing, take this cup from me;
yet not my will, but yours be done.
Luke 22:42

Some people have an evil will. It's easy to spot because it doesn't tolerate any opposition. Other people have another type of will that appears to be good but is actually evil. It can be recognized by its fruit—impatience. A truly good will, if it's hindered, says, "O God, I thought what I wanted would be good. If it's not to be, I'm satisfied. Let your will be done." Wherever there's conflict and impatience, there's nothing good—no matter how good it may seem.

Besides these two types of evil wills, there's also a good will that God doesn't want us to do. This is the kind of will David had when he wanted to build a temple for God. God praised him for it, and yet God didn't let it happen (2 Samuel 7:2–29). This was the kind of will that Christ had in the garden of Gethsemane. Even though it was good, his will had to be set aside (Luke 22:42). So if you would like to save the whole world, raise the dead, lead yourself and everyone else to heaven, and perform miracles, you should first seek God's will and submit your own will to his will. You must pray, "Dear God, this or that seems good to me. If it pleases you, let it be done. If it doesn't please you, let it remain undone."

God often breaks a good will in order that a false, evil will won't sneak in by appearing good. He does this so we learn that as good as our will might be, it's still immeasurably inferior to his will. So our inferior good will must yield to the infinitely good will of God.

WILLING TO LET GO

❦

*Naked I came from my mother's womb, and naked
I will depart. The LORD gave and the LORD has taken away;
may the name of the LORD be praised.*
Job 1:21

Isn't it true that your money, property, body, spouse, children, and friends are good things created and given to you by God himself? Ultimately, they all belong to God and not to you. What if he were to test your loyalty by taking them away from you? What if he wanted to learn whether you were willing to let go of them for his sake? What if he wanted to see whether you would hold tighter to him or to his gifts? What if you became separated from your loved ones? Do you think you would have the right to rant and rave, forcibly attempt to get them back, or sulk until they were returned to you? If you argue that these are God's good gifts to you and that you want to get them back no matter what the cost, then you would be making a big mistake.

If you want to do the right thing, don't rush ahead without thinking. You must fear God and say, "Dear Lord, the people and things you have given me are good, as you have said in Scripture. Yet I don't know whether you will let me keep them. If I knew that you didn't want me to have them, I wouldn't even try to get them back. However, if I knew that you wanted me to have them, I would do what you want by taking them back. But I don't know what you want me to do. All I can see now is that you have allowed them to be taken away from me. So I'll turn the whole matter over to you. I'll wait until I know what to do. I'm ready to live either with them or without them."

LOVING THE WORLD

Do not love the world or anything in the world.
If anyone loves the world, the love of the Father is not in him.
1 John 2:15

Being in the world, seeing the world, and experiencing the world are all different from loving the world, just as having sin and feeling sin are both different from loving sin. Abraham certainly had property, but he didn't love it. He recognized that God made him a steward over these possessions, and he managed them accordingly. David was a mighty king but didn't demand his own way. Rather, he governed according to God's will. For he said of himself, "I dwell with you as an alien, a stranger, as all my fathers were" (Psalm 39:12). In other words, he considered himself to be a traveler, merely a guest on this earth. David didn't rule his kingdom according to his own will, but according to God's will and for God's honor. So he didn't love the world. But when someone oppresses and troubles the poor and uses other people's possessions as their own, then we see someone loving the world. This is unjust. Christ doesn't take us out of the world. Rather, he leaves us in the world after baptism so that others will be strengthened and encouraged by our example. So anyone who flees the world lives in a godless way.

Christ says that the Holy Spirit "will convict the world of guilt in regard to sin" (John 16:8). The world is filled with people who have turned away from God and know nothing about God. They have turned instead to what God has created and have used his creation for their own honor.

KEEP YOUR EYES OPEN

❧

The wise man has eyes in his head, while the fool walks in the darkness;
but I came to realize that the same fate overtakes them both.
Ecclesiastes 2:14

I've noticed that the same kinds of things happen to both wise and foolish people. Both end up making mistakes. Nevertheless, wisdom is better than foolishness. You may be familiar with the expression "If you want to play chess, don't hide your eyes in your pocket." That means you not only have to know the game well, but you also have to be an observant and careful player. The author of Ecclesiastes says here, "The wise man has eyes in his head." In other words, wise people aren't merely clever managers, but they're also alert, conscientious, and watchful. They see how things ought to be done even though they can never assure the outcome. Foolish people, on the other hand, don't use the eyes in their heads, because they let themselves be swept up by boldness and audacity. In the end, the affairs of both appear to be determined by coincidence and luck. In reality, God directs everything. Neither wisdom nor boldness determines how things will turn out.

Both wise and foolish plans sometimes fail and sometimes succeed. But God doesn't want us to base our rules for living on whether or not something is successful. That's because what God has created is in his hands, not ours. He allows us to use these things, but he accomplishes what he wants through us. It's pointless to add anything to what God wants or to try to determine how God should do things. In this way, God teaches us not to rely on our own wisdom and insight, but to deal with matters as they come along. If they don't turn out well, then we should simply commit them to God.

GENUINE FORGIVENESS

*When they kept on questioning him, he straightened up
and said to them, "If any one of you is without sin,
let him be the first to throw a stone at her."*
John 8:7

The poor woman caught in adultery was in dire need. Her predicament was no joke to her. She had been brought before the judge and sentenced according to what the law stated: "Stone her to death." This was not music to her ears. Her heart froze in fear. Her only hope was in the man who was writing on the ground. But she was surprised when he said, "If any one of you is without sin, let him be the first to throw a stone at her."

Sinners, like this woman, are the ones who belong in Christ's kingdom. Christ doesn't want sinners who refuse to admit that they're sinners. They think that because they haven't sinned notoriously, they don't need the help of God. I used to act like this when I was a monk. I would say, "Today I did nothing evil. I was obedient to my superior. I fasted and prayed. Therefore, may God be merciful to me." I thought God should forgive me for the sins that I didn't really consider sinful. In fact, these sins weren't real sins at all. Yes, I was inventing them.

Sins that we invent ourselves are stupid sins. God's compassion isn't concerned with made-up sins. They must be real sins—such as not fearing, trusting, or believing God; not loving your neighbor; not praying; not listening to sermons; not doing what the law of Moses commands. In other words, real sins break God's law, which no one can ignore. These are the sins that require genuine forgiveness, not meaningless forgiveness. Let's go back to the woman caught in adultery. She was caught, not merely in imaginary sins, but in adultery. So we must guard against real sins. But it's also to real sinners that the gospel reaches out.

THE BENEFITS OF SUFFERING

*Joseph had his chariot made ready and went to Goshen
to meet his father Israel. As soon as Joseph appeared before him,
he threw his arms around his father and wept for a long time.*
Genesis 46:29

Israel, or Jacob, didn't despair even though he faced many troubles. He appeared to be rejected, but God didn't abandon him. He remained God's child, and God remained in him in a hidden and wonderful way. Much later, when the events had played themselves out, Jacob saw that his son Joseph was still alive and had become an important leader in Egypt. Then Jacob was happy to have gone through so much suffering. He thought, "I wouldn't have experienced this much happiness if my family had been taken care of the way I had planned. Joseph would've been just a shepherd like the rest of my sons. But now he has been elevated to a position of royalty, and he will save many people."

So when we are being disciplined and feel sad, we shouldn't fight against our troubles, but rather remind ourselves, "I will not die but live" (Psalm 118:17). Even when the opposite seems to be true, we should be able to say, "Whenever I feel helpless, I can put my trust in God, who is able to make everything out of nothing. When I am totally devastated, no one can lift me up again the way he can."

The more severe the suffering, the greater the wonderful benefits to God's holy people. Being tested through suffering is a sure sign of God's grace and mercy to his faithful people. When they faithfully cling to God's promises, unbelievable blessings result. James says, "Blessed is the man who perseveres under trial, because when he has stood the test, he will receive the crown of life that God has promised to those who love him" (James 1:12).

THE FRUIT OF FAITH

The law is not based on faith; on the contrary,
"The man who does these things will live by them."
Galatians 3:12

You can't show me one person in the whole world, outside the promise of the gospel, whom you could rightfully call "a doer of the law." Therefore, the expression "doer of the law" is an imaginary term that no one understands unless he or she is a true believer— one who is above the law and in the blessing and faith of Abraham. True doers of the law are people who have received the Holy Spirit through faith in Christ and begin to love God and do good to their neighbors. The good that these people do includes faith at the same time. In other words, faith brings about a tree, and then the fruit, which is good works, grows. First, the tree must be there; then the fruit will follow. The fruit doesn't produce the tree, but the tree produces the fruit.

Similarly, faith first transforms the person into someone who can then do good works. So if someone wants to fulfill the law without faith, it's like producing fruit without a tree or making fruit out of wood and clay. The result isn't real fruit but simply an illusion. After the tree is planted—after faith in Christ creates a new person—then the works will follow. The doer must come before the work, not the work before the doer.

KNOWING GOD

*The wrath of God is being revealed from heaven against all
the godlessness and wickedness of men who suppress the truth
by their wickedness, since what may be known about God is
plain to them, because God has made it plain to them.*
Romans 1:18–19

We are so horribly corrupted by sin that, on our own, we are no longer aware of God. We have strayed from the righteousness of the law and have fallen into a pit of lies. We think we can reconcile ourselves to God through the works we invent. Using our human reason, we can recognize God in the laws of Moses, as Romans 1:19 teaches. But the gospel message shows that we can't truly know God through our human reason. The gospel is a new revelation that came from heaven. It not only teaches us about the Ten Commandments, but also tells us that all of us were conceived in sin and are hopelessly lost. No one fully obeys the laws of Moses. We will be saved only by the grace and truth of Jesus Christ. This is the depth of his nature and the will of God.

Whether they're tempted to cling to the laws of Moses or to their own righteousness, all people must acknowledge that no one can be saved or even know God apart from Christ. No one is justified unless that person is first covered by the grace and truth of the Son. This truth is hidden from our human reason; therefore, many people don't know anything about it.

We must find protection in Christ by crawling to him in humility, attaining everything through his grace and truth. This is what God intends and wants. This is what it means to know God in the right way. So we can't see God through the laws of Moses or through our human reason. No one can imagine what he is like. No one can climb to his heights. He is too exalted for us. Only those born of God will see God.

THE PURPOSE OF WORSHIP

And God blessed the seventh day and made it holy, because on it
he rested from all the work of creating that he had done.
Genesis 2:3

Human beings were created primarily to know God and to worship him. The day of worship was established, not for sheep and cows, but for people so that they might learn to know God. Even after the human race lost its knowledge of God because of sin, God intended his command to set apart the day of worship as holy to stay in effect. Furthermore, God wanted people to use the seventh day for studying his Word and for participating in the kind of worship he established. He did this so that first and foremost we would realize that our fundamental calling and purpose in life is acknowledging and praising God.

In addition, this day was established to assure us of eternal life in the future. Everything that God commands us to observe on the day of worship gives us clear indications of another life to follow. Why would God bother to talk to us through his Word if we were not going to receive eternal life in the future? If there was no hope of any future life, why wouldn't we live our lives as if God had nothing to say to us? Wouldn't we rather pretend that we didn't know him? Because the Lord of all speaks only to humans, and they are the only ones who can know him and know about him, it follows that there must be a life beyond this one. In order to reach the next life, we need to know God and his Word in this life.

PATIENCE IN SUFFERING

꒰꒷꒦

Now I rejoice in what was suffered for you, and I fill up
in my flesh what is still lacking in regard to Christ's afflictions,
for the sake of his body, which is the church.
Colossians 1:24

All Christians should know they won't be spared from suffering. But it should be the kind of suffering that is worthy of its name. It should really hurt us and weigh us down, such as a serious threat to our possessions, bodies, or lives. We should really feel it, for it wouldn't be suffering if it didn't hurt. Moreover, we shouldn't choose our own suffering, as some people do. It should be the kind of suffering the devil or the world sends our way. We would want to be spared of it, if at all possible. Then we need to hold on tight and reconcile ourselves to this suffering. As I have said before, we have to suffer so that we will become more and more like Christ. It cannot be any different. Everyone will face Christ's cross and suffering.

If you know this, then the suffering is easier and more bearable for you. You can comfort yourself by saying, "Well now, if I want to be a Christian, I must wear the colors of the team. Our dear Christ doesn't give out any other clothing for his side. I must endure this suffering."

People who insist on choosing their own cross cannot do this. They become upset and fight against it. What commendable behavior that is! Yet they criticize the way we teach about suffering as if they were the only ones who could teach how to handle it. Nevertheless, we still teach that none of us should choose our own suffering. But when the cross comes, we should patiently endure it and carry it.

FINDING THE MIDDLE WAY

It is good to grasp the one and not let go of the other.
The man who fears God will avoid all extremes.
Ecclesiastes 7:18

Reading Ecclesiastes tends to have the same effect on foolish people that preaching the gospel has on unbelieving people. When unbelievers hear about freedom in Christ and about God's approval coming from faith instead of what they do, they conclude that they don't need to perform any good works. They think they can go on sinning because faith is enough. On the other hand, when we preach that good works are the fruit of faith, they think this is how they are saved. Then they try to earn their salvation by doing these works. So hearing God's Word often leads to either arrogance or despair. It's very difficult to avoid either extreme and find the middle way.

The same thing happens when foolish people hear the teaching of Ecclesiastes on having a calm and quiet heart and leaving everything in God's hands. They infer that they don't have to do any work if everything is in God's hands. Others, who are just as foolish, do the opposite. They are much too worried and always try to control everything in every way.

However, we must find the middle way. We should work diligently, doing whatever we can that doesn't go against God's Word. But we shouldn't evaluate our work on the basis of our own efforts. Rather, we should commit all of our accomplishments, solutions, and successes to God. The author of Ecclesiastes speaks both to those who are lazy in their work and to those who are too worried about it. He tells them to submit themselves fully to God's Word, as well as to work diligently. So the author of Ecclesiastes provides a good warning to those who aren't sticking to the middle way.

TRUE DISCIPLES

❦

To the Jews who had believed him, Jesus said,
"If you hold to my teaching, you are really my disciples."
John 8:31

Christ preaches about true and false followers of God's Word. He is saying, "Many hear the gospel and stick with it because it's useful to them. They gain money, possessions, and honor from it. Yes, dear friends, who wouldn't want that? This is why I teach that if you live by what I say, you are truly my disciples. For I have two kinds of disciples. The first kind believes in me. They praise and listen to the gospel and say, 'This is the real truth.' I consider these people excellent disciples. They continue to believe. Then there are others who hear the gospel. But when the battle heats up, they say, 'Oh my, I don't know whether I should give up this or that thing for the sake of the gospel.' There are only a few who hold tightly to the gospel when there's a cross to carry. Where can I find those who will stand firm? Therefore, I say, 'If you hold to my teaching, you are really my disciples.'"

People would gladly believe in Christ if it meant becoming rich and acquiring a kingdom. But if it involves suffering, then their faith is finished. So Christ knows many of them won't keep on following his teaching. Remaining true to his teaching is rare, especially when evil winds begin to blow. Many become Christians and hold to the gospel in the beginning. Afterward, they fall away just as the believers in this passage did. It's similar to the parable about the seed that fell on the rock. When the heat of the sun beat down on it, it withered and dried up (Luke 8:6). But those who stick with the gospel are true disciples of Christ.

HOW THE WORLD REWARDS SERVICE

*When his master heard the story his wife told him, saying,
"This is how your slave treated me," he burned with anger.
Joseph's master took him and put him in prison,
the place where the king's prisoners were confined.*
Genesis 39:19–20

Losing his good reputation and being thrown in prison was certainly Joseph's worst hardship. What disgraceful wages he received for his years of faithful service! His impeccable character and hard work were rewarded with punishment and a ruined reputation. We serve, teach, counsel, comfort, and do what God tells us to do. For the most part, we do this for undeserving people from whom we get nothing in return except hatred, envy, and suffering. It seems that our lives are wasted on being kind to people who don't appreciate it.

Don't ever expect the world to acknowledge or reward your faithfulness and hard work. The opposite often happens, as Joseph's life shows. Therefore, make sure that you direct your service and life elsewhere. Don't look for favor and kindness from the world. Its favor can quickly turn into furious anger.

If you are called as a pastor or teacher, or if you are in some other position, set this goal for yourself: I will do my job faithfully without expecting any reward from the people I serve. I won't assume that they will be grateful to me. Rather, I will bless others the same way my heavenly Father hands out his blessings. He gives money, talents, peace, and health even to the most ungrateful and evil people. I will remember Christ's command, "Be perfect, therefore, as your heavenly Father is perfect" (Matthew 5:48). This means that we must serve people who are wicked, undeserving, and ungrateful. A few will acknowledge our service and thank us. But the others might even threaten our lives. Joseph's example shows us what reward we can expect from the world for even the greatest of kindness—being tied up and thrown in prison.

WE ARE GOD'S CHILDREN

❦

You are all sons of God through faith in Christ Jesus.
Galatians 3:26

Paul, as an extremely good teacher of the faith, always has these words on his lips: "through faith," "in faith," "by faith in Christ Jesus." He doesn't say here, "You are God's children because you are circumcised, have listened to the law, and have obeyed it." This is what the Jews imagined and the false apostles taught. Instead, he says, "You are all sons of God through faith in Christ Jesus."

The law, much less human laws, doesn't make us children of God. It can't create a new creature or produce a new birth. But it places before our eyes the old birth by which we are born into the kingdom of the devil. By doing so, the law prepares us for the new birth, which takes place through faith in Jesus Christ, not through the law. Paul testifies to this in the clearest way: "You are all sons of God through faith." It's as if he were saying, "Although you are tormented, humiliated, and killed by the law, it still has not made you righteous. But faith has made you righteous. Which faith? Faith in Christ." It's faith in Christ, not the law, that creates children of God. The book of John testifies to this: "Yet to all who received him, to those who believed in his name, he gave the right to become children of God" (John 1:12).

TRUE AND FALSE CHRISTIANS

When Jesus saw Nathanael approaching, he said of him,
"Here is a true Israelite, in whom there is nothing false."
John 1:47

The Lord Christ does not want us to brag about being a Christian or, as in the case of Nathanael, being an Israelite. It's not enough to say, "I am baptized," or even to say, "I am a bishop," "I am a cardinal," or "I am a preacher." You must believe in Christ and live like a Christian. You must be righteous both on the inside and on the outside. You must not be embarrassed of the Lord Christ and the Christian faith. If you are, then you are a false Christian. If you don't believe in your heart, your entire life is a lie and you remain in darkness. You aren't righteous, and you only appear to be a Christian. Your actions don't reflect your Christian faith.

If we could separate Christians from one another and divide them into true and false Christians, how many true Christians would we find? The world is crazy, foolish, and wild. It's filled with all kinds of evil—adultery, drunkenness, vindictiveness, and other sins. Some people no longer consider it a sin for people to cheat each other. Yet these same people want to be considered good Christians.

Believe me, you're not fooling anyone but yourself. God isn't fooled or mocked. He will know what you are really like in an instant, just as he knew that Nathanael was a true Israelite who believed in the prophets. He will look at you and say, "Yes, here is a true Christian!"

THE PATTERN OF TEMPTATION

*When the woman saw that the fruit of the tree was good for food
and pleasing to the eye, and also desirable for gaining wisdom,
she took some and ate it. She also gave some to her husband,
who was with her, and he ate it.*

Genesis 3:6

All of Satan's temptations follow the same pattern. First, Satan tests the faith of people and lures them away from God's Word. This leads them to commit sins against others. We can see from our own experience that Satan always works this way.

When an idea first strikes us, we don't think that we're about to do something wrong. If we did, we might have second thoughts and consider the potential results. We would think about the harm and misery we would cause. We might even change the way we were thinking and acting. But such thoughts are usually kept hidden. So we go right ahead with our sinful action and abandon our faith.

Eve picked the fruit from the tree. She was convinced that she would not die, even though God said she would. She believed what Satan had told her. She thought her eyes would be opened and she would gain wisdom. After the devil's poisonous words entered her ears, she reached out with her hand, took hold of the forbidden fruit, and tasted it with her mouth. Therefore, she sinned with every part of her body and soul. Still, she was not yet aware of the terrible sin she had committed. She cheerfully ate the fruit and brought some to her husband, who also ate it.

Lust, anger, and greed all work the same way. While sin is working, we don't feel it. Sin doesn't scare us. It doesn't sting. Instead, it seems friendly, kind, and cheerful. We often don't feel guilt as we're sinning. But later, when God's law exposes sin, the consequences crush us.

THE WORD WAS WITH GOD

❦

In the beginning was the Word, and the Word was with God,
and the Word was God. He was with God in the beginning.
John 1:1–2

Notice that John strongly emphasizes the word *with*. He repeats the word again so that he may clearly express the difference between the separate persons of God. He does this to counteract natural reason and future heretics. Natural reason clearly understands that there is only one God. Many verses in Scripture support this, and of course it's true. But reason struggles against the idea that three persons can be the same God.

This is why the heretic Sabellius claimed that the Father, Son, and Holy Spirit are all one person. Then another heretic, Arius, admitted that the Word was with God but didn't confess that the Word was true God. Sabellius teaches too great a simplicity in God. Arius teaches too great a multiplicity. Sabellius mixes the persons together, while Arius divides the nature of God into three parts.

But the truth of the Christian faith stays in the middle, teaching and confessing the individuality of the persons and the indivisibility of God's nature. The Father is a different person from the Son, but he is not a different God. Whether or not our natural reason comprehends it, it's still correct. Faith alone must grasp it. Natural reason leads to heresy and error. Faith teaches and holds to the truth. Faith simply clings to the Scripture, which never deceives us or lies to us.

HARDSHIPS BEFORE HONOR

Joseph named his firstborn Manasseh and said, "It is because God has made me forget all my trouble and all my father's household." The second son he named Ephraim and said, "It is because God has made me fruitful in the land of my suffering."
Genesis 41:51–52

Joseph became an important ruler in Egypt, and Jacob eventually saw his descendants become a large nation. But both men had to go through hardships first. Joseph learned this lesson firsthand. When naming his sons, he thought, "I was the firstborn son and an heir of a noble mother. But I lost everything, and I had no hope of inheriting anything. One must totally forget any material gain he might find in this world." So Joseph named his son Manasseh in God's honor, because God had brought him to his knees and to the point where he forgot all about his father's family. Joseph named his other son Ephraim, because God had lifted him up again and given him children. Later, Ephraim received a wonderful blessing from his grandfather Jacob. Ephraim's descendants would become the powerful tribe we read about in Joshua, Judges, 1 Kings, and 2 Kings.

We learn from this passage that we are brought down before we are raised up. We must become like Joseph. We must be reduced to nothing. Our human natures find this idea very painful and hard to take. All of creation hates destruction and decay. You can't cut down a tree or a bush without hearing a loud crash. Even Christ himself was brought low. He cried out from the cross, "My God, my God, why have you forsaken me?" (Matthew 27:46). That's why we should have the same modest attitude as Joseph. Even after receiving honor, he didn't become proud, but remained humble.

SERVING EACH OTHER

You, my brothers, were called to be free. But do not use your freedom
to indulge the sinful nature; rather, serve one another in love.
Galatians 5:13

If grace or faith is not preached, then no one will be saved, for faith alone justifies and saves. On the other hand, if faith is preached as it should be preached, then the majority of people understand this teaching about faith in a worldly way. They turn the freedom of the Spirit into the freedom of the sinful nature. One can see this today in all classes, whether higher or lower. All boast that they are evangelical and praise Christian freedom. Meanwhile, they follow their own desires, turning to greed, lust, pride, envy, and so on. No one faithfully carries out his or her duty. No one serves others in love. This shameful behavior makes me so impatient that I often wish that such pigs who trample the pearls with their feet were still under the tyranny of Rome. It's practically impossible for these people of Gomorrah to be ruled by the gospel of peace.

We know that the devil hounds those of us who have God's Word. For he holds everyone else captive and is eager to take away this freedom of the Spirit or at least to turn it into unrestrained living. Christ acquired this freedom of the Spirit for us through his death. Therefore, we follow Paul's example by teaching and encouraging people that this freedom of the Spirit gives them an opportunity to serve, not an opportunity to act on their evil desires. As Peter says, "Live as free men, but do not use your freedom as a cover-up for evil; live as servants of God" (1 Peter 2:16).

WHEN WE DON'T UNDERSTAND

※☙❧

"How can a man be born when he is old?" Nicodemus asked. "Surely he cannot enter a second time into his mother's womb to be born!"
John 3:4

Christ isn't talking about physical birth in this passage; rather, he is talking about spiritual birth, which is accomplished through water and the Spirit. If Nicodemus didn't understand what Christ was saying up to this point, how much less would he understand this spiritual rebirth? Our opponents think it's ridiculous to teach that a person must be born anew by water and the Spirit—nothing else. They don't understand or believe this teaching. That is why they shout, "You must do good works!" In this way, they discredit what's most important: If a person isn't reborn by water and the Spirit, then all is lost. Don't think that anyone will enter the kingdom of God unless they first are born anew by water and the Spirit. These are plain but powerful words: "You must be born again" (John 3:7). We have to pass from the birth of sin to the birth of righteousness. Otherwise, we will never go to heaven. After this new birth, good works will naturally follow.

Christ tells Nicodemus much about this new birth. But Nicodemus can't understand it. You won't be able to understand it either, unless you have been born anew and have experienced spiritual rebirth. Let these words stay as they are. Don't try to reinterpret them, even though they might seem foolish and strange to human reason. Understand the simple meaning of these words, the way they are usually read.

You shouldn't dare to reinterpret the Word of God your own way. It's better to think, "I don't understand these words. But before I change them, take something away from them, or add to them, I would rather leave them alone. I'll give them to God." The Scriptures should always be handled with reverence and respect.

ETERNAL LIFE IS CERTAIN

Enoch walked with God; then he was no more,
because God took him away.
Genesis 5:24

The first people of the earth eagerly anticipated eternal life because they knew that Abel and Enoch were living with God. We have an even greater anticipation because we know that Christ has already come and has gone back to the Father to prepare a place for us. Our human nature spends all of its energy pursuing the fleeting things of this world but doesn't look forward to the joys of eternal life. Nothing could be more certain than eternal life. We have so much evidence! We know that Abel, Enoch, and Elijah are living with God—even with Christ himself. Christ is the first of those who have died to come back to life (1 Corinthians 15:20, 23).

People who are devoted to seeking worldly pleasures are worthy of contempt. Similarly, our own human nature, which makes us look for pleasure, is worthy of contempt. Because we are so wrapped up in the concerns of this world, we care little for the riches of eternal life.

We should pay attention to this passage and keep it in our hearts. Enoch was not taken from this world by one of his devout ancestors or an angel. He was taken by God himself. This is the comfort that relieved the pain of death for the Old Testament believers. They had so little fear of death that they didn't even call it *death*. Instead, they referred to it as mere sleep from which they would awaken into eternal life. For believers, death is not death but simply sleep. When death no longer brings dread and fear—when it no longer has sting and power—it can no longer be called *death*. Consequently, when faith becomes stronger, death becomes proportionately weaker. Lack of faith, on the other hand, increases the bitterness of death.

GOD'S HOLY NAME

❧

This, then, is how you should pray:
"Our Father in heaven, hallowed be your name."
Matthew 6:9

Although it's short, the Lord's Prayer is delightful and profound when prayed from the heart. Among the seven parts of the Lord's Prayer, the greatest part is "Hallowed be your name." Notice, however, that God's name is holy in and of itself. It's not made holy by us. God is the one who makes all things holy and makes us holy as well. So "Hallowed be your name" means that God's name should be made holy in us. When this happens, God becomes everything, and we become nothing. The other six parts of the Lord's Prayer point to the same end—keeping God's name holy. When we keep God's name holy, we do everything well.

To learn how to keep God's name holy in us, we should first look at how it's dishonored and made unholy in us. Clearly, it's dishonored in us in two ways. First, we dishonor God's name when we misuse it to sin. Second, we dishonor his name when we steal it from him. To illustrate, consider a holy object at church. We can desecrate it in two ways: we can use it for human purposes instead of God's purposes, or we can steal it from the church.

God's name is made unholy through misuse. Instead of using it for improving our souls and making us more faithful, we might actually use God's name to sin and damage our souls. This happens in various ways—through witchcraft, magic, lies, oaths, curses, and deceptions—which are all covered in the commandment "You shall not misuse the name of the LORD your God, for the LORD will not hold anyone guiltless who misuses his name" (Deuteronomy 5:11). In summary, we dishonor God's name when we fail to live as God's children.

RESPONDING TO GOD'S PROMISES

Rend your heart and not your garments. Return to the LORD
your God, for he is gracious and compassionate, slow to anger
and abounding in love, and he relents from sending calamity.
Joel 2:13

Promises like this one are very beautiful, rich, and far-reaching. The Holy Spirit holds them before us so that people who are deeply discouraged in their souls may find refuge and comfort in these promises when they sense the Lord's anger. It's wonderful to see the way the Holy Spirit works. He highlights the threat in order to show us the goodness and mercy of God. This is what all the prophets do: They frighten us with the strongest and most severe threats. Then they immediately add the greatest promises of the mercy and grace of God.

But the effect of these threats and promises is different for God-fearing people than for ungodly people. The ungodly don't apply the promises or the threats correctly. When they hear the threats, they don't think these threats pertain to them. They continue in their hypocrisy and godless ways and even consider their ways to be very spiritual. Therefore, these rich promises have no effect on them. Because the threats don't result in troubled hearts for the godless, the promises are equally ineffective for them.

On the other hand, God-fearing people apply these promises to themselves in the right way. They are disheartened and crushed by the anger of God and the threats of punishment. They know they deserve divine judgment. They recognize the seriousness of their sin and its condemnation. So when they hear these promises, they turn to God's mercy and their consciences are lifted up again and calmed. So this is the way our God works: He leads his faithful people to hell before he brings them back. After terrifying them with threats, he comforts them with his promises.

COME TO THE FATHER

Jesus answered, "I am the way and the truth and the life.
No one comes to the Father except through me."
John 14:6

What does it mean to come to the Father? It means nothing else but to come from death to life, from sin and condemnation to innocence and godliness, from distress and sorrow to eternal joy and blessedness. Christ is saying, "No one should try to come to the Father through a different way than me. I alone am the way and the truth and the life." Christ clearly rules out and powerfully disproves all teaching that salvation can be obtained by works. He completely denies that we can get to heaven by any other way. For Jesus says, "No one comes to the Father except through me." There is no other way.

Salvation can be obtained only by a faith that clings to Christ. No work of ours—or of any other person or saint—can have this same honor. On the other hand, we shouldn't think that we don't have to do good works. Rather, we must first come to Christ in order to receive God's mercy and eternal life. After that, we should do good works and show love. We should make this distinction clear. We should never consider the way we live or the works we do as powerful enough to take us up to the Father.

Though everyone else may abandon me and leave me lying in ruins, I will still have an eternal treasure that can never fail me. This treasure isn't the result of my own works or efforts. The treasure is Christ—the way, the truth, and the life. Only through Christ do I come to the Father. I will hold to this, live by this, and die by this.

WAITING FOR GOD

*The Lord is not slow in keeping his promise, as some
understand slowness. He is patient with you, not wanting
anyone to perish, but everyone to come to repentance.*
2 Peter 3:9

God sometimes postpones answering prayers. He doesn't do this in order to destroy or abandon his people. Instead, he does it to fulfill his promises even more generously. Paul tells us that God "is able to do immeasurably more than all we ask or imagine" (Ephesians 3:20). Therefore, God wants us to wait patiently during the delay, trusting with certainty that he will give us even more than he has promised.

Human nature makes us so overconfident and wicked that we distrust God's promises and ignore his threats. Because punishment doesn't come right away, we don't take God's warnings seriously. Foolish people hear that sin will bring judgment and punishment, but they just brush it off and say, "That won't happen for a long time. I wish I had lots of money to count in the meantime." But God wants us to fear his warnings and wait for his promises to be fulfilled. Of course, that can be done only if we have faith.

People of the world couldn't care less about God's warnings. They take his warnings about as seriously as a goose hissing at them. But God is patient. He postpones both fulfilling his promises and carrying out his threats. That doesn't mean he's lying. God will eventually punish the wicked and shower even greater and richer blessings on the faithful because of the delay. But in the end, he will certainly come.

Unbelievers don't fear God, don't believe in him, don't hope in him, and don't even care about him. Believers, on the other hand, pay attention to God's warnings and trust his promises.

THE INTERNAL BATTLE

*For the sinful nature desires what is contrary to the Spirit,
and the Spirit what is contrary to the sinful nature. They are
in conflict with each other, so that you do not do what you want.*
Galatians 5:17

You shouldn't despair when you feel that the sinful nature continuously struggles against the Spirit. You shouldn't despair if you can't immediately force the sinful nature to be subject to the Spirit.

Don't be surprised or frightened when you become aware of this conflict between the sinful nature and the Spirit in your body. But you should take courage when Paul says the desires of the sinful nature are contrary to the Spirit. "They are in conflict with each other, so that you do not do what you want." With these words, he comforts those who are being tested. It's as if Paul wanted to say, "It's impossible to follow the Spirit as your leader in all situations without the sinful nature interfering. The sinful nature will get in the way so that you can't do what you really want to do. At that point, it's enough to resist the sinful nature so that you won't gratify its desires. Follow the Spirit, not the sinful nature, which quickly becomes powerless because it's so impatient. It doubts, complains, seeks revenge, hates God, fights against him, and despairs."

If you are aware of this battle with the sinful nature, don't lose heart, but resist in the Spirit and say, "I am a sinner and feel sinful because I am still in this body. As long as I live, sin will cling to this body. I will obey the Spirit, not the sinful nature. I will grasp Christ by faith, hope in him, and find comfort in his Word." You won't gratify your evil desires when you are strengthened this way.

JESUS IS BOTH GOD AND MAN

The Father loves the Son and has placed everything in his hands.
John 3:35

How do we bring together the two truths that Jesus is Lord over all and at the same time is a human being? If Jesus is God, how could God put everything in Jesus' hands? If Jesus is God, he already has everything. So how can anything else be given to him?

You already know there are two natures in Jesus Christ, but there is only one person. These two natures keep their characteristics but also transfer them to each other. This has caused some confusion. For example, Mary gave birth to Jesus 1,539 years ago. So some ask, "If he's only 1,539 years old, then how can he be eternal?" Jesus suffered on the cross when Pontius Pilate was governor in Judea. So some wonder, "If he suffered under Pilate, then how can he have everything in his power?" How do we reconcile all of this?

The two natures of Christ, the human and divine, are inseparable, and they are united in one person. The characteristics of one nature are attributed to the other nature. For instance, dying is a part of being human. When human nature is united with the divine in one person, death also becomes a divine attribute. Therefore, we can say, "God became a man. God suffered. God died." If you separate the human from the divine, that statement would be a lie, for God cannot die. But if we say that two natures reside in one person, then we have spoken correctly.

REAL BLESSINGS

May God give you of heaven's dew and of earth's richness—
an abundance of grain and new wine. May nations
serve you and peoples bow down to you.
Genesis 27:28–29

Wishing you good things or nice, obedient children could hardly be considered giving you a blessing because of the uncertainty of the outcome. But the blessing Isaac gave Jacob was neither empty words nor good wishes from one person to another. Isaac's blessing was definite and would certainly come to pass. It wasn't just a wish. Isaac actually gave Jacob something, telling him in effect, "Take the gifts that I am promising with my word."

Saying, "I wish you a strong and healthy body and mind," doesn't mean much. But if I were to hand you a thousand dollars and say, "I would like you to have this money," now that would be different. Similarly, Jesus told the paralyzed man, "Get up, take your mat and go home" (Matthew 9:6). If he were merely wishing the best, he would have said, "Poor man, I wish you were healthy and strong." But that wouldn't have cured or strengthened the sick man. Those good wishes would have accomplished little.

The Bible isn't filled with good wishes. It contains real blessings that actually come to pass. We have these kinds of blessings in the New Testament through Christ. We receive a blessing when the pastor says, "Receive forgiveness for your sins." If he were to say, "I *wish* that God would show you favor and mercy, give you eternal life, and forgive your sins," it would be merely an expression of love. Instead, he says, "I forgive you all your sins in the name of the Father, the Son, and the Holy Spirit." These words have the power to actually forgive you, if you believe.

BELIEVE IN GOD

Do not let your hearts be troubled. Trust in God; trust also in me.
John 14:1

Christ is saying here, "You have heard that you should trust in God. But I want to show you how to really find him so you won't start worshiping something you made up in your head. If you want to trust in the true God, then trust in me. If you want to invest your faith and trust in the right place, where it will never fail, then invest in me. For all of God lives in me." Later he tells them, "I am the way and the truth and the life" (John 14:6). In other words, "Whoever sees me sees the Father. Whoever hears me hears the Father. Therefore, if you want to meet God, then take hold of him in me and through me. If you have me, you also have the Father. The Father himself testifies about me." In the Gospels, Jesus repeatedly declares that he is from the Father. He doesn't speak and act on his own. Instead, the Father commands the whole world to believe that Christ is God. No one should believe in any other person or accept any other way to know God than Christ.

So it's certain that whoever tries to go around Christ won't meet the true God. God is completely in Christ and places himself in Christ for us. No one will be able to succeed in dealing with God apart from Christ. No one will find God on the basis of human thoughts and devotion.

Whoever wants to take the right path with their faith and not lose their way should begin where God has placed the path and where God wants to be found. Otherwise, everything they do and believe is useless.

IN NEED OF COMFORT

Never again will I curse the ground because of man, even though
every inclination of his heart is evil from childhood. And
never again will I destroy all living creatures, as I have done.
Genesis 8:21

God is speaking here as if he is sorry that he punished the earth because of humans. It almost sounds as if he is criticizing himself for dealing so harshly with the world. We shouldn't take this as meaning that God changed his mind about his creation. Instead, we should take comfort from this passage. God, in effect, blames himself in order to encourage and lift the spirits of his little flock. He tells his people that he wants to be merciful from this point on.

Noah and his family needed comfort. They were terrified by God's anger, which had just destroyed the world. Because their faith was shaken, God wanted to show himself in a way that would make them expect nothing else but his good will and mercy. So he was present at their sacrifice, talked to them, and told them he was pleased with them. He told them he was displeased about destroying the human race and promised never to do it again. God wasn't being inconsistent or changing. No, he wanted these people, who were witnesses of the effects of his anger, to change their attitudes and perceptions of him.

People who are going through spiritual trials know how important it is to hear words of comfort. They need to be told to hope in God's good will and dismiss discouraging thoughts of impending doom. A whole day, even an entire month, may not be enough time to comfort them. Recovery from sickness often takes a long time. In the same way, wounded hearts can't be quickly healed with one little word. Because God is aware of this, he uses a variety of ways—even blaming himself—to show people his good will and mercy.

WHY WE SAY AMEN

*For no matter how many promises God has made,
they are "Yes" in Christ. And so through him
the "Amen" is spoken by us to the glory of God.*
2 Corinthians 1:20

The little word *Amen* indicates strong affirmation and means "Let it be so." It expresses the faith we should have when we pray. Christ said, "If you believe, you will receive whatever you ask for in prayer" (Matthew 21:22). He also said, "Whatever you ask for in prayer, believe that you have received it, and it will be yours" (Mark 11:24). The Samaritan woman received what she asked for because she didn't stop asking and firmly believed. In response, the Lord said to her, "You have great faith! Your request is granted" (Matthew 15:28). James also said, "But when he asks, he must believe and not doubt, because he who doubts is like a wave of the sea, blown and tossed by the wind" (James 1:6).

So as the author of Ecclesiastes said, "The end of a matter is better than its beginning" (Ecclesiastes 7:8). For at the end of your prayers, you say, "Amen," with heartfelt confidence and faith. When you say, "Amen," the prayer is sealed, and it certainly will be heard. Without this ending, neither the beginning nor the middle of the prayer will be of any benefit.

GROWING UP IN CHRIST

*Until we all reach unity in the faith and in the knowledge
of the Son of God and become mature, attaining to the whole
measure of the fullness of Christ. Then we will no longer be infants.*
Ephesians 4:13–14

Human reason enjoys finding fault with the messengers of God's Word. It can quickly detect if these teachers' lives and habits aren't consistent with the absolutely pure teachings that they proclaim. Somehow, reason can judge their lives on the basis of their doctrine while, at the same time, rejecting their doctrine. In this way, our enemies complain that they're always hearing the gospel from us but not seeing behavior that matches it. They say we preach one thing and do another.

But our critics should remember that human beings are merely creatures with the ability to reason. Yet God has given these human beings the authority to rule over all of creation (Genesis 1:28). Now look at little babies. Where is this mighty authority God has given to them? Infants are the most pitiful of all living beings. They can't help themselves in the least. They depend solely on outside help; otherwise, they would die. Despite their helplessness, babies still possesses authority over all creation. Although we can't easily see this authority, the hope and promise of it remain. So the parents cherish, nourish, and take care of the children so that when they grow up and become strong, they can take on this authority.

Just as all people begin life as a weak baby does and mature over time, the same is true for all believers regarding spiritual matters. Day by day, we grow in our faith and by our faith. We keep growing until we eventually meet our Lord as mature people, just as Paul wrote in Ephesians 4:13. Meanwhile, God, our merciful Father, watches over us in our weakness and continually forgives us.

REMAINING ON THE VINE

I am the vine; you are the branches. If a man remains in me and I in him, he will bear much fruit; apart from me you can do nothing.
John 15:5

By saying that believers remain in him and he in them, Jesus is making it clear that Christianity is not something we put on externally. We don't put it on like clothes. We don't adopt it as a new lifestyle that focuses on our own efforts, as do those who practice a holy lifestyle they have invented themselves. Rather, Christian faith is a new birth brought about by God's Word and Spirit. A Christian must be a new person from the depths of the heart. Once the heart is born anew in Christ, these fruits will follow: confession of the gospel, love, obedience, patience, purity, and so on.

In this passage, Christ warns his disciples that they must remain in his Word. Remaining in the Word leads to genuine, newborn Christians. These true Christians produce much fruit. They guard themselves from the teaching that perverts God's Word and that tries to make grapes from thistles and thorns. This will never happen, however, because each kind produces its own kind. Even if you teach about, strive for, and pile up good works, your nature won't change. You must first possess a new nature. You won't accomplish anything by striving and exhausting yourself.

The two types of works remain vastly different. The one type of work is produced by human effort, while the other grows naturally. The works we make up always require us to strive harder, but they never do as well as natural growth. In contrast, natural growth stands, moves, lives, and does what it should naturally. So Christ says, "All other human teaching cannot succeed, because it instructs people to make up works. But if you remain in me, as natural branches remain on the vine, you will certainly produce good fruit."

GOD WILL TAKE CARE OF YOU

*He humbled you, causing you to hunger and then feeding you
with manna, which neither you nor your fathers had known,
to teach you that man does not live on bread alone but on
every word that comes from the mouth of the LORD.*
Deuteronomy 8:3

How does providing manna show that people should live on every word that comes from the mouth of the Lord? Is this manna God's Word? No, but God uses this example to explain what he said about hunger: "He humbled you, causing you to hunger and then feeding you with manna." He did this to show you that even if you don't have manna, God's Word can keep you alive. God's Word promises that he will never leave you and he will always take care of you. For even in times of hunger, faith in what God says nourishes, not only the soul, but also the body—the whole person. God will never abandon you. In his own time, he will provide food for your body the same way he used ravens and the widow of Zarephath to feed Elijah, and manna to feed the Israelites.

When Moses says that a person can't live on bread alone, he isn't only talking about manna. These words apply both to times when you're hungry and to times when you have plenty of food. The point is that God wants to show you his goodness through all your experiences. When you're hungry, you should learn to trust God's Word. God promises to take care of you and not let you die of hunger. When you trust in him, he will provide nourishment to your body because of your faith. He does all this to prevent you from worshiping your appetites and to teach you that life doesn't depend on a full stomach. God sustains both the body and the soul. You never would have learned this truth if your stomach had always been full. This is how you learn to trust in God.

BE AWARE OF SINFUL TENDENCIES

Those who belong to Christ Jesus have crucified
the sinful nature with its passions and desires.
Galatians 5:24

It's very advantageous for believers to be aware of the corrupt tendencies of their sinful nature. This awareness keeps them from becoming filled with pride through the useless, godless delusion of trying to become righteous by works, as if this would make them acceptable to God. Puffed up by this delusion, the monks believed they were so holy because of their self-chosen works that they sold their righteousness and holiness to others. In their own hearts, however, they were convinced that they were impure. Trusting in our own righteousness and imagining ourselves to be pure are very damaging behaviors.

But if we are aware of the sinfulness in our own hearts, we cannot trust in our own righteousness. This awareness humbles us so that we let go of our pride and stop trusting in our own works. It compels us to run to Christ, our Reconciler. He doesn't have a sinful, impure nature, but a completely clean and holy one, which he gave for the life of the world. In him we find a trustworthy and complete righteousness. So we remain humble—not with false humility, but with true humility—because of the corrupt tendencies and shortcomings of our sinful nature. Therefore, we would be guilty of eternal death if God were to judge us strictly. But we are not proud in the sight of God. We humbly acknowledge our sins and desire forgiveness with a broken heart. Trusting in the work of Christ as Mediator, we enter God's presence and plead for forgiveness of sins. Consequently, God spreads his immeasurable heaven of kindness over us, and for the sake of Christ, he does not credit our sins to us.

NOT TO CONDEMN THE WORLD

*For God did not send his Son into the world
to condemn the world, but to save the world through him.*
John 3:17

A father and mother don't scold, spank, or punish their children because they want to see their children die. They discipline their children so that they won't fall into the hands of the executioner later. In the same way, God doesn't want us to run wild. He directs and disciplines us in order to restrain us and keep us from being punished. God wants to protect us and make us heirs in the kingdom of heaven.

God disciplines his chosen ones and even sends them many trials and troubles. When you find yourself thinking, "Oh, God is so angry with me," then say to yourself, "I believe in you and in your Word. You won't deceive me. Even if you send me many troubles, it's not because you are condemning me. You will never throw me out. As Psalm 143:2 says, 'Do not bring your servant into judgment,' for you haven't been sent to judge the world." Even if God was to send plagues, don't think that he wants to destroy everything. When the Corinthians behaved foolishly at the Lord's Supper and God allowed many to become ill and die, Paul declared, "But if we judged ourselves, we would not come under judgment. When we are judged by the Lord, we are being disciplined so that we will not be condemned with the world" (1 Corinthians 11:31–32).

We should understand that God disciplines us so that we will be saved, not condemned. By disciplining us, he hopes to pull us back from the condemnation and judgment reserved for the world. He doesn't want us to be judged along with the world. Christ didn't come to judge. We shouldn't look on him as an executioner. He isn't angry. He doesn't want to condemn us. Instead, Christ wants to help us.

USING POSSESSIONS WISELY

Abram had become very wealthy in livestock and in silver and gold.
Genesis 13:2

People have many wrong ideas about wealth and material possessions. The Bible gives us numerous examples, such as this passage,
for countering these errors. The Scriptures teach us that riches are
not wrong in and of themselves, because they are gifts from God.
Rather, the problem begins with the people who own and use
them.

No good philosopher or theologian would find fault with
what God has created and given to his people. Instead, they would
condemn the misuse of God's gifts. David says, "Though your
riches increase, do not set your heart on them" (Psalm 62:10). It's
as if he meant to say, "Riches are good, but be careful that you
don't use them in the wrong way." Similarly, it isn't necessarily
wrong to admire a woman. After all, she is one of God's beautiful
creatures. But desiring someone you're not supposed to desire is
sinful. In order to remain pure, monks shut themselves up in
monasteries to avoid seeing any women. But even when they were
alone, they would burn with desire for women because they had
sinful hearts. Refusing to look at women can't stop these improper
thoughts, just as abstaining from certain things doesn't put an end
to sinful longings. Rather, we learn how to control ourselves by
interacting with people and actually using our possessions.

Your primary goal in life should be devotion to God. After
that, strive to make use of what you own with a pure heart. Keep
in mind that material possessions aren't evil in and of themselves.
Those who use their possessions wrongly are like fools who slouch
when they stand in the sunlight and then become upset because
their shadows are crooked. These people don't realize that the problem is inside of them.

PERSECUTED AND BLESSED

We are hard pressed on every side, but not crushed; perplexed, but not in despair; persecuted, but not abandoned; struck down, but not destroyed.
2 Corinthians 4:8–9

If the world cannot enthrall us with its delights and draw us into its sins, then it tries to drive us out with suffering and torment. The whole time we are on earth, the world tries to deceive us by showing us examples of sin or by cruelly torturing us. It's like a mythical monster with the head of a beautiful maiden, the body of a lion, and the tail of a poisonous serpent. The final destiny of the world, with its pleasures and cruelty, is poison and eternal death.

Therefore, God has ordained matters so that the sins of the world end up bringing us blessing. So also the persecutions of the world aren't useless, but God intends for them to increase our blessings. When the world tries to harm us, it ends up serving us and making us better people.

So we see that the entire Bible and all the early church fathers agree that those who try to harm us end up being very useful to us if we patiently endure the suffering. That is why Peter says, "Who is going to harm you if you are eager to do good?" (1 Peter 3:13). And we read in the Psalms, "No enemy will subject him to tribute; no wicked man will oppress him" (Psalm 89:22). But how can our enemies not harm us when they try so hard to kill us and sometimes even succeed? It's precisely when they harm us that they do us the most good. If we are wise, we understand we're living in the middle of blessing and evil at the same time. It's amazing how God in his goodness moderates it all!

CRYING OUT TO GOD

*[Jonah] said: "In my distress I called to the LORD,
and he answered me. From the depths of the grave
I called for help, and you listened to my cry."*
Jonah 2:2

We should cry out to God in such a way that we're convinced in our hearts that he will answer. It should be a cry that allows us to boast, as Jonah did, that God answers when we cry out in our need. This is simply crying out with the heart's true voice of faith. Unless we first lift up our hearts to God, we are unable to lift up our heads or hold up our hands.

With the help and support of the Spirit, we run to an angry God, looking for his undeserved kindness in the middle of his anger. When we lift our hearts in this way, we willingly endure punishment from God and we continue to look for his mercy. Notice what strong character such a heart must have. Though surrounded by God's anger and punishment, it doesn't seem to be aware of them. Instead, it sees and feels only God's kindness and grace. Though the heart is clearly aware of God's anger and punishment, it simply doesn't *want* to see or feel them. Rather, it's determined to look for God's kindness and grace—no matter how hidden they might be.

Turning to God is difficult. Breaking through his anger, punishment, and displeasure is like running through a row of thorns or even through a line of spears and swords. It's only with a sincere cry of faith that we can break through. When we cry out in this way, we know in our hearts that God hears us.

THE PRAYERS OF BELIEVERS

If you remain in me and my words remain in you,
ask whatever you wish, and it will be given you.
John 15:7

This is a miserable world for unbelievers. They work so hard yet accomplish nothing. They may even pray a lot, search all over, and knock at the door. Yet nothing is gained, found, or achieved, for they're knocking on the wrong door. They do all these things and even pray as if they were doing any other work. In other words, they do all this without any faith. That's why they can't really pray.

Prayer is the work of faith alone. No one except a believer can truly pray. Believers pray, not on their own merits, but in the name of the Son of God, in whom they have been baptized. They're certain that their prayers please God, because he commanded them to pray in the name of Christ and promised he would listen to them. But unbelievers don't know this. Instead, they pray in their own names and believe they can prepare themselves. They think they can read enough to make themselves worthy and smart enough to make prayer into an acceptable work. And when we ask them whether their prayers have been heard, they reply, "I prayed, but if my prayers were heard, only God knows." If you don't know what you are doing or whether God is listening, what kind of a prayer is that?

But Christians don't approach prayer this way. We pray in response to God's command and promise. We offer our prayers to God in the name of Christ, and we know that what we ask for will be given to us. We experience God's help in all kinds of needy situations. And if relief doesn't come soon, we still know that our prayers are pleasing to God. We know that God has answered us because he gives us the strength to endure.

PRAY FOR GOD'S RICH BLESSINGS

*Surely goodness and love will follow me all the days of my life,
and I will dwell in the house of the LORD forever.*
Psalm 23:6

The devil never stops tormenting believers. On the inside, he afflicts them with fears. On the outside, he torments them with the tricks of false teachers and the power of tyrants. So at the conclusion of this psalm, David earnestly prayed that God, who had given him rich blessings, would continue to take care of him until the end. He was asking God to grant him favor so that "goodness and love will follow" him all the days of his life. Then David explained how God would show his goodness and love: "I will dwell in the house of the LORD forever." He was saying, "Lord, you are the one who started all this. You gave me your holy Word and made me one of your people who know, honor, and praise you. Continue to show me your favor so that I may stay close to your Word and never be separated from your holy kingdom."

David asked for the same in Psalm 27. He said, "One thing I ask of the LORD, this is what I seek: that I may dwell in the house of the LORD all the days of my life, to gaze upon the beauty of the LORD and to seek him in his temple" (v. 4).

By his example, David teaches all believers that they should not become overconfident, proud, or presumptuous. Instead, they should be afraid and pray that they don't lose God's rich blessings. David's example should wake us up so that we will pray diligently.

BELIEVERS ARE STILL SINNERS

If, while we seek to be justified in Christ, it becomes evident
that we ourselves are sinners, does that mean
that Christ promotes sin? Absolutely not!
Galatians 2:17

How can those who are justified in Christ not be sinners and yet be sinners at the same time? For the Scripture asserts both conditions about the person who is justified. John writes in 1 John 1:8, "If we claim to be without sin, we deceive ourselves and the truth is not in us." He also writes in 1 John 5:18, "We know that anyone born of God does not continue to sin." He says the same in 1 John 3:9, "No one who is born of God will continue to sin, because God's seed remains in him; he cannot go on sinning." In other words, John is saying that believers don't sin. But if they were to claim they had no sin, they would be lying.

We can see a similar difficulty in the book of Job. God, who cannot lie, says Job is a man of integrity in Job 1:8. Yet Job confesses later in Job 9:20 and other passages that he is a sinner. In Job 7:21 he says, "Why do you not pardon my offenses and forgive my sins?" Job must be telling the truth, because if he were lying to God, God wouldn't call him a righteous person. So Job is at the same time righteous and sinful.

If we look at faith, God's laws are fulfilled, sin is destroyed, and no law is left. But if we look at our sinful nature, there is nothing good. Therefore, we must always remember that all of us who are righteous through faith are still sinners.

ETERNAL FOOD

*Do not work for food that spoils, but for food that endures
to eternal life, which the Son of Man will give you.
On him God the Father has placed his seal of approval.*
John 6:27

In this passage, Christ compares what perishes with what endures forever. If we were truly concerned about this difference, we would keep holding on to what is eternal and stop clinging to what is temporary. Christ is saying here, "If I were to give you right now the type of things you already have, such as the bread you get from the baker, and if I were to give you enough of it to satisfy the entire world, how much would it really help you? If I had more wheat, barley, oats, money, and property than the richest person in the world to give you, what would be gained? I would have food to give you, but it would be perishable food that wouldn't last forever."

There isn't a farmer who would be so foolish as to give one hundred bushels of grain for a crumpled piece of paper. There isn't a merchant who would exchange a hundred bottles of beer for a glass of water. Both would rather sell their possessions at a premium price.

Christ, however, is saying that everything we own is perishable and that we should willingly give it all away in order to get eternal food. But in this world, we tend to be more concerned about what will pass away than what will last forever. We grab for a handful of food and end up letting go of the gospel.

PRESERVING HARMONY

❦

"Your servant is in your hands," Abram said. "Do with her whatever you think best." Then Sarai mistreated Hagar; so she fled from her.
Genesis 16:6

In the dispute between Hagar and Sarai, Abram sided with his childless, elderly wife instead of her pregnant servant. Abram didn't want to make his godly wife sad. So he allowed Sarai to deal with her servant as she pleased, despite the fact that Hagar was pregnant with Abram's child. This little incident describes the hazards, struggles, and conflicts that are a part of marriage. Sarai was being tested, yet God comforted her through Abram. The fact that God always watches over marriages and families shows us that he is pleased with these institutions.

Family life often leads to quarreling and conflict between husbands and wives. Furthermore, frequent disagreements and disputes occur in government. Splinter groups form in the church. Anyone who has watched all these conflicts would assume that nothing good could come from all of this.

This passage is warning us to be prepared for troubles and to patiently tolerate them. Don't think that you will escape marital conflicts or political disputes. Only foolish people, who are naive about life, think this way. Problems are common in church administration as well. Splinter groups and other troublemakers in the church cause all kinds of disruptions. Here on earth we live among unappreciative, stubborn people who will never stop spreading confusion and bitterness. In light of this, we must remember this story and believe and trust in God, just as faithful Abram did. We must try to get along in peace and preserve harmony as best we can.

CONCENTRATING ON PRAYER

The end of all things is near. Therefore be clear minded
and self-controlled so that you can pray.
1 Peter 4:7

If it were possible to see into a person's heart, nothing would be more ridiculous than seeing the thoughts of a cold, undevoted heart in prayer. When someone forgets what they just said, they aren't praying a good prayer. Praise God that I now understand this clearly. In true prayer, one remembers all the words and thoughts from the beginning to the end of the prayer.

To illustrate, a good barber must keep his thoughts, mind, and eyes on the razor and on the hair he's cutting. He can't forget where he is. If he starts chatting away, thinking about something else, or looking somewhere else, he might cut his customer's mouth, nose, or throat. So doing anything well requires total concentration of the whole person. As the saying goes, "Whoever thinks about many things thinks about nothing and doesn't do anything right." Praying a good prayer requires even more concentration than this. It demands the whole heart.

This is how I pray the Lord's Prayer. For even today I keep on eating and drinking from the Lord's Prayer as if I were a hungry baby or a famished adult who can never get enough. It's the best prayer of all.

IN A SINGLE DAY

"See, the stone I have set in front of Joshua! There are seven eyes on that one stone, and I will engrave an inscription on it," says the LORD Almighty, "and I will remove the sin of this land in a single day."
Zechariah 3:9

The stone was going to be engraved, and God promised he would take away all sin in one day. We know very well, of course, that sin isn't taken away by anything except Christ's suffering. His suffering would result in the forgiveness of sins, as Isaiah 53 states. Peter and Paul also teach the same in many places. So the engraving of the stone symbolizes the suffering of Christ, not his conception or birth.

God's promise to remove the sin of the land shows that the sacrifices of the old priesthood were incapable of providing forgiveness of sins. Only Christ's suffering can take away sin, nothing else. All good works are worthless and are even sinful before God. Only the engraved foundation stone can achieve forgiveness of sins for us, nothing else.

God shows us just how strong and powerful this forgiveness is when he said he wanted to accomplish it all "in a single day." This phrase means he wanted to accomplish this in one day—once and only once. The forgiveness and reconciliation achieved on that day would be enough for the sins of the entire world—from its very beginning into eternity. God didn't want to continually arrange for forgiveness of new sins on a daily or yearly basis, as was true under the old priesthood. The people of Israel had to regularly seek forgiveness through sacrifices and worship. But God wanted to provide complete forgiveness in one day. Christ's suffering would be enough, satisfying everything. The author of Hebrews sums this up beautifully: "By one sacrifice he has made perfect forever those who are being made holy" (Hebrews 10:14).

JOY AND SORROW

I tell you the truth, you will weep and mourn while the world rejoices.
You will grieve, but your grief will turn to joy.
John 16:20

We must see the sadness, crying, and wailing described in this passage from a Christian perspective, not a worldly one. This sadness accompanies all of the positions in life that are ordained by God.

God designed the world in such a way that he places people in positions in life before they understand everything that goes with those positions. For example, young people are hurried into marriage with music and dancing. They joyfully approach marriage and imagine it will be as sweet as pure sugar. In the same way, God gives great honor and glory to princes and lords. He hangs gold chains around their necks, sets them on velvet cushions, and allows people to bow before them and call them "Your Honor." He gives them large castles and great fame. Those who haven't experienced this lifestyle would think these people's lives are filled with nothing but joy and pleasure. Then, having caught them, it's as if God tosses a rope over their horns. When they are caught in their positions, they discover their lives are far different than they thought they would be. The thrill fades. Misfortune and sorrow spoil the joy and pleasure.

This is nothing compared to the lofty truths Christ is talking about in this passage. This is how life goes. It alternates between good and bad, joy and sorrow, summer and winter, sun and rain, good years and bad years, times of sadness and times of laughter and then times of trouble again. This is the way it is for all people in their positions in life. It's very difficult and unpleasant, but we all must patiently endure part of the punishment placed on Adam.

WHITER THAN SNOW

Cleanse me with hyssop, and I will be clean;
wash me, and I will be whiter than snow.
Psalm 51:7

How can we become whiter than snow when sin remains in us and sticks to us? Because of our sins, we are never as clean and holy as we should be. But we have received baptism, which is pure. We have received God's Word, which is also pure. And through baptism and God's Word, we have received Christ's blood, which is absolutely pure. Because of the purity we receive in faith through Christ, we can certainly say that we are whiter than snow. We are purer than the sun and stars, even though sin still sticks to us. Our sin is covered by the purity and innocence of Christ, which we receive when we hear and believe God's Word. We should keep in mind, though, that this purity comes completely from outside ourselves. In other words, Christ clothes us with his own perfection.

If we look at Christians apart from Christ and see them as they really are, we would notice how much they are contaminated by sin. Even if they were fine people, we would see not only that they're thoroughly contaminated, but also that they're covered over with a thick, dark film of sin. If someone tried to separate us from Christ and take away our baptism and God's promises, we would no longer have Christ's purity. We would be left with nothing but sin.

So when someone asks you, "If sin always sticks to people, how can they be washed so clean that they are whiter than snow?" you can answer, "We should view people, not as they are on their own, but as they are in Christ."

CARRY EACH OTHER'S BURDENS

꩜

Carry each other's burdens, and in this way
you will fulfill the law of Christ.
Galatians 6:2

Everywhere love turns, it finds burdens to carry and ways to help. Love is the law of Christ. To love means to wish another person good from the heart. It means to seek what is best for the other person.

What if there were no one who made a mistake? What if no one fell? What if no one needed help? To whom would you show love? To whom could you show favor? Whose best could you seek? Love would not be able to exist if there were no people who made mistakes and sinned. The philosophers say that each of these people is the appropriate and adequate "object" of love or the "material" with which love has to work.

The sinful nature—or the kind of love that is really lust—wants others to wish it well and to give it what it desires. In other words, it seeks its own interests. The "material" it works with is a righteous, holy, godly, and good person. People who follow this sinful nature completely reverse God's teaching. They want others to bear their burdens, serve them, and carry them. These are the kind of people who despise having uneducated, useless, angry, foolish, troublesome, and gloomy people as their life companions. Instead, they look for friendly, charming, good-natured, quiet, and holy people. They want to live, not on earth, but in paradise; not among sinners, but among angels; not in the world, but in heaven. We should feel sorry for these people, because they are receiving their reward here on earth and possessing their heaven in this life.

LIFE AFTER DEATH

For my Father's will is that everyone who looks to the Son and believes in him shall have eternal life, and I will raise him up at the last day.
John 6:40

This passage is a glorious promise to us. It's repeated twice because we tend to think, "That doesn't quite make sense. These words are difficult to believe." No one could foresee that faith would be so important until Christ actually said, "Everyone who believes in me will have eternal life." Now Jerome, Ambrose, and Cyprian all believed in Christ, yet they were executed. How do we fit this together with the promise of eternal life? When we see how people who believe in Christ are cursed, condemned, exiled, even beheaded and burned, it's like having the rug pulled out from under us. Christians aren't allowed to live in peace. This promise about eternal life seems like a lie to us. If this is what eternal life means—that one is pursued and killed—then let the devil have that type of life.

But faith must close its eyes and refuse to pass judgment on what it sees or feels in the world. You won't become aware of eternal life until Christ raises you from the dead. Meanwhile, your eternal life is hidden in death. It's covered up and out of sight. But remember that as long as you live, and even when you're dying, you have forgiveness. If you feel the weight of sin crushing you, you can still say, "My sins are forgiven." When your sins hunt you down, bite at you, and terrify you, you can look to Christ, put your feeble faith in him, and hold on tightly.

LOT'S PRAYER

You have shown great kindness to me in sparing my life. But I can't flee to the mountains; this disaster will overtake me, and I'll die. Look, here is a town near enough to run to, and it is small. Let me flee to it.
Genesis 19:19–20

Take a look at the different parts of Lot's prayer. The first part of a good prayer is giving thanks to God. Giving thanks includes acknowledging God's wonderful acts of kindness and praising God. When we pray the Lord's Prayer, we certainly do ask for daily bread. But we first address God as our Father right at the beginning of the prayer. With these very words, we are acknowledging that he has already provided food and protection for us, as a father would, up to that very day. Praising and thanking God are good ways to acknowledge his kindness.

The second part of a prayer is to pour out our deepest concerns to God about personal problems and needs. In Lot's case, he was saying, "I'll be in danger if I do what you say and run for the mountains. In the past, I have gotten into trouble for being too slow. I could be in bigger trouble now if I'm too slow. Please give me what I'm asking, for I know you are merciful."

In the third part of Lot's prayer, he proposed his own solution to the problem and asked God's permission to carry it out. He wanted to run to a nearby city where he thought he would be safe. He pointed out that it was a small town, which would provide a safe place to stay.

This was Lot's prayer. Think carefully about this incident and what happened as a result. Lot prayed, and then God changed his plan. At this point, we shouldn't debate about whether or not God changes his mind. Rather, we should learn what Psalm 145:19 teaches: "He fulfills the desires of those who fear him; he hears their cry and saves them."

WHAT IT MEANS TO SEE GOD

Blessed are the pure in heart, for they will see God.
Matthew 5:8

It's very important for believers to have pure hearts that follow God. They need be pure on the basis of God's pure and holy Word. What reward will they have? What has God promised to those who are pure in heart? We are told, "They will see God." Surely this is wonderful—an excellent treasure! But what does it mean to "see God"?

Some people have their own ideas about how to see God. They crouch in a corner, lift their thoughts toward heaven, and engage in a life of idle speculation. Is this any way to try to see God? They use their own ideas to try to stroll into God's presence. They try to climb up to heaven under their own power. They insist on using their own intellect to figure out everything about God and his Word.

However, if you believe that Christ is your Savior, you'll soon realize that you have a gracious God. Faith leads you to heaven and lets you see inside of God's heart. There you will get a glimpse of his infinite kindness and love. This is what it really means to "see God." You can't physically see him with your eyes, because no one can see God in this life. Instead, you see God by faith.

GOD'S POWER

In his great mercy he has given us new birth . . . into an inheritance
that can never perish, spoil or fade—kept in heaven for you,
who through faith are shielded by God's power.
1 Peter 1:3–5

Peter addresses those "who through faith are shielded by God's power." He uses this description because when certain people hear the gospel—how faith alone without works makes us godly—they jump in and say, "Yes, I believe too." They confuse their own thoughts, which they make up, with faith. We have previously taught from Scripture that none of us can do even the smallest works without God's Spirit. How then out of our own strength could we do the greatest work—to believe? Such thoughts are nothing but a dream. If we are to believe, then God's power must be working in us. Paul says, "I keep asking that the God of our Lord Jesus Christ, the glorious Father, may give you the Spirit of wisdom . . . that you may know . . . his incomparably great power for us who believe" (Ephesians 1:17–19). Not only is it God's will, but he also has the power to spend a great deal on us. For when God creates faith in us, it is a great work. It's as if he were creating heaven and earth again.

People are being foolish when they say, "How can faith alone save us?" There are some people who believe, yet they don't do any good works. For they think that their own thoughts are faith and that faith can exist without good works. In contrast, we agree with Peter, who says faith is a power that comes from God. When God gives faith, the individual is born again and becomes a new creature. As a result, good works naturally flow from faith.

BETWEEN ARROGANCE AND DESPAIR

But he gives us more grace. That is why Scripture says:
"God opposes the proud but gives grace to the humble."
James 4:6

We shouldn't become proud in times of prosperity nor despair in times of trouble. On the one hand, we must keep our arrogance in check by fearing God. On the other hand, we should cling to his mercy in those times when we think he is angry with us. By doing so, we won't crash into heaven with our big heads or fall flat on our faces on the earth.

The person who is humble and has a broken heart is neither proud nor full of despair. Yet it's difficult for us to avoid both arrogance and despair. In our weakness, we sometimes swerve to the right and sometimes to the left. Whenever we feel overconfident or full of despair, we must make an effort to resist such tendencies. We cannot give in to either one. When an archer misses the bull's-eye, the archer is still awarded points for hitting the target. Similarly, God is pleased when we at least fight against arrogance and despair. Even if we may not show enough joy in times of trouble or enough reverence for God in times of prosperity, he won't hold it against his faithful people. We have Christ as our mediator. Through him, we are considered true saints even though we have barely started to act like holy people.

In summary, those with many troubles should lift their spirits by acknowledging God's mercy and remembering what Christ has done for them. Those with few troubles should drive out arrogance by living in the fear of God.

LETTING GO OF OUR POSSESSIONS

The very fact that you have lawsuits among you means
you have been completely defeated already. Why not rather
be wronged? Why not rather be cheated?
1 Corinthians 6:7

Unfortunately in this world, we have lawsuits. It would be better if there were none. But God allows them to exist in order to avoid greater evil. He permits lawsuits because people are imperfect. When someone takes something from people, they don't want to let go of it and give it back to God.

Nevertheless, we should strive toward the goal of keeping God's name holy. We should learn from day to day how to give God's honor and goods back to him. This includes giving back to God anything that is taken away from us. In this way, we are made completely holy. The Lord's Prayer was given to us to help us remember that we should always want to keep God's name holy.

It shouldn't surprise Christians if they have everything taken away from them—all of their property, honor, friends, health, wisdom, and so on. For ultimately all their possessions will be destroyed, and they will be separated from all things before they can be made holy and keep God's name holy. For if something exists, its name also exists. So everything must be taken away so that only God, the things of God, and the names of God remain.

DOING IN FAITH

Clearly no one is justified before God by the law,
because, "The righteous will live by faith."
Galatians 3:11

We are used to speaking about faith in two ways. We sometimes speak about faith apart from works, and at other times we speak about faith accompanied by works. Just as a craftsman speaks about the material in various ways and a gardener speaks of a tree sometimes being barren and sometimes bearing fruit, so the Holy Spirit speaks in Scripture in various ways about faith. Sometimes Scripture refers to an abstract or absolute faith. Other times it refers to faith as it appears outwardly, as it relates to other things, or as we live it out. Faith is absolute and not connected to other things when the Scripture speaks absolutely about justification or those who are justified, as we can see in Romans and Galatians.

But when Scripture speaks of rewards and works, it's speaking of faith as it relates to other things—how it appears or how we live it out. The Bible gives several examples of this faith. "The only thing that counts is faith expressing itself through love" (Galatians 5:6). "Do this and you will live" (Luke 10:28). "If you want to enter life, obey the commandments" (Matthew 19:17). "The man who does these things will live by them" (Galatians 3:12). "Turn from evil and do good" (Psalm 34:14). There are countless verses like this in Scripture. In these and similar verses where "doing" is mentioned, Scripture always speaks of "doing in faith." If you have faith, then you are able to do good works.

THE BEST PRAYER OF ALL

❦

This, then, is how you should pray:
"Our Father in heaven, hallowed be your name."
Matthew 6:9

After having denounced showy and meaningless prayers, Christ introduced a splendid short prayer of his own. With it, he instructed us on how to pray and what we should pray for. He gave us a prayer that touches on a variety of needs. By themselves, these needs should compel us to approach God daily with these few, easily remembered words. None of us can excuse ourselves by saying we don't know how to pray or what to pray for.

Praying the Lord's Prayer every day is certainly a worthwhile habit, especially for ordinary people and children. We can pray it in the morning, in the evening, and at the dinner table—at any time for that matter. As we pray this prayer together, we bring our needs before God.

As has been said many times before, the Lord's Prayer is the finest prayer that anyone could have ever thought up or that was ever sent from heaven. Because God the Father gave his Son the words for the prayer and sent him to introduce it, we know beyond a doubt that this prayer pleases the Father immensely.

Right at the beginning of the prayer, with the words "Our Father," Jesus reminds us of what God demands and promises. God insists that we give him the respect, honor, and reverence he deserves, just as earthly fathers expect this from their children. Also, God the Father wants us to trust that he will meet our needs. We are overjoyed to be his children through Christ. And so, because we trust that he will give us what he promised, we can pray to him with confidence in the name of Christ our Lord.

ANGELS HEAR THE HARMONY

꧁ ꧂

Jacob also went on his way, and the angels of God met him.
Genesis 32:1

Angels are spirits who serve all of creation. Their job on earth is to fight for the good of the world and the welfare of God's people. Their job in heaven is to sing, "Glory to God in the highest," and "Lord God, we praise you." Christ says that the "angels in heaven always see the face of my Father in heaven" (Matthew 18:10).

The angels have a good understanding of how the world works. They know that there's a correlation between the fortunate circumstances of wicked people and the adverse conditions of faithful believers. While we Christians are still on earth, we cannot fully understand this or see how it can be true. At the end of the world, after this life, we will understand how all of this fits together.

People who are unfamiliar with the principles of musical harmony have trouble appreciating how the various sounds produced by an organ or harp can result in such beautiful music. In this life, we hear the sounds, not the symphony. It appears to us that God is asleep and the devil is wide-awake and ruling everything. Human reason concludes that neither God nor people are in control of the world, but that everything on earth happens by chance. Human wisdom can't comprehend the infinite, heavenly truth that God is in charge and allows many more things in this world to succeed than fail. God's kindness is more widespread than the devil's cruelty. But human reason makes us uncertain because we experience so much disorder and injustice. We feel uncertain because we don't see by the same light the angels do. We can't understand how right and wrong, life and death, light and darkness all harmonize.

HOLD ON TO CHRIST

For God so loved the world that he gave his one and only Son,
that whoever believes in him shall not perish but have eternal life.
John 3:16

In this passage, Jesus tells us how he destroyed death and how we will survive it. Jesus is the antidote for death. Nevertheless, death and the law condemned Jesus so that he had to die and be buried. Yet Jesus rose again from the dead.

But how do we approach our Redeemer and Savior? Do we approach him with personal sacrifice and religious rules? No! Just hold on to the Son in faith. He has overcome death and stabbed the devil's stomach. Although he was crucified under Annas and Caiaphas, Jesus will rule and reign. So we must remain in him. Then we will be able to tear right through death and the devil, for the passage says, "Whoever believes in him shall not perish but have eternal life." Accept it as true. Accept this wonderful truth that God loved the world and say, "I believe in the Son of God, who was also the son of Mary, who was nailed to the cross and lifted up." Then you will experience the new birth. Death and sin will no longer condemn you. They will no longer bring you harm, sorrow, or pain. Whoever believes in the Son will have eternal life.

Cling to Christ's neck, or hold on to his clothes. This means believing that Jesus became a man and suffered for you. Make the sign of the cross and say, "I am a Christian, and I will prevail." Death won't prevail. Death couldn't hold on to Christ. "It was impossible for death to keep its hold on him" (Acts 2:24) because deity and humanity were united in one person, Jesus Christ. In the same way, we won't remain dead. We will destroy death if we remain in the faith and cling to the destroyer of death, Jesus Christ.

OPPOSING EVIL

꧁ ❦ ꧂

*But I tell you, Do not resist an evil person. If someone strikes you
on the right cheek, turn to him the other also. And if someone wants
to sue you and take your tunic, let him have your cloak as well.*
Matthew 5:39–40

Getting involved in secular matters isn't a sin for Christians. Believers are simply carrying out the responsibilities that all citizens have—whether Christian or non-Christian. Yet believers have to consciously avoid sin and do what Christ expects of them. In contrast, the people of the world don't do what Christ requires.

That's why when Christians fight in a war, file a lawsuit, or impose a punishment, they are functioning in their role as a soldier, lawyer, or judge. But within these roles, Christians will want to keep their consciences clear and their motives pure. They don't want to hurt anyone. So they live life simultaneously as Christians and as secular people. They live as Christians in all situations, enduring hardships in this world. They live as secular people obeying all national laws, community regulations, and domestic rules.

In summary, Christians don't live for visible things in this life. These things fall under the authority of secular government, which Christ doesn't intend to abolish. Outwardly and physically, Christ doesn't want us to evade governmental authority or expect us to abandon our civic duties. Instead, he wants us to submit to and make use of the organizational and regulatory powers of the government, which keep society intact. But inwardly and spiritually, we live under Christ's authority. His kingdom isn't concerned with governmental authority and doesn't interfere with it but is willing to accept it. So as Christians and as individuals, we shouldn't resist an evil person. On the other hand, as citizens with responsibilities in society, we should oppose evil to the full extent of our authority.

OPEN TO CORRECTION

*Everyone who does evil hates the light, and will not come
into the light for fear that his deeds will be exposed.*
John 3:20

The world doesn't want to be punished. It wants to remain in darkness. It doesn't want to be told that what it believes is false. If you also don't want to be corrected, then you might as well leave the church and spend your time at the bar and brothel. But if you want to be saved—and remember that there's another life after this one—you must accept correction.

If you don't want to be saved, what's the use of me being concerned about it? If you aren't sure you believe in hell, the devil, death, eternal condemnation, and the wrath of God, then just ask your neighbor about it. Anyone can tell you that all of us will die.

In short, if the church and secular government are to exist, they must shed light on evil. The civil authorities must punish the obvious darkness of public vices and the offensive ways of people, while we preachers in the church must bring to light the subtle darkness of false teachers and false belief. We must confront those who teach and think that they are righteous because of what they do.

If the church and government stopped admonishing people, the whole world would collapse in a heap. If you want to be saved and be a Christian, then stay open to correction. Preachers have to rebuke, or they should leave their position. The Christian who won't accept correction is only pretending to be a Christian.

THE GOOD OLD DAYS

Do not say, "Why were the old days better than these?"
For it is not wise to ask such questions.
Ecclesiastes 7:10

When people are ungrateful to us, we often start complaining, "Things are worse now than they ever were." But we shouldn't talk like this. Elderly people tend to say, "When I was a child, everything was better." They are the "people who praise the days gone by," as one poet calls them. But the author of Ecclesiastes says this isn't true. Things never really went that well. We only realize how bad things are now because as we grow older, the number of things that annoy us also increases.

Children don't pay much attention to news about someone deceiving or murdering someone else. They keep on playing, running, and riding. They think it's the worst thing in the world when someone steals another's marbles. Only then do they become angry. But when they become adults, they become sensitive to the troubles and disloyalty of people around them. They get angry when a horse breaks a leg, when the cattle don't fatten properly, and so on.

The world has always been filled with troubles, but we haven't always been aware of them all. When we were children, nothing bothered us. Our lives remained relatively calm. But the world has always been wicked. Therefore, make sure that you have a quiet and peaceful heart. Don't become upset when you see these evils. Though you can't change the world, make sure you are changed into a new person.

THE LIMITS OF GOVERNMENT

*Show proper respect to everyone: Love the brotherhood
of believers, fear God, honor the king.*
1 Peter 2:17

The secular government doesn't extend any further than external and physical matters. God can tolerate secular government because it doesn't concern itself with sin, good works, or spiritual matters. Instead, it handles other matters, such as guarding cities, building bridges, collecting tolls and taxes, providing protection, defending the land and the people, and punishing criminals. So Christians should obey government officials as long as these officials don't command them to do something against their consciences. Christians obey without having to be forced because they're free in all matters.

If an emperor or prince were to ask me about my faith, I surely would tell him, not because of his governmental authority, but because I should confess my faith publicly. If, however, he ordered me to believe this or that, I would say, "Sir, take care of the secular government. You have no authority intruding on God's kingdom. I will not obey you. You cannot tolerate anyone intruding on your domain. If someone oversteps their boundary without your permission, you shoot them. Do you think that God should tolerate your desire to push him off his throne and seat yourself in his place?"

Peter calls the secular government merely a human institution. It has no power to interfere with the way God has arranged the world. It has no power to give orders about faith.

ETERNAL LIFE BEGINS NOW

I tell you the truth, he who believes has everlasting life.
John 6:47

One could preach a hundred thousand years about these words and emphasize them again and again. Yes, one can't speak enough about these words. Here Christ explicitly promises eternal life to the believer. He doesn't say that if we believe in him we *will have* eternal life. Rather, he says that as soon as we believe in him, we *already have* eternal life. He is speaking, not of future gifts, but of present ones. He is saying, "If you believe in me, you are saved. You already have eternal life."

This passage is the cornerstone of our justification. With it, we can settle the disputes we're having about how we receive God's approval. Good works don't lead us to heaven or help us in the sight of God. Only faith can do this. Of course, we should do good works and live holy lives in obedience to God. But these efforts won't help us earn salvation. We already have eternal life. If we don't receive it while here on earth, we'll never receive it after we leave. Eternal life must be attained and received in this body.

Yet how do we acquire eternal life? God becomes our teacher, for he tells us about eternal life through those who preach his Word. He convinces us that we should accept his Word and believe in him. That is how it begins. Those same words that we hear and believe will lead us to none other than the person of Christ, born of the Virgin Mary. God will take us nowhere else. If we believe in Christ and cling to him, we are redeemed from both physical and spiritual death. We already have eternal life.

BOUGHT AT A PRICE

You were bought at a price; do not become slaves of men.
1 Corinthians 7:23

Here Paul forbids us to become slaves. No doubt he says this as a general guideline against people who try to destroy the freedom and equality of belief and clamp down too tightly on consciences. For example, if someone teaches that a Christian man absolutely cannot marry a non-Christian woman or stay married to her, as some churches teach, then that person hinders the freedom taught here by Paul. That person actually steers people to be more obedient to him than to God's Word, which Paul says is serving human beings. The people following this teacher think they are God's slaves and serving him when in fact they are serving human teaching and becoming slaves of others. This is also true of those who preached that Christians must be circumcised, nullifying Christian freedom as a result.

So in every way, Paul is concerned about Christian freedom and guards it against the chains and prison of human rules. Paul verifies this when he says, "You were bought at a price." Paul means that Christ bought us with his own blood and set us free from all sins and laws, as it says in Galatians 5:1.

The freedom Christ purchased, however, isn't what the world means by freedom. It doesn't affect the roles people have with one another, such as a servant with a master or a wife with a husband. God doesn't want these roles to be changed. Instead, he wants them to be honored. He changes us inwardly and spiritually. Before God, no law binds us or holds us captive. We are truly free in all things. Before, we were caught in our sins, but now all of our sins are gone. So whatever outward roles or relationships still exist, they have nothing to do with sin or merit before God.

LISTEN TO CHRIST

But blessed are your eyes because they see, and your ears because they hear.
Matthew 13:16

Some people listen to what Jesus says but don't believe that the Father is speaking. They don't believe that his words are the words of the Father. That's why God must draw them further along. When they hear the Word, God impresses it on their hearts. Then they're able to believe that they're hearing the Father's words when they hear Christ speaking.

I plead with you to learn what it means for the Father to draw you. This means you must listen to the words from Christ's mouth. You must learn from him. You must not stray from his words.

It's not reason that brings you to faith. Christ overthrows your own self-deceit and reason. He condemns people who reject his spoken word and want to wait for something special to happen. They hope the Father will speak personally to them from heaven and give them the Spirit directly. They want to hear an audible voice from heaven, but it won't happen.

The only way to hear the Father speak is through the Son. You will hear the words of Christ, but these aren't enough to draw you. Your reason says that Christ is only a man, and his words are only the words of a man. But if you delight in reflecting on the Word—reading it, listening to it being preached, and loving it— soon you will come to the point where you say, "Truly this is God's Word!" In this way, faith comes alongside reason.

GOD CAN FIX MISTAKES

The fear of the LORD is the beginning of wisdom; all who follow his
precepts have good understanding. To him belongs eternal praise.
Psalm 111:10

You should beware of two extremes. One is becoming arrogant about your wisdom and plans. The other is becoming depressed when things go wrong. God forgives and even blesses the mistakes of faithful people. In my ignorance, I often made the biggest mistakes and did the most foolish things when I was sincerely trying to help people and give them good advice. When I made these mistakes, I prayed fervently to God, asking him to forgive me and correct what I had done. Important and faithful leaders often cause great harm through their advice and actions. If God didn't have mercy on them and didn't straighten everything out, the world would be in a terrible mess.

All of us make mistakes. We consider ourselves wise and knowledgeable. Yet in our sincere desire to help, we can end up causing a lot of damage. If God in his wisdom and compassion didn't correct our mistakes, we would make a mess out of our lives. We are like the farmer whose horses had trouble moving a heavy load. Thinking the wheels on the wagon were too wide, he sharpened them. This only made the load sink so deep into the mud that the wagon couldn't be moved at all.

Does that mean that people should do nothing and just run away from all their responsibilities? Not at all. You should faithfully do the job that God has given you to do. Don't rely on your own wisdom and strength, and don't pretend to be so smart and important that everything has to be done your way. Don't be ashamed to get on your knees and pray, "Dear God, you gave me this job. Please teach and guide me. Give me the knowledge, wisdom, and strength to perform my duties tirelessly and well."

WORRYING ABOUT DAILY NECESSITIES

꒰ ꒱

Therefore I tell you, do not worry about your life, what you will eat
or drink; or about your body, what you will wear. Is not life more
important than food, and the body more important than clothes?
Matthew 6:25

In this passage, Jesus delivers a scathing sermon against worry.
Worry shows lack of trust, and therefore it's opposed to the gospel
of Christ. Worry is a problem for the world at large as well as for
Christians.

The devil hates anyone who wants to live a Christian life and
declares that Christ is Lord. The devil, the ruler of this world, keeps
opposing and antagonizing believers. He can't attack them through
God's Word and faith, so he attacks them with what is under his
authority and control. Believers are trapped in their bodies, which
are still in Satan's kingdom. So he harasses and imprisons them,
deprives them of food and drink, and constantly threatens to take
away all their wealth and possessions. As this is happening, believers naturally try to find ways to escape these calamities and avoid
losing their property.

The people of this world, however, praise those who strive
for wealth and possessions. Instead of seeing striving for wealth
as a failure to trust God, they consider it a commendable virtue
and a praiseworthy character trait.

Take note of what it means to serve wealth. It means undue
concern about the needs and necessities of life, such as worrying
about what you will eat and what you will wear. In short, it means
thinking only about this life and accumulating a large fortune
under the mistaken notion that this life will go on forever. We
don't have to consider daily necessities, such as eating, drinking,
and buying clothes, as serving and worshiping wealth. Purchasing
and storing food are essential for life. The sin, however, is being
concerned about daily necessities and setting our hearts on them
as sources of comfort and security.

EVIL DESIRES WITHIN US

*Dear friends, I urge you, as aliens and strangers in the world,
to abstain from sinful desires, which war against your soul.*
1 Peter 2:11

Peter points out here that no believer is completely perfect and pure. Some think this passage refers only to sinners, as if believers don't have any evil desires. But study Scripture carefully and take note: On one hand, the prophets sometimes speak of believers as if they were pure in every respect. On the other hand, they also speak of them as still having evil desires and struggling against sin. Some people cannot get comfortable with both truths. So look at Christians as having two parts—the inner being, which is faith, and the outer being, which is the sinful nature. If you look at Christians only according to faith, they appear pure and totally clean, for the Word of God finds nothing impure in them. When faith enters a person's heart and the heart accepts it, the Word makes it completely clean. Therefore, all things are perfect in faith, and we are kings, priests, and God's people. But because faith lives in us and we still live on earth, we at times feel evil inclinations, such as impatience, fear of death, and so on. These are still short-comings of the sinful nature, for faith doesn't yet have full power over our outer being.

In Luke 10:30–37, a man was traveling from Jerusalem to Jericho and fell among robbers who beat him and left him lying half-dead. Later, a Samaritan bound his wounds, took him, and had him cared for. Because this man was being taken care of, he was no longer deathly ill and was sure to live. He had life, but he didn't have complete health. In the same way, we have Christ and we are certain of eternal life, but we don't yet enjoy total health. Some of our evil desires still remain with us.

GOD IS GOOD

Give thanks to the LORD, for he is good; his love endures forever.
Psalm 118:1

You shouldn't read the words *good* and *love* in a dispassionate way. Don't skim over these words. Don't say them too quickly or irreverently in church. Instead, remember that these are vibrant, relevant, and meaningful words that emphasize the goodness of God.

God is good—much better than humans. God, from the very bottom of his heart, is inclined to help people and continually do what is good. He doesn't like to get angry or punish people. He does so only when it's necessary—when he's forced into it by a person's wickedness and stubborn refusal to change. People could never be as patient as God is. They would punish a hundred thousand times sooner and more severely than God does.

God proves beyond a shadow of a doubt that he is good and loving. His daily and continual goodness shows this in rich and powerful ways. This psalm says, "His love endures forever." In other words, God continually does what is best for us. He provides for our bodies and souls and protects us day and night. He continues to preserve our lives. He lets the sun and moon shine for us and allows the sky, fire, air, and water to serve us. The Lord causes the earth to give us everything we need—grain, food, cattle feed, wood, and the resources for making wine and clothes. He gives us gold and silver, homes and families, spouses and children, animals, birds, and fish. Who can count all the Lord's blessings?

STRENGTH IN WEAKNESS

*Not until halfway through the Feast did Jesus go up
to the temple courts and begin to teach.*
John 7:14

Jesus traveled to the festival secretly. This made his opponents proud. But Jesus was obedient to God and wasn't afraid of their defiance. He didn't merely go to Jerusalem; he went to the middle of the temple. This was the place where his worst enemies, the priests and Pharisees, had great power and ruled. Setting aside all fear, Christ took them on at their own game. He didn't ask if it was okay with them if he could preach. He ignored their religious authority and civil status and didn't ask for permission. Instead, he entered the temple with enthusiasm and spiritual power and began to teach. Christ didn't ask, "Mr. Annas, Mr. Caiaphas, do you mind if I preach?" Instead, he took over the priestly ministry for himself. He was very brave to walk up right before their eyes. Earlier they had challenged him and called him afraid and timid. Now they had to stand there and listen to him preach.

John describes this event for our comfort. No one should become worried when God allows himself to appear weak while the world boasts and struts around. The same is true for all Christians, especially preachers. They are often weak and timid while their powerful adversaries stomp their feet and threaten. This is nothing new. We have to get used to it. It doesn't happen only to us. It happened to all the prophets and apostles. They appeared weak compared to their oppressors. Yet it was in their weakness that they were the strongest.

PRETENDING TO BE SORRY

꧁ ✦ ꧂

Then God came to Laban the Aramean in a dream at night and said to him, "Be careful not to say anything to Jacob, either good or bad."
Genesis 31:24

Laban was warned in his dream not to treat Jacob harshly. But he continued to chase Jacob anyway. He was told not to harm Jacob, but he was so angry that he still threatened to hurt him. Laban didn't want to be called a failure. He didn't want people to think that his plans went wrong and that he had to return without doing what he intended to do. He felt he would be disgraced if he didn't carry out all the furious threats he had made in front of everyone.

Laban is a good example of a hypocrite pretending to repent. Unbelievers often pretend to be truly sorry and say they're going to change the way they think and act, but inside they know it's a lie. When David admitted he had sinned (2 Samuel 12:13), it was entirely different from the time when Saul admitted he had sinned (1 Samuel 15:24). They used the same words, probably even the same tone of voice, and showed the same feeling of remorse, but the motivation was quite different.

When unbelievers say they're sorry for their sins, their sorrow is really the expression of disappointment that they will no longer be able to do what they want. They don't really want to change their behavior. When thieves express sorrow, they mean they're sorry they can't steal anymore. Laban is portrayed in this same way. Deep down, he didn't really repent. His sorrow was only an outward show. Those who are truly repentant aren't afraid of anything except God's anger and displeasure. They aren't concerned about being humiliated and disgraced in front of other people as long as they know that God is on their side.

FAITH BRINGS FREEDOM

*[We] know that a man is not justified by observing the law, but
by faith in Jesus Christ. So we, too, have put our faith in Christ Jesus
that we may be justified by faith in Christ and not by observing the law.*
Galatians 2:16

Don't make the mistake of thinking that Christians are people who
never sin or feel sinful. Rather, because of their faith in Christ,
God simply doesn't attribute their sin to them. This teaching is
comforting to those who have terrified consciences. For good reason, we often try to impress on people that sins are forgiven and
that righteousness is attributed to believers for the sake of Christ.
Similarly, Christians should not have anything to do with the law
or with sin.

To the extent we are Christians, we stand above the law and
sin. Christ is the Lord of the law. He is present and locked in our
hearts, just as a precious stone is firmly mounted in a ring. When
the law accuses us and sin terrifies us, all we need to do is look to
Christ. When we have taken hold of him in faith, we have the victor over the law, sin, death, and the devil with us. Because Christ
rules over all of these, we won't be harmed.

That's why a Christian, correctly defined, is free from all laws
and subject to no one, either inwardly or outwardly. But notice
that I said, "to the extent we are Christians," not just to the extent
we are human and have consciences. We are free to the extent we
have consciences that are transformed and made rich through
faith. This faith is a great and immeasurable treasure—as Paul says,
an "indescribable gift" (2 Corinthians 9:15), a gift that cannot be
raised high enough or praised enough. It makes us children and
heirs of God.

JESUS IS THE LIGHT

He came as a witness to testify concerning that light,
so that through him all men might believe. He himself was
not the light; he came only as a witness to the light.
John 1:7–8

My opponents accuse me of teaching that God alone should be respected and revered. They claim that I treat the saints as though they had never done anything good or useful in their lives. They ask, "Wouldn't you at least say that John the Baptist was worth something?"

I haven't snubbed John. I honor and respect him. However, John is a servant of the Lord and is not the Lord himself. John points to the true Light and leads people to it, but he is not the Light. He certainly had a more important role than the prophets did. John didn't prophesy, as others did, that the Lord would come one of these days. Instead, he pointed with his finger at the Lord who was standing right there and said, "Look, there he is!" That's why I greatly respect John. I am thankful that God gave us such a faithful prophet, whose mouth spoke about the true Light and whose finger pointed out the Lamb of God. Yet I won't depend on John to save me. I can't rely on his holiness, ascetic life, and good works. John admitted that he wasn't the Messiah when he said, "I am not the Christ" (John 3:28). But regarding Christ, he said, "He must become greater; I must become less" (John 3:30).

Christ said that John was the greatest of all people ever born (Matthew 11:11) and that he was far more than a prophet (Matthew 11:9). Yet John was not the Light. So if John's holiness, ascetic life, strange clothes and food, and refusal to drink wine can't help me obtain eternal life and salvation, then any saint who is less significant than John will be able to do even less for me.

PRAYING IN TIMES OF TROUBLE

Hezekiah received the letter from the messengers and read it.
Then he went up to the temple of the LORD and spread it out
before the LORD. And Hezekiah prayed to the LORD.
Isaiah 37:14–15

This chapter of Isaiah contains an interesting story about King Hezekiah. The Assyrians were attacking Jerusalem with a large army and beginning to overpower it. The situation looked hopeless. King Sennacherib ridiculed Hezekiah mercilessly. Sennacherib made fun of Hezekiah's misfortune by writing him a letter filled with insults about God in order to make the devout king lose all hope. Instead of losing hope, Hezekiah went into the temple, spread out the letter in front of God, bowed down with his face touching the ground, and prayed a heartfelt prayer.

Learning to pray when there's an emergency or when something is frightening us requires a lot of discipline. Instead of praying, we tend to torture ourselves with anxiety and worry. All we can think about is trying to get rid of the problem. The devil often tricks us when temptation or suffering first begins, whether we are dealing with spiritual or physical matters. He immediately barges in and makes us so upset about the problem that we become consumed by it. In this way, he tears us away from praying. He makes us so confused that we don't even think about praying. When we finally begin to pray, we have already tortured ourselves half to death. The devil knows what prayer can accomplish. That's why he creates so many obstacles and makes it so inconvenient for us that we never get around to prayer.

On the basis of this story in Isaiah, we should get into the habit of falling on our knees and spreading out our needs in front of God the moment we have an emergency or become frightened. Prayer is the very best medicine there is. It always works and never fails— if we would just use it!

WHATEVER YOU ASK

And I will do whatever you ask in my name,
so that the Son may bring glory to the Father.
John 14:13

What does Christ mean when he says, "I will do whatever you ask in my name"? I would think he should say, "What you ask the Father in my name, he will do." But Christ is pointing to himself in this passage. These are peculiar words coming from a human being. How can a mere man make such lofty claims? With these simple words, Christ clearly states that he is the true and almighty God, equal with the Father. For whoever says, "Whatever you ask, I will do," is saying, "I am God, who can and will give you everything." Why else should Christians pray in Jesus' name?

Why do people call on saints as helpers in times of need—Saint George for protection in war, Saint Sebastian for protection from pestilence, and on others for other circumstances—unless they believe that these saints will answer their prayers? But Christ claims this role for himself. In other words, he is saying, "I won't command others to do whatever you ask for. I will do it myself." So he is the one who can help in every situation with what we need. He is mightier than the devil, sin, death, the world, and all creation.

No being—whether human or angelic—has ever had or ever will have such power. Christ possesses all of God's power and strength. Here Christ sums up what we can ask him for in prayer. He doesn't limit his promise by adding, "That is, only if you ask for gold and silver or for something that other people can give you." Rather, he says that he will do "whatever you ask."

GOD'S CALLING AND CHOOSING

Therefore, my brothers, be all the more eager to make your calling and election sure. For if you do these things, you will never fall.
2 Peter 1:10

Although the calling Peter talks about here is strong enough by itself, it doesn't feel strong and firm enough to you. This is because you're not yet certain that it's meant for you. So Peter wants to make this calling and election feel firmer with good works.

Peter considers the fruit of faith to be very important. This fruit is directed toward our neighbors in service to them. But the fruit doesn't remain outside of us. Faith is strengthened by the fruit so that we do more and more good works. So this power is very different from physical strength. We get tired and injure ourselves if we overuse our physical strength. But with spiritual power, the more we use it, the stronger it becomes. And if we don't exercise it, it diminishes.

We shouldn't let faith rest. It becomes more powerful with cultivation and practice until we become certain of our calling and election. We become certain that we cannot fail. In addition, this passage gives us a guideline for dealing with election. There are many frivolous spirits who don't know what strong faith feels like. They jump in, start at the top, and want to find out through their human reason whether God has chosen them. They do this so that they can feel certain of their position. We should quickly back away from this approach, because it's not the correct way. If we want to become certain, we must approach it the way Peter suggests here. If we choose a different way, we have already failed. But if we cultivate and practice our faith over time, we will become certain so that we will never stumble.

SHOWING CONTEMPT FOR THE WORLD

"Meaningless! Meaningless!" says the Teacher.
"Utterly meaningless! Everything is meaningless."
Ecclesiastes 1:2

The book of Ecclesiastes condemns, not what God has created, but rather people's evil tendencies and desires. We aren't satisfied with what God created and gave us to use. So we concern ourselves with accumulating more possessions and achieving more fame as if we were going to live on this earth forever. We become bored with what we currently have, then we strive for more things, and then strive for even more. Depriving ourselves of what we presently have because we're desperately concerned about acquiring more for the future is shameful and pointless.

These twisted tendencies and human striving are what the author is condemning in this book, not the things themselves. Later, in Ecclesiastes 5:18, the author says that nothing is better for people than being happy and making their lives pleasant by eating, drinking, and finding joy in their work. The author would be contradicting himself if he condemned these same things in this passage. Instead, he's only condemning the misuse of these things, which comes from having a wrong attitude.

Some foolish people haven't understood this very well and have taught nonsensical ideas about hating the world and avoiding anything to do with it. But living alone or isolating ourselves from others doesn't show the proper contempt for the world. Neither does throwing money away or refusing to touch it show the proper contempt for money. Those who live surrounded by what the world has to offer and yet don't become attached to these things are the ones who display the proper attitude.

A HIGHER AUTHORITY

*Finally the temple guards went back to the chief priests
and Pharisees, who asked them, "Why didn't you bring him in?"
"No one ever spoke the way this man does," the guards declared.*
John 7:45–46

The words of the temple guards were humble yet powerful. The guards didn't arrogantly say, "You scoundrels, you want to kill the man who is from God." Instead, the guards remained humble and deferred to the authority of the chief priests and Pharisees. They didn't grab their swords or resort to force. They remained servants who knew their place. Their dispute was not about earthly matters. They didn't raise themselves higher than they were. Their dispute concerned the spiritual realm. The heart of the matter was that the faith and beliefs of the temple guards were different from those of the Pharisees. They refused to go along with the Pharisees.

We must distinguish between civil and spiritual authority. A servant shouldn't run away from his master even though one believes differently from the other. God doesn't want them separated. The servant shouldn't resist or murmur against the master but should recognize his authority. Even though the servant humbly serves his master, he has still another Master—Christ, who is Lord over the conscience and soul. Christ also should be served, for the earthly master has no authority over the servant's conscience. The servant can say to his master, "I have put myself in your service with body, hand, and foot, but not with my conscience. I don't get paid for learning God's Word and believing in it. In spiritual matters, I am free. There, I answer to someone else."

So if two people disagree about what to believe, they should remain unified in external matters of the world even though they may be divided in matters of faith and conscience.

PEOPLE WHO HAVE IT ALL

*Esau took his wives and sons and daughters and all the members
of his household, as well as his livestock and all his other animals
and all the goods he had acquired in Canaan, and moved
to a land some distance from his brother Jacob.*
Genesis 36:6

The account of Esau's family is appropriately included in the history of Isaac and Jacob. In this passage, we see that unbelievers have honor and fame on earth. They are wealthy and successful, and they rule the world. They either look down on believers or oppress them, as Esau's descendants did. Because of their arrogance, they despised and oppressed Jacob and his descendants in later years.

On the other hand, Jacob had God's blessing. He was an important leader in the world and among God's people. Yet he had to endure many tragedies in his life. He had so many problems and so much misery that it seemed as if all spiritual blessings and even God's favor had been taken away from him. Yet in the end, God worked out everything the way Mary described in her song: "He has brought down rulers from their thrones but has lifted up the humble" (Luke 1:52). Christ described the end for the godless when he said, "But woe to you who are rich, for you have already received your comfort. Woe to you who are well fed now, for you will go hungry" (Luke 6:24–25). And Christ described the end for believers when he said: "Blessed are those who mourn, for they will be comforted" (Matthew 5:4).

Unbelievers will be fortunate for a while. But in the end, they will be destroyed. Believers, on the other hand, will have to suffer for a while. But they will find protection, help, and comfort in God. He sustains sad people and relieves their misery. In the end, God will take his little flock away from their suffering and reward his people with eternal life and happiness.

NO LONGER CONDEMNED

Therefore, there is now no condemnation for those who are in Christ Jesus.
Roman 8:1

Christians are truly humble when they genuinely feel their sin and recognize that they are worthy of the wrath and judgment of God and eternal death. So in this life, Christians will be humbled. At the same time, however, they possess a pure and holy pride, which makes them turn to Christ. By turning to Christ, they can pull themselves out from under this feeling of God's wrath and judgment. Christians believe that any remaining sin is not counted against them. They also believe that they are loved by the Father. Christians are loved, not for their own sake, but for the sake of Christ—the one whom God loves.

From this it becomes clear how faith justifies us without works. It becomes clear why we still need Christ's righteousness credited to us. The sin, which God thoroughly hates, remains in us. Because this sin still remains in us, Christ's righteousness must be credited to us. God gives us that righteousness for the sake of Christ—the one given to us, the one we grasp by faith.

Meanwhile on this earth, we still have sin and godless people. Even believers continue to sin. That's why Paul, in Romans 7:23, complains about how believers still have sin within them. Yet Romans 8:1 says, "There is now no condemnation for those who are in Christ Jesus." Who can reconcile these diametrically opposed statements: that the sin in us is not sinful, that those worthy of condemnation will not be condemned, that the wicked will not be rejected, that those worthy of wrath and eternal death will not be punished? The only one who can reconcile these is the "one mediator between God and men, the man Christ Jesus" (1 Timothy 2:5). As Paul says, "There is now no condemnation for those who are in Christ Jesus."

THE GRACE AND TRUTH OF CHRIST

For the law was given through Moses;
grace and truth came through Jesus Christ.
John 1:17

We need to learn how to clearly distinguish the laws given through Moses from the grace that came through Christ. We must always keep the role of Christ separate from the role of Moses and make a clear distinction between the two. We need to know precisely what purpose each one fulfills so that we don't become confused. I was confused about this distinction myself for over thirty years. I just couldn't believe that Christ wanted to show his kindness to me.

The first commandment teaches us that God wants us to sincerely trust him. Yet we also must fear him above everything else. In other words, Christians are like children who have been punished but who still love their father and are confident their father still loves them. The good works required by the first commandment are far better than wearing special clothes, fasting, praying, and all the other good works religious people have invented. So the good works required by the first commandment are holy and must be obeyed. But who can live up to them? Certainly no one can completely obey the first commandment. Everyone is a sinner except for Christ.

Christ, however, comes to us and says, "I have shed my blood for you. My blood cries out on your behalf." Out of his grace and kindness, he brings us the forgiveness of our sins at no cost to us whatsoever.

GOD'S PERFECT TIMING

There is a time for everything,
and a season for every activity under heaven.
Ecclesiastes 3:1

No one can change the future, no matter how hard they might try. How could someone who doesn't know what's coming change something that hasn't happened yet? God wants us to use what he has given us without telling him when or how he should provide it. All of that is in God's hands. We shouldn't think everything is in our hands to use in whatever way we wish. After all, God must provide everything first.

"There is a time for everything" means that everything happens when God wants it to occur. If people try to plan and do everything themselves without acknowledging that God is in control, they will experience nothing but failure. Many people work hard at getting rich but don't succeed. Others acquire wealth without trying at all. That's because God provided the right time for some of them but not for the others.

So people on earth strive for what they want to have. But all their striving only leads to frustration. They don't accomplish anything because they don't wait for the right time. Knowing this, we should leave everything up to God, use what we presently have, and avoid yearning for things we want in the future. If we don't follow this advice, our lives will be full of trouble and disappointment.

THE FATHER POINTS TO CHRIST

Then they asked him, "Where is your father?"
"You do not know me or my Father," Jesus replied.
"If you knew me, you would know my Father also."
John 8:19

When the Pharisees asked, "Where is your father?" they were saying, "We don't hear the testimony of the Father. The miracles that you have performed, such as raising the dead, don't amount to anything." The Pharisees wanted Jesus to place the Father right before their eyes so that they might feel and touch him as they would a wall. Otherwise, they wouldn't believe or accept what he was saying. But Christ pointed to the Father's testimony, not so that they might see and touch the Father, but so that they would believe. The Father's testimony should have led them all to his Word. Philip also said to Christ, "Show us the Father" (John 14:8). But Christ doesn't show us the Father the way we might want him to. Rather, the Father shows us Christ, who says, "The Father points you to me, not the other way around. He is the one who shows you Christ. He testifies of me. You must do what he says and listen to my words and testimony."

This is the main point of the argument: we should always keep Christ before our eyes. The devil continually tempts us to abandon Christ and seek the Father, saying to us, "This or that will please him." Meanwhile, we ignore Christ—the one the Father sent—so that we might listen to him alone. We respond as the Pharisees did and reject Christ. We wonder, "Where is the Father?" That is the question the world asks.

This is the greatest temptation to our faith. We must devote ourselves to the Word of Christ and train ourselves to hold on to it so that we never lose sight of Jesus.

BECOMING LAZY

We want each of you to show this same diligence to the very end,
in order to make your hope sure. We do not want you to become lazy,
but to imitate those who through faith and patience
inherit what has been promised.
Hebrews 6:11–12

God's blessings don't come to those who are sleepy and lazy. Solomon didn't mean to prohibit work when he said that the Lord gives food to those he loves while they sleep (Psalm 127:2). He wanted to say that we should have peaceful, rested consciences. Work shouldn't disturb the restful sleep God gives to those who have faith and confidence in him. We should have peace of mind and clear consciences. Christ says, "Do not worry about tomorrow. . . . Each day has enough trouble of its own" (Matthew 6:34). Don't create your own unhappiness. Sleep well, and don't ask, "What shall we eat? . . . What shall we drink?" (Matthew 6:31).

I don't mean people should be lazy loafers. They should work. God doesn't give his blessings to those who are lazy and lie around snoring. He wants our sinful natures to be controlled and killed. As Paul says, "Those who belong to Christ Jesus have crucified the sinful nature with its passions and desires" (Galatians 5:24).

Although it is God's blessing that brings us what we need, not our work, God still wants us to do our duty and work diligently at the jobs we are called to do. That way we'll get our exercise so that we don't become lazy. As a non-Christian poet once said, "By nature all people would prefer not to work and would like to do what they want." We can't give in to loafing and laziness. Instead, we should work diligently and faithfully to do what is required of us. Even in times of hardship, exhausting work, and persecution, we should wait cheerfully for the Lord's blessing.

HAMMERED BY THE LAW

What, then, was the purpose of the law? It was added because of transgressions until the Seed to whom the promise referred had come.
Galatians 3:19

Although the law doesn't justify us, it's still useful and necessary. First, in society, it holds the lawless people in check. Second, it shows people that they are sinners guilty of death and worthy of eternal wrath.

Why does the hammer of the law smash us to pieces and crush us? Of what use is this humiliation? It shows us that the way of grace stands open to us. So the law is a servant and prepares us for grace. For God is a God of the humble, the miserable, the troubled, the oppressed, the despairing, and those who have become totally nothing. He lifts the lowly, feeds the hungry, heals the blind, comforts the miserable and troubled, justifies the sinner, raises the dead, and saves the despairing and the condemned. For he is the almighty Creator who makes everything from nothing. Most of all, he protects us from the most harmful corruption—presuming we're righteous. No one wants to be a sinner who is impure, miserable, and condemned. But everyone wants to be righteous and holy. So God uses this hammer of the law to break, crush, and annihilate this beast with its empty confidence, wisdom, righteousness, and power. As a result, it will learn through its misfortune that it is lost and condemned. When the conscience has been terrified in this way by the law, there's a place for the teaching of the gospel and of grace, which restores and comforts the conscience. This teaching says that Christ came into the world, not to break a bruised reed, not even to snuff out a smoldering wick (Isaiah 42:3), but "to preach good news to the poor. . . . bind up the brokenhearted, to proclaim freedom for the captives and release from darkness for the prisoners" (Isaiah 61:1).

THE SIN OF THE WORLD

*The next day John saw Jesus coming toward him and said,
"Look, the Lamb of God, who takes away the sin of the world!"*
John 1:29

From this passage, we learn that all people have been plunged into sin by the devil and that only the Lamb can lead us out. Our unbelief isn't Jesus' fault. The guilt is ours. If we don't believe, then we're stuck in our own sins. In short, the Lamb of God has carried the sins of the world.

You should believe and confess this all of your life. You may think, "Yes, I know that Jesus carried the sins of Peter, Paul, and other saints. They were holy people. But who knows if Christ will carry my sins, too? If only I were as good as Peter or Paul." Can't you hear what John is saying? "This is the Lamb of God who takes away the sin of the world." You must admit that you too are a part of this world. You were born of a human mother and father—you aren't a cow or pig! It follows, then, that your sins are paid for, just as the sins of Peter and Paul are paid for. You are unable to pay for your own sins. They couldn't pay for their own sins either. There are no exceptions.

Therefore, don't listen to your own thoughts. Listen to God's Word. It promises forgiveness of sins to anyone who believes that this Lamb carried the sins of the whole world. Did you hear that? The Lamb didn't miss any of it. He carried all the sins of the world from the beginning of time. Therefore, he carried your sin too, and he offers his grace to you.

SATAN SNATCHES THE WORD

❧

Some people are like seed along the path, where the word is sown.
As soon as they hear it, Satan comes and takes away
the word that was sown in them.
Mark 4:15

When the gospel is taught clearly, believers are confirmed in their faith, and they are able to guard themselves from idolatry. Satan is upset when the truth of the gospel is taught. He uses various methods to distort the Word and keep people from hearing it. In the early church, a number of heresies appeared. One claimed that Christ isn't the Son of God. Another claimed that he isn't Mary's son. In Basil's time, some denied that the Holy Spirit is God.

We have examples of Satan snatching away God's Word in our own day. When I and my followers began to preach the pure message of the gospel, many people arose who were against God's Word and his work in the world. Of course, none of the other temptations lessened. Satan keeps on tempting people to commit sexual sins and other terrible crimes because he doesn't want people to believe in what God says and does. But the church and God's people should regard Satan's attacks on God's Word and work as especially dangerous.

This is how Satan deceived Adam and Eve. They lost their trust in God and no longer believed what he said. Instead, they believed Satan's lies. When Satan deprives people of their trust in God, it's not surprising that they become proud and despise God and other people. Eventually they will turn to adultery, murder, and so on. Letting go of God's Word is the root of all temptations. It results in the destruction and violation of all God's commandments. Unbelief is the source of every sin. If Satan is able to tamper with God's Word or snatch it out of people's hearts, he will achieve his goal—people will no longer believe in God.

STUCK IN THE MUD

It does not, therefore, depend on man's desire or effort, but on God's mercy.
Romans 9:16

Even with extreme effort, learning to depend on God's mercy is difficult—especially for we who have been raised in the doctrine of works and have been told to look to the law and our own efforts. Moreover, our nature leans toward doing works. We are so rooted in our habits, and our hearts are so used to it, that we can't stop thinking this way: "If I have lived a holy life and done great and many works, then God will be merciful to me." So we struggle against both our nature and our ingrained habits. It's extraordinarily difficult to change our thinking and clearly distinguish between faith and love.

Even if we already have faith, the mud still sticks and clings to us. We keep wanting to brag, "I have preached so long, have lived so well, and have done so much. Surely God will take note of that." We want to bargain with God. We want him to look at our lives and change the judgment seat into the mercy seat because of what we have done. But nothing will come of this. You may be able to tell other people, "I have tried to do good to everyone. Where I have fallen short, I will try to make it up." But when you come before God, leave such bragging at home. Remember that you are appealing for grace, not justice. Let anyone try this. They will see how difficult and troublesome it is. Those who have been stuck in their own works their whole lives find it difficult to pull themselves out and let themselves be lifted by faith.

HELPING OTHERS IN NEED

※C～c

If anyone has material possessions and sees his brother in need
but has no pity on him, how can the love of God be in him?
1 John 3:17

If we should be willing to die for our fellow believers, shouldn't
we be even more willing to give up our property and belongings?
If we have possessions and don't share them, if we don't give food,
drink, clothing, and so on—in other words, if we are greedy and
stingy—then we aren't Christians.

Today, people are loudly complaining that those who have
come to know Christ are the ones hoarding money. This is happening to such an extent that they fear God may unleash his wrath
soon. Of course, God is merciful, but he isn't idle. He doesn't let
sinners go unpunished. He's merciful to the humble who fear him.

It's foolish to interpret this passage as referring only to people
in extreme need. Besides, there are several degrees of love: we
shouldn't offend an enemy; we should help out a fellow believer;
and we should support a member of our household. We know
Christ's commandment about loving our enemies. But we owe
even more to a believer who loves us in return. We should help
out whoever doesn't have enough to live on. But what should we
do if that person betrays us? We should help them again. We owe
the most, however, to the ones related to us. "If anyone does not
provide for his relatives, and especially for his immediate family,
he has denied the faith and is worse than an unbeliever" (1 Timothy 5:8). It's a general rule that if a person who has property and
belongings doesn't take the need of a neighbor to heart, then that
person has no love.

ENJOYING WHAT YOU HAVE

꧁ ❧

Better what the eye sees than the roving of the appetite.
This too is meaningless, a chasing after the wind.
Ecclesiastes 6:9

Enjoying what you currently have is better than letting your heart wander. You should make use of what is in front of you instead of wandering around full of desires. This is what the dog in Aesop's writings did when it chased after the reflection in the water and lost the meat it had in its mouth. You should use what God has placed before you and be satisfied with it. You shouldn't try to satisfy your own desires, because they will never be satisfied. Instead, you should use whatever God has placed in front of you. All of it is very good (Genesis 1:31).

Faithful people are pleased with what they currently have and consider it all to be a gift from God. Unbelievers, however, act differently. Everything they see in front of them is nothing but a nuisance. They don't use these gifts or enjoy them. Rather, they allow their hearts to roam in discontent. If they have money, they don't find pleasure in it or enjoy it. They always want something different. If they have a spouse, they want someone else. If they acquire a kingdom, they aren't satisfied with just one. Alexander the Great, for example, wanted another world to conquer.

We should keep our eyes on what we already have in front of us. We should delight in all of it. We should enjoy it and give thanks to God for it. God doesn't want our hearts to wander to thoughts of other things. This passage points out that we should make use of what we currently have. Letting our hearts wander around filled with desires is meaningless.

FREEDOM FROM SIN

So if the Son sets you free, you will be free indeed.
John 8:36

True freedom is being free from sin. How does this happen? It happens when we hear his Word—Christ was born of Mary, suffered, was crucified, died, was buried, and rose again from the dead on the third day. "Oh," we might say, "I know that message well. It is a very familiar sermon." But let's learn this lesson again from our children, for it tells us how we can be saved and be set free. "Yes," we might even say, "This teaching is too simple. That's why it won't work." But it's a virtue that children can pray these words and understand them so easily. We are old fools. The more educated and intelligent we become, the less we know and understand.

We must preach this message again and again so that all of us may be satisfied and filled with its teaching. My hunger, however, has not yet been satisfied. This teaching is like bread. No one ever grows tired of eating bread. We fill ourselves with all kinds of food, but we never have enough bread, unless we are ill and can't eat. A healthy person will never grow tired of bread. In the same way, Christians will never learn this completely during their lifetimes, whether they are saints or even Mary or John the Baptist.

So we must sit with the children by the stove and learn the lesson again. There are some who say they have already been taught the message and think they know everything about it. But when troubles come, they desperately need someone to recite these words to them again. They end up needing a four-year-old child to show them how to believe.

MORE THAN WE CAN IMAGINE

*So Pharaoh said to Joseph, "I hereby put you in charge of
the whole land of Egypt." Then Pharaoh took his signet ring
from his finger and put it on Joseph's finger.*
Genesis 41:41–42

Paul is absolutely correct when he says that God "is able to do immeasurably more than all we ask or imagine" (Ephesians 3:20). In contrast, our prayers tend to be weak and insignificant. Joseph didn't dare ask for what he finally received. His heart was like a bruised reed and a smoldering wick. His groaning was like smoke that rises straight to heaven. His heart was a real incense burner! The sweet aroma that comes from a humble, groaning heart pleases God. Though Joseph may have felt like he was dying, his groaning didn't cause any real harm.

Hang on. God will remain faithful. Don't despair. Cling to the truth the psalmist proclaims: "Wait for the LORD; be strong and take heart and wait for the LORD" (Psalm 27:14). The Lord won't extinguish a smoldering wick but instead will make it glow brightly. He won't break the bruised reed but instead will strengthen it (Isaiah 42:3).

God wants to give us more than we ask for, not just fulfill our weak prayers. Joseph asked for nothing more than to be rescued, released from prison, and returned to his father. God in heaven let him pray that for a long time. In effect, God was saying, "You don't know what you are asking [Matthew 20:22]. I will give you more than all you ask or imagine [Ephesians 3:20]. That's why you have to wait a little longer. I want more of the smoke that rises straight to heaven." But later, Joseph received what he never could have imagined. He never would have had the confidence or courage to ask for it. We must recognize that God's wisdom, grace, mercy, and power are most certainly with us, as they were with Joseph. However, God usually doesn't give them to us in the way we ask for them.

A FLICKER OF FAITH

*But by faith we eagerly await through the Spirit
the righteousness for which we hope.*
Galatians 5:5

Very few people know how weak and feeble faith and hope can be when they are suffering and struggling under a cross. At such times, faith and hope appear to be "a smoldering wick" that a strong wind could easily blow out (Isaiah 42:3). But during these terrifying struggles, some continue to believe and hope, even when it seems there is nothing left to hope for (Romans 4:18). Trusting in the promises of Christ, they fight against the feelings of sin and God's wrath. Eventually they will experience this little flicker of faith; at least this is how faith appears to their human reason, because they can hardly sense it. They will watch this flicker of faith become a great fire that will fill the entire heavens and devour all terror and sin (2 Peter 3:10–12).

Truly faithful people have nothing more precious in the whole world than this teaching on faith. They hold on to it tightly, and they know what the whole world doesn't. They know that sin, death, misfortune, and physical and spiritual evils work for the good of God's chosen ones. Likewise, they know that God is nearest to them when he seems to be farthest away. He is the most merciful and truly a Savior when he seems to be angry and punishing them. They know that they have eternal righteousness when they are feeling the terrors of sin and death the most. With hope, they look for eternal righteousness as their certain possession laid aside for them in heaven. They are lords over all things when they are the poorest—as Paul says, "having nothing, and yet possessing everything" (2 Corinthians 6:10). This is what Scripture calls receiving comfort through hope. But we can't learn this skill without going through many great trials.

BORN TO DO GOOD WORKS

In reply Jesus declared, "I tell you the truth, no one can
see the kingdom of God unless he is born again."
John 3:3

A child who will be born two years from now doesn't yet exist.
The woman who will carry and give birth to the child is still a virgin, and the child hasn't even been conceived. That child can do
nothing, for that child does not yet exist. Everyone can understand that. In the same way, all works, no matter how precious
and good they might be, amount to nothing if a person does them
before they have been spiritually born. These works lead only to
sin and death. This is why Jesus said that Nicodemus and all the
Pharisees were nothing if they didn't accept him, for they hadn't
been born anew.

But what will become of those who do even less than Nicodemus? What will happen to all those religious people whose works
are nothing compared to those of Nicodemus? None of those
people will be able to do good works that please God, because they
haven't been born anew. We aren't condemning good works.
People first have to be made ready to do good works by being born
anew. Only then will they be capable of doing good works.

If you want to have a carpenter build a house, the carpenter
must first exist. For what can be built if the carpenter hasn't been
born yet? The same is true for good works. Doing good works
doesn't make anyone good. First, ask yourself if you have been born
anew. Then after that, ask yourself what works you should do.
Many people, however, don't go about it this way. They mistakenly
assume that their good works can save them. Just make sure that
you are born again. Because if you are not, your good works are
worthless.

GOD'S APPROVAL OF US

※⟨⌒⟩⊂

The LORD looked with favor on Abel and his offering,
but on Cain and his offering he did not look with favor.
So Cain was very angry, and his face was downcast.
Genesis 4:4–5

God's approval isn't based on what a person does. Rather, he accepts what a person does because he already approves of the person. The person hasn't earned God's approval through the good that he or she does. Because God looked with favor on Abel, he also accepted Abel's offering. God did not look with favor on Cain, so he didn't accept his offering. So Abel had God's approval even before he had done anything.

The author of Hebrews writes, "By faith Abel offered God a better sacrifice than Cain did. By faith he was commended as a righteous man, when God spoke well of his offerings" (Hebrews 11:4). Cain also brought an offering. In fact, he brought his offering before Abel brought his. But he brought his offering with an arrogant and overconfident attitude. He assumed that God would be pleased with his sacrifice for the simple reason that he was the firstborn. Because he lacked faith and didn't acknowledge his sinfulness, he felt no need to pray and didn't place his confidence in the mercy of God.

This is exactly how those who rely on their own efforts to be justified still act today. They concentrate on the good that they do, which they hope will please God. They don't trust in God's mercy and his grace. They aren't hoping that God will forgive their sins through Christ. This passage is definite proof that God cannot be influenced by outward appearances or impressed by the good that people do. He looks only at the faith of the individual. Yet God doesn't reject any acts of human kindness, no matter how insignificant or meaningless they seem to be. Indeed, the only thing God hates and condemns is unbelief.

PRAYING WITHOUT WORDS

*But you, dear friends, build yourselves up in your most holy faith
and pray in the Holy Spirit. Keep yourselves in God's love as you wait
for the mercy of our Lord Jesus Christ to bring you to eternal life.*
Jude 1:20–21

All teachers of Scripture conclude that the essence of prayer is
simply the lifting up of the heart to God. But if this is so, it follows that everything else that doesn't lift up the heart to God is
not prayer. Therefore, singing, talking, and whistling without this
lifting up of your heart to God are as much like prayer as scare-
crows in the garden are like people. The name and appearance
might be there, but the essence is missing.

Jerome confirmed this truth about prayer when he wrote about
an early church leader named Agathon. Agathon lived in the desert
for thirty years and carried a stone in his mouth so that he would
learn to stay quiet. But how did he pray? In his heart, undoubtedly.
This is the kind of prayer God likes the best. In fact, this is the only
kind of prayer God regards and wants. But hearing the words helps
us think about what we're saying and helps us pray correctly. We
should consider our spoken words to be like a trumpet, drum,
organ, or other kind of sound that moves our hearts and lifts them
up to God.

We shouldn't attempt to pray without words, relying on our
own hearts, unless we are well trained spiritually and skilled in
removing stray thoughts from our minds. Otherwise, the devil will
lead us astray and quickly destroy the prayers in our hearts. So we
should cling to the words and let them lift us up—lift us until our
feathers grow and we're able to soar high without the help of
words.

CHRIST WILL REIGN FOREVER

I will be his father, and he will be my son. I will never take my love away from him, as I took it away from your predecessor. I will set him over my house and my kingdom forever; his throne will be established forever.
1 Chronicles 17:13–14

Human reason objects to this passage. Considering itself ten times wiser than God, reason asks, "How can God give his eternal power to someone else? What would he be keeping for himself?" Now, it's true that God has said, "I will not give my glory to another or my praise to idols" (Isaiah 42:8). It would be especially difficult for God to give his glory to a mere human being, who was born in time and not eternal. But Christians do acknowledge that Jesus was a human being. He was Mary's son and David's descendant. He was born, and he died.

Furthermore, people of other religions deduce that God can't have a son because he doesn't have a wife. Why do these people think they can contain the incomprehensible nature of God in the nutshell of their human reason? Shame on you, Satan, as well as all others who are students of blind, foolish, miserable human reason. No one can fully understand these lofty matters but God alone. All we know about them is what the Holy Spirit has revealed to us through Scripture.

Christians can answer these objections correctly, clearly, and accurately because they have insight from the New Testament. God's Son has two natures in one inseparable person. He is one Christ, not two Christs. The Father gave Christ, his Son, eternal divinity—not in time, but from all eternity. The Father gave his divinity to Christ completely and fully, just as the Father himself possessed divinity from eternity. When he gave it to Christ, the Father didn't lose any divinity himself. Rather, he gave to the Son the same power, which he still retains in eternity. There are not two deities. Rather, God the Father and Christ are united in one deity.

PATHS IN LIFE

Jesus answered, "I am the way and the truth and the life.
No one comes to the Father except through me."
John 14:6

"I am the way." You should learn what this eloquent statement of Christ means. Don't think of a path that you walk on with your feet. Instead, think of one that you travel on by faith—a faith that clings only to the Lord Christ.

There are various ways of walking and wandering through life. First, there are many roads and footpaths for physically walking from one place to another, as cows and horses do. The Scripture teaches nothing about these paths. But there are other kinds of paths in this life. A second kind of path pertains to everyday life. On this path, we lead a good and moral life before the world and seek to preserve government, peace, honor, and order. Living in this way brings possessions and respect. Philosophers have given us good principles, and rulers have issued various laws, for walking on this path. But these two kinds of paths are still limited to this life, which is passing away.

Over all of these ways is still another path, about which the Scripture and Christ speak here. This third path is the way to get from this life to the next. For this journey, we need a much different way, a much different path. Here Christ is saying, "When you have come to me in faith, you are on the right way. This path is reliable and won't mislead you."

GOD'S TRAINING METHODS

Joseph said to his brothers, "I am Joseph! Is my father still living?"
But his brothers were not able to answer him,
because they were terrified at his presence.
Genesis 45:3

The emotional climax to Joseph's story was this sudden revelation to his brothers. They had thought Joseph was a horrible, terrifying tyrant because he had treated them like strangers and scared them to death. Even though he had left them many clues, they couldn't imagine any kindness hidden under his hostile appearance. But then he came straight to the point. Without using an interpreter, he said, "I am Joseph!"

This story is a beautiful example of how God treats his faithful people. He sometimes punishes us and acts as if he weren't our God and Father. Sometimes he even appears to be a tyrant or a strict judge who wants to torture or even destroy us. But at the right time—when he is ready—he will say to us, "I am the Lord your God. Up to now, I treated you as if I wanted to reject you or send you to hell, but it was only an exercise I use to train my people. I never would have trained you this way if I didn't love you from the bottom of my heart."

In this Bible story, God shows us the training methods he uses with his people. This should comfort us. We must get used to the way God tests and instructs us. We also should humble ourselves so that the horrible evil called original sin may be restrained. God doesn't want to condemn or reject us, even when our suffering and punishment nearly destroy and kill us. Rather, he wants to sweep away the sin that clings to us. Only then will we understand what God means when he says, "The LORD brings death and makes alive; he brings down to the grave and raises up" (1 Samuel 2:6).

COMMANDED TO LOVE

❧

The entire law is summed up in a single command:
"Love your neighbor as yourself."
Galatians 5:14

People who think they have a good understanding of the command to love are badly mistaken. To be sure, they have this command written on their hearts. By nature, they know that they should do to others what they want done to them (Matthew 7:12). That doesn't mean they truly understand it; otherwise they would also show it in their actions and prefer love above other works. They wouldn't make such a big deal about their antics and superstitions, which amount to nothing. Some examples of such behavior include walking around with a sad face and hanging head, being celibate, eating only bread and water, living in the desert, dressing shabbily, and so on. These are strange and superstitious works, which they choose for themselves and which God neither commands nor accepts. They consider these works so glorious and holy that they cast a dark shadow over love, which is the sun that shines over all works. The blindness of human reason is so limitless and incomprehensible that reason cannot come to a correct understanding of faith, much less make correct judgments about life and works.

Therefore, we must strongly resist our own opinions. In matters of salvation, we by nature would rather base our opinions on our hearts than on the Word of God. We also should strongly object to the mask and halo of self-chosen works. Instead, we must learn to value our calling and the responsibilities that go with it. Although these works may appear puny and contemptible, they are commanded by God. In contrast, we should despise the works that reason chooses to do apart from God's command no matter how glorious, meaningful, great, or holy they appear.

CHRIST IS THE CENTER

Just as Moses lifted up the snake in the desert,
so the Son of Man must be lifted up.
John 3:14

When Moses lifted up the snake on a pole, many Israelites disapproved of God's command to look at it because it wasn't pleasant. Only believing Israelites—and no one else—understood and were healed because of their faith in the Word. Who else but our Lord could have used this story to point to Christ? I never would have been so bold to interpret this story the way Christ did. He explains it by pointing to himself and saying, "That is the bronze snake. But I am the Son of Man. The Israelites had to look at the snake with their eyes. But you must look at me with the eyes of faith. They were cured of a physical poison. But through me, you will be redeemed from an eternal poison. Looking at the snake means believing in me. Their bodies were healed. But I will give eternal life to those who believe in me." These are strange statements and an extraordinary teaching.

With these words, the Lord gives us the proper way to interpret the Old Testament. He helps us understand that the writers and prophets of the Old Testament point to Christ with their stories and illustrations. Christ shows us that he is the center point from which the entire circle is drawn. Everyone looks toward him. Whoever follows Christ belongs in that same circle. All the stories in Holy Scripture, if they are interpreted correctly, point toward Christ.

FEELING FORGOTTEN

*But God remembered Noah and all the wild animals
and the livestock that were with him in the ark,
and he sent a wind over the earth, and the waters receded.*
Genesis 8:1

Being trapped inside that floating container for such a long time was no joke and could hardly be described as fun. Noah and his family saw the torrential downpour and were tossed back and forth on the rising floodwaters. Noah felt that God had forgotten them. Moses makes a point of this when he wrote that God finally remembered Noah and his family. Through faith, Noah and his family were able to overcome their feelings of abandonment. But they had to struggle with their human natures. Because Noah had never experienced anything this serious in the past, he wondered if God would show compassion and remember him and his family. In the end, they conquered their anxieties. But it came with a tremendous struggle. In the same way, young people who want to live a pure and virtuous life must make a determined effort to control their sinful desires.

Our human nature is weak. It cannot tolerate the idea that God may have forgotten or abandoned us. We even want to brag and take the credit for ourselves when God remembers us, looks on us with kindness, and gives us success. Is it any wonder that we become hopeless when we feel as though God has abandoned us and everything seems to be going wrong?

Don't forget that this story gives us a model of faith, patience, and perseverance. It teaches us that we must believe and trust God. It also makes us aware of our need for patience. Yet patience is unnecessary if we have no personal struggles and doubts. Even Christ calls us to persevere in difficult situations when he says in the New Testament, "But he who stands firm to the end will be saved" (Matthew 24:13).

LET YOUR KINGDOM COME

Your kingdom come, your will be done on earth as it is in heaven.
Matthew 6:10

We shouldn't pray, "Dear Father, let us come into your kingdom," as though it's a place to which we travel. Instead, we pray, "Your kingdom come." For if we're to receive it at all, God's grace and his kingdom with all its virtues must come to us. We will never be able to go to him. In the same way, Christ came to us—from heaven down to earth. We didn't go up to him from earth to heaven.

Another mistake of those who pray the Lord's Prayer is that they think only about their eternal happiness. They understand the kingdom of God to mean nothing but joy and pleasure in heaven. Thinking from an earthly, physical perspective and fearing hell, they seek only their own benefit and advantage in heaven. These people don't realize that God's kingdom is nothing but godliness, chastity, purity, gentleness, tenderness, and kindness. His kingdom is full of every virtue and grace. They don't know that God must have his way and that he alone lives and reigns in us. This should be our first and foremost desire. We are saved only when God reigns in us, and we become his kingdom.

We don't have to seek or ask for joy, happiness, or anything else we may desire. Rather, all of this comes along with God's kingdom. So to help us avoid wanting what is false and selfish, Christ tells us to seek first God's kingdom itself, not the fruits of the kingdom. But those who seek the fruits of God's kingdom seek the back end of God's kingdom. They seek the last part first, and the first part they value only because of its ultimate benefits.

WALK HUMBLY WITH YOUR GOD

He has showed you, O man, what is good.
And what does the LORD require of you? To act justly
and to love mercy and to walk humbly with your God.
Micah 6:8

Even the most spiritually minded people have a difficult time escaping the temptation to love themselves. As soon as they see that they are better than others in some way, they begin to love themselves and look down on others. The Scripture provides us with a frightening example of this in the story of Saul. He was well thought of and had no equal in Israel (1 Samuel 9:2). He was filled with the Spirit of the Lord. But he didn't do what Micah demanded in this passage. Therefore, he fell into terrible disgrace and was rejected by God.

The church fathers spoke about the temptation to love ourselves in the following way: "No matter where you throw the head of a thistle, it will stand straight up." Similar to a thistle, this wicked attitude easily takes root in the hearts of believers. It's difficult for believers to avoid self-love. As Augustine stated, this is the only evil that sticks to good works. That's why God allows his people to slip into sin, just as he allowed Peter and David to fall. Shocked by their fall into sin, believers humble themselves. They're fearful of thinking of themselves too highly, and they want to keep in mind how weak they still are. This is why David cried out, "My sin is always before me" (Psalm 51:3).

Believers humble themselves by recognizing and looking at their weaknesses and sin. They try to avoid feeling proud of their works or of the gifts of the Spirit they have received from God. This is what it means "to walk humbly with your God." We should be genuinely modest and humble, wanting to remain in the background. We should never look for honor and praise for the good works we do.

OUR COUNSELOR

And I will ask the Father, and he will give you
another Counselor to be with you forever.
John 14:16

It's correct to say that the Holy Spirit is our Counselor, because that's what he does and is supposed to do. Right now, I don't want to debate about his divine being or substance. Christ indicates here that the Spirit is a distinct person—the Holy Spirit is neither the Father nor the Son. But in John 15, we also see that the Spirit is God—the Holy Spirit is one in essence with the Father and the Son. For now, it's enough to learn that he is called a counselor for us.

The word *counselor* shows us how we should think of the Holy Spirit. A counselor is not a lawgiver or someone like Moses, who frightens us with the devil, death, and hell. No, a counselor fills a troubled heart with joy toward God. A counselor encourages us to be happy that our sins have been forgiven, death has been conquered, heaven has been opened, and God is smiling upon us.

Whoever understands what it means for the Spirit to be our Counselor will have already won the battle. That person will find nothing but pure comfort and joy in heaven and on earth. Because the Father is the one who sends him to help us, and because Christ is the one who asks him to do so, this sending is certainly not done out of anger. Instead, it flows from a fatherly, heartfelt love. So Christians should remind themselves of this name for the Holy Spirit. He is a counselor, and we are the troubled and timid ones whom he helps.

TRUSTING GOD IN TIMES OF NEED

⊰⊱

Do not test the LORD your God as you did at Massah.
Deuteronomy 6:16

Deuteronomy 6 teaches us to trust that God will take care of us in good and bad times. We shouldn't become overconfident in times of plenty, but we also need to patiently endure times of adversity. God will never leave us. He will be near us in our troubles. Unbelievers don't have this confidence in God, because they put their trust in earthly things.

If what we need isn't available to us, we have to rely on God's promises. If we don't rely on God, we are testing him. This is what Moses was writing about when he said, "as you did at Massah." At Massah, Israel complained and asked, "Is the LORD among us or not?" (Exodus 17:7). The people didn't trust God's promises because he didn't fulfill them in the time, place, or manner they expected. Therefore, they gave up and stopped believing. When we try to dictate to God the time, place, and manner for him to act, we are testing him. At the same time, we're trying to see if he is really there. When we do this we are putting limits on God and trying to make him do what we want. It's nothing less than trying to deprive God of his divinity. But we must realize that God is free—not subject to any limitations. He must dictate to us the place, manner, and time that he will act.

RESIST THE SINFUL NATURE

_So I say, live by the Spirit, and you will not gratify
the desires of the sinful nature._
Galatians 5:16

Sometimes believers fall and gratify the desires of the sinful nature. David fell terribly, committing adultery and causing the murder of many when he wanted Uriah to die in battle. He gave God's enemies opportunity to criticize the people of God, give the credit to idols, and blaspheme the God of Israel. Peter also fell dreadfully when he denied Christ. But as great as these sins were, they were not committed intentionally out of contempt for God; rather, they were committed out of weakness. In addition, when these men were confronted, they did not stubbornly persist in their sins but repented. Paul commands that we should accept, instruct, and restore such people (Galatians 6:1). So those who sin and fall because of weakness will not be refused forgiveness if they stand up again and do not persist in their sin. Persisting in sin is disastrous. Those who do not repent but stubbornly continue to gratify the desires of the sinful nature show that their spirits are filled with dishonesty.

We will not be without sinful desires as long as we live in these bodies. Consequently, none of us will be free of temptation either. But each person is tempted in a different way according to individual differences. One person will be attacked emotionally, such as with depression, blasphemy, unbelief, or despair. Another will be attacked with coarser sins, such as sexual desire, anger, or hatred. But Paul demands that we live by the Spirit and resist the sinful nature. Those who obey the sinful nature and continue to gratify its desires should know that they don't belong to Christ. Even though people may label themselves with the name "Christian," they are only deceiving themselves.

CHRIST CAME TO SAVE THE WORLD

❦

For God did not send his Son into the world to condemn the world,
but to save the world through him.
John 3:17

No one should run from Christ or from God the Father. God wants us to stay close to him in the same way that chicks gather under the wings of a hen. Just as children cling to their parents, we also should find refuge in Christ and the heavenly Father.

The world is already judged because of original sin, the fall, and the laws of Moses, for it was led astray by the devil. The laws of Moses, our consciences, and our hearts already judge us. Paul says that our own consciences accuse and condemn us (Romans 2:15). No additional judge is necessary. The world has always been full of judgment and death. It has never been worthy of love. That's why no other judge is needed. But the Son was sent to silence these thoughts.

In the past, no one saw the glory of this passage or took these words to heart: "God did not send his Son into the world to condemn the world, but to save the world through him." Christ is not a judge. He is a mediator, helper, comforter, and throne of mercy. He is our bishop, brother, and intercessor. He is both our gift and our helper in times of need. We have no reason to run away from him. But we still have wounded hearts that have not yet healed. We, by nature, tend to distrust God. Yet all of us should study this passage again, as a young child would. We must learn that Christ didn't come to judge the world.

FAITH CHANGES PEOPLE

*By faith he made his home in the promised land like a stranger
in a foreign country; he lived in tents, as did Isaac and Jacob,
who were heirs with him of the same promise.*
Hebrews 11:9

Faith changes people. It makes them see everything in a new light. Their ears hear, their eyes see, and their hearts feel something completely different from what everyone else perceives.

Faith is living and powerful. It's not a simpleminded idea. It doesn't float around in the heart like a goose on the water. Rather, it's like water that's been heated. After heating, the water is different. It's still water, but it's warm. The same thing happens when the Holy Spirit gives us faith. Faith transforms the mind and attitudes. It creates an entirely new person.

Faith is active, profound, and powerful. If people were to describe faith correctly, they would say it's a process, not a result. In other words, faith changes the heart and mind.

Reason tends to concentrate on what is present—the here and now. Faith concerns itself with things that are intangible and, contrary to reason, regards them as actually being present. That is why faith isn't as common among people as the five senses are. Considering the number of people in the world, there are relatively few believers. Most people concern themselves with what they can see, touch, and handle rather than listening to God's Word.

THE EVIL WITHIN US

What comes out of a man is what makes him "unclean."
For from within, out of men's hearts, come evil thoughts,
sexual immorality, theft, murder, adultery, greed, malice,
deceit, lewdness, envy, slander, arrogance and folly.
Mark 7:20–22

Whether people believe it or not, no agony, pain, or burden could be worse than feeling all of the evil that lies within themselves. The evil they don't feel is even greater and worse than the wickedness they do sense. For if people were able to feel all of their evil, they would get a taste of what hell is like.

So when the all-powerful God disciplines us in his mercy, he only shows us our lesser evils. He knows that if he shows us all of our wickedness, we would be ruined and would die in an instant. According to the author of Hebrews, God shows us some of the evil within us as a part of fatherly instruction or discipline: "He punishes everyone he accepts as a son" (Hebrews 12:6). By showing us our lesser evils and disciplining us, God wants to drive out the greater evils so we will never have to see them. As Proverbs says, "Folly is bound up in the heart of a child, but the rod of discipline will drive it far from him" (Proverbs 22:15).

Isn't it true that devout and faithful parents experience more suffering, grief, and distress when their children become thieves or are otherwise bad than if their children were wounded? Faithful parents would much rather severely discipline their children than allow them to become bad.

What prevents us from feeling all the evil within us? God has established matters so that people won't die by seeing the evil in their innermost selves. So God is the one who hides our wickedness from us. He wants us to see it only through the eyes of faith.

FEAR OF SIN AND PUNISHMENT

[Jonah] answered, "I am a Hebrew and I worship the LORD,
the God of heaven, who made the sea and the land."
This terrified them and they asked, "What have you done?"
Jonah 1:9–10

From the story of Jonah, we learn how to free ourselves from all anxiety and fear. Above all, we should confess our sin. Openly acknowledging our sin decreases the immediate danger and lessens our anxiety. Our hearts must be helped first. Confessing sin makes our hearts lighter and allows them to breathe. Then we can find help for the rest of our bodies. Only after our consciences have been released from their heavy load and are able to breathe freely can we find relief for other areas of distress.

When God's anger is poured out, we immediately become aware of our sin and become afraid. Foolish people cope with this situation in the wrong way. They ignore their sin and only try to get rid of their fear. That doesn't work, so they eventually fall into despair. This is the way human reason always tries to handle the problem in the absence of God's grace and the Spirit. Wise people, however, try to ignore their fear and focus instead on their sin. They acknowledge their sin and try to get rid of it, even if it means that their fear will remain with them forever. They willingly accept their punishment, as Jonah did in this story.

But godless people do just the opposite. They pay attention to the *punishment* and are afraid of it, but they aren't concerned about their *sin*. If there were no punishment, they would never stop sinning. But this isn't what happens, because punishment consistently follows sin. In contrast, godly people pay attention to their *sin* and are afraid of it. They aren't as concerned about the *punishment*. In fact, it's almost as if they would rather endure the punishment without sinning than commit the sin without facing any punishment.

EXTRAORDINARY FRUIT

I am the vine; you are the branches. If a man remains in me and I in him, he will bear much fruit; apart from me you can do nothing.
John 15:5

False Christians cannot understand what Jesus is saying in this passage. They wonder, "What kind of Christians are these people? They can't do anything more than eat and drink, work in their homes, take care of their children, and push a plow. We can do all that and better." False Christians want to do something different and special—something above the everyday activities of an ordinary person. They want to join a convent, lie on the ground, wear sackcloth garments, and pray day and night. They believe these works are Christian fruit and produce a holy life. Accordingly, they believe that raising children, doing housework, and performing other ordinary chores aren't part of a holy life. For false Christians look on external appearances and don't consider the source of their works—whether or not they grow out of the vine.

But in this passage, Christ says that the only works that are good fruit are those accomplished by people who remain in him. What believers do and how they live are considered good fruit—even if these works are more menial than loading a wagon with manure and driving it away. Those false believers can't understand this. They see these works as ordinary, everyday tasks. But there is a big difference between a believer's works and an unbeliever's works—even if they do the exact same thing. For an unbeliever's works don't spring from the vine—Jesus Christ. That's why unbelievers cannot please God. Their works are not Christian fruit. But because a believer's works come from faith in Christ, they are all genuine fruit.

THE SHEPHERD'S ROD AND STAFF

Even though I walk through the valley of the shadow of death, I will fear no evil, for you are with me; your rod and your staff, they comfort me.
Psalm 23:4

Even though David couldn't see or hear the Lord, David said, "You are with me." The Lord's presence can't be perceived by the five senses. Only faith enables us to know that he's there. Faith convinces us that the Lord is nearer to us than we are to ourselves. In what way is God near? He is near to us through his Word.

When David said, "Your rod and your staff, they comfort me," it's as if he wanted to say, "Nothing else on earth can help me through my worries and troubles. God's Word alone is my rod and staff. I will hang on to it and use it to pull myself up again. I will be certain that the Lord is with me and that he gives me courage in all anxieties and troubles. He defies the devil and the world and rescues me from my enemies."

With the words "your rod and your staff," David was referring to the image of a shepherd with his sheep. He wanted to say, "A shepherd guides his sheep with his rod and staff and leads them to graze in the meadow and drink fresh water. He also uses his staff to protect them from all dangers. This is the way the Lord, the true Shepherd, leads and guides me with his staff. In other words, he leads me with his Word. Then I can walk with him on the right path in firm faith and with a clear conscience. I can also protect myself from false doctrine and false piety. In addition, the Lord protects me from all spiritual and physical dangers and uses his staff to rescue me from all my enemies. God's Word so richly strengthens and comforts me that no spiritual or physical trial is too much to endure and overcome."

WATCH YOURSELF

Brothers, if someone is caught in a sin, you who are spiritual should restore him gently. But watch yourself, or you also may be tempted.
Galatians 6:1

This passage gives us a very serious warning. It's meant to restrain the severity of those who don't help or console those who have fallen into sin. Augustine says, "There is no sin committed by a person which could not also be committed by someone else." We are always walking on a slippery path. It's very easy to fall off if we become proud or get out of line. "So, if you think you are standing firm, be careful that you don't fall!" (1 Corinthians 10:12).

David was a holy man, full of faith and of the Spirit of God. He received glorious promises from God and did great things for God. But he fell in such a shameful way. After successfully enduring many trials that God used to test him, and even though he was advanced in age, he was carried away by the passion of youth. If this could happen to such a man as David, how can we ever take for granted our own ability to remain steady? Through this example, God shows us our own weakness so that we will not exalt ourselves but stand in fear. God also shows us his judgment. He finds nothing more intolerable than pride, whether against him or against a brother or sister. So Paul does not uselessly say, "Watch yourself, or you also may be tempted."

Those who have faced temptations know how important this is. Some haven't, so they don't understand what Paul is saying, and they lack compassion for those who have fallen.

FOLLOWING FOR WRONG REASONS

Jesus answered, "I tell you the truth, you are looking for me,
not because you saw miraculous signs but because
you ate the loaves and had your fill."
John 6:26

Christ tells the people that they're following him, not because of his teaching, but because of their stomachs, which they hold dear. They were thinking to themselves, "Jesus is a great teacher for us! He'll give us freedom. We will all be full and satisfied, getting whatever we want." In this passage, the Lord reveals what type of followers the gospel will attract. Even today, the gospel attracts people who think it will fill their bellies, satisfy their desires, and help them here in this life.

This idea is so common today that I have almost become tired of preaching and teaching it. People, pretending to be sincere disciples, come to hear a sermon. But under this guise, they come only for personal gain. However, the gospel wasn't sent from heaven in order to allow people to fill their own bellies, take whatever they want, and do whatever they please. Christ didn't shed his blood for this purpose!

The gospel proclaims God's glory and teaches us how to praise the Lord. God wants us to praise him. He wants us to do what pleases him. If we make God's honor and kingdom our first priority, then not only will he give us life and everything we need in this world, but he will give us eternal life as well.

LIVING WITH INGRATITUDE

He slept with Hagar, and she conceived.
When she knew she was pregnant, she began to despise her mistress.
Genesis 16:4

As a slave, Hagar owned nothing except the food and clothes that Sarai, out of kindness and generosity, had given her. Sarai was even the one who chose her to be the mother of Abram's child. Yet Hagar began to be disrespectful to Sarai, Abram's true wife. The Holy Spirit relates this story about the quarrel between Sarai and Hagar for our comfort. He wants us to understand what God's people had to go through in their lifetimes. The entire family was affected by the fact that Hagar treated Sarai with disrespect.

On the surface, this story seems to be trivial and insignificant. Nevertheless, the Holy Spirit considered it so worthwhile as to describe it in great detail. This was done so that believers would be comforted and learn the lesson that they should be patient as they wait to be delivered from similar problems.

Hagar owed everything she had, even life itself, to Sarai. Yet she was rude and disrespectful to the person who generously provided for her. So we should learn to do good to others but be prepared to put up with ingratitude. Many situations in our lives don't turn out the way we expect. Our hopes for other people aren't always fulfilled. After all, human nature is corrupt, and people are unpredictable. When life suddenly starts going well, it's difficult for anyone to avoid the temptation of becoming rude and disrespectful to others.

TAKING TIME TO PRAY

Pray continually; give thanks in all circumstances,
for this is God's will for you in Christ Jesus.
1 Thessalonians 5:17–18

It's good to let prayer be the first thing you do in the morning and the last thing you do at night. Be on guard against false, deceitful thoughts that say, "Wait awhile; you can pray in an hour. First, you must finish this or that." For with such thoughts, you turn away from prayer toward the business at hand, which surrounds you and holds you back so that you never get around to praying that day.

Of course, some tasks are as good as or better than prayer, especially during an emergency. Nevertheless, we should pray continually. Christ says to keep on asking, seeking, and knocking (Luke 11:9–11). And Paul says that we should never stop praying (1 Thessalonians 5:17). Likewise, we should continually guard against sin and wrongdoing, which can't happen if we don't fear God and keep his commandments in mind at all times. In Psalm 1 we read about the one who is blessed: "His delight is in the law of the LORD, and on his law he meditates day and night" (v. 2).

We shouldn't neglect the habit of true prayer and get caught up in necessary work—which usually isn't all that necessary anyway. We can end up becoming lazy about prayer, cold toward it, and tired of it, but the devil doesn't get lazy around us.

RETURN TO GOD

❧

The LORD was very angry with your forefathers. Therefore tell the people: This is what the LORD Almighty says: "Return to me," declares the LORD Almighty, "and I will return to you," says the LORD Almighty.
Zechariah 1:2–3

In this passage, we see that Zechariah's message was primarily concerned with belief and unbelief. He pointed out that the greatest sin of the Israelites' ancestors was not trusting in God when they were undergoing trials. Rather, they looked to other people for help. In this way, they were rebellious and idolatrous. Zechariah wanted the people of Israel to understand that the words "Return to me" should penetrate their hearts deeply.

People "return to God" when they trust in and find comfort in God at all times, especially in times of need. On the other hand, people have turned away from God when they don't trust in God. When people don't trust God, their good works and sacrifices won't be able to help them. This is what happened to Israel's ancestors.

In Zechariah's time, when the Israelites were trying to rebuild the temple, they needed to turn to the Lord Almighty because of all the trials and troubles they were facing. They had to cling to God and depend on him even if rebuilding the temple angered the emperor of Persia or the neighboring people. God spoke. He wanted to help, could help, and would help them so that Israel's enemies wouldn't overpower them again.

We too need to hear these warnings in the book of Zechariah. Let everyone return to Christ, cling to him, and not fall away. Let no one become scared or be led astray. God speaks. And God will do what he says.

SINS THAT LEAD TO DEATH

But the man who has doubts is condemned if he eats, because his eating is not from faith; and everything that does not come from faith is sin.
Romans 14:23

After coming to faith, no one should think that sin can be taken lightly. Sin is truly sin, whether it is committed before or after one comes to know Christ. God always hates sin. Every sin is a mortal sin—a sin that leads to death—as far as the act itself is concerned. But it's not a mortal sin for the believer. Christ the Reconciler atoned for sin by his death. For unbelievers, not only are all of their sins mortal ones, but even their good works are sins. As Paul says in Romans, "Everything that does not come from faith is sin."

The philosophers make a fatal error when they classify sins according to the acts themselves rather than according to the person who commits the sin. Believers have the same sin and just as great a sin as unbelievers. But the sin of the believers is forgiven and not credited to them. The sin of the unbelievers, however, is retained and counted against them. For the believer, the sinful act is a sin that can be easily forgiven. For the unbeliever, it's a mortal sin that leads to death. This is not because of the difference in the sin itself as if the believer's sin is less and the unbeliever's sin is greater. It is because of the difference in the person who committed it.

By faith, believers see that their sins are forgiven for the sake of Christ. Christ offered himself for their sin. So they remain righteous in spite of their sin, although they have sin and continue to sin. But unbelievers remain unrighteous. Although believers aren't free from sin, they know that their sin isn't credited to them because of their faith in Christ. This is the wisdom and the comfort of true believers.

FILTHY IN GOD'S SIGHT

The angel said to those who were standing before him,
"Take off his filthy clothes."
Then he said to Joshua, "See, I have taken away your sin,
and I will put rich garments on you."
Zechariah 3:4

Joshua, the chief priest at this time, was selected by God to lead the people. In these verses and the ones that follow, God linked his promises to Joshua's obedience. By doing this, God guarded against Joshua becoming too proud as a result of his receiving visions, comfort, and promises earlier. Rather than assuming that God was bound by his promises and had to fulfill them, Joshua needed to remain humble and continue to live in the fear of God.

We who live on this earth are such poor people. We become easily discouraged and fainthearted when God punishes us and sends us problems. Then God has plenty of work to do to comfort and lift us up again. After he comforts us and allows us to experience good times, we become proud and overconfident. Then he has to threaten and frighten us. So we are too weak and fragile to endure what God allows to happen to us—whether good or bad. No matter what he does for us, he ends up having more work to do. We can't hold up under the bad times, and we can't hold on during the good times.

After giving Joshua great promises, God needed to humble him. God couldn't allow Joshua to become arrogant in the light of such wonderful promises. Similarly, Saul and many other kings of Israel were blinded by God's promises. They became too proud and were destroyed as a result. Though their ancestors were completely dependent on God and his promises, they didn't want to obey him. Oh, if only we could recognize how poor and filthy we are in God's sight!

GOD CHOSE YOU

*You did not choose me, but I chose you and appointed you
to go and bear fruit—fruit that will last.
Then the Father will give you whatever you ask in my name.*
John 15:16

A fierce battle has been raging in this world since the very beginning. Cain wanted to choose God on his own terms. He wanted God to value his work and his offering instead of his brother's. The world has followed Cain's example from that day until now. The world always wants to turn this verse in John around and say, "I don't want to be chosen by God; I want to choose him first." But God cannot and will not tolerate this. He turns their words back around and says, "You cannot and should not choose me. I must choose you. It won't happen the way you imagine, but the way I want it to. I want to be your Lord and Master. I don't want to be mastered by you." That's why throughout Scripture God condemns and throws away this type of choosing that goes against what he commands.

Even Paul condemns this vice. He says, "Do not let anyone who delights in false humility and the worship of angels disqualify you" (Colossians 2:18). Likewise, he says, "Such regulations indeed have an appearance of wisdom, with their self-imposed worship, their false humility and their harsh treatment of the body, but they lack any value" (v. 23). With these words, he describes those who practice useless, self-chosen worship and justify it by saying, "I mean well and am doing it for God and to honor him. It will please him, and so he will be merciful to me." These people are twice as bad as God's enemies. God called the Israelites out of Egypt and gave them the Ten Commandments, telling them what they should and shouldn't do so that they wouldn't invent ways to serve him. In the same way, God wants to tell us what it means to serve him.

PRAYING FOR GOD'S MERCY

※⟨⟩⟩⟨⟨

Have mercy on me, O God, according to your unfailing love;
according to your great compassion blot out my transgressions.
Psalm 51:1

We naturally think, "I'm frightened by the sight of God, so I can't
look to heaven for help. I know that I'm a sinner and that God
hates sin. How can I pray?" With these thoughts, an intense battle begins inside us. Because we know we are sinners, we may
think we have to postpone praying until we feel worthy. Or we
look for other people to assure us that we have done enough good
works to have confidence in our own worthiness. Only then do
we pray, "God, have mercy on me." But we were born in sin. If
we had to wait until we felt pure and free from all sin before we
prayed, we would never pray.

We must shake off these kinds of unchristian thoughts. When
surrounded by our own sinfulness—even while drowning in our
sins—we should cry out to God, just as David did in this psalm.
Then we won't have to postpone our prayer. What purpose do the
words "Have mercy on me, O God, according to your unfailing
love" serve if the only people who pray them are pure and don't
need any mercy? No matter how sinful we feel, we must encourage ourselves to cry out to God, "Have mercy!"

I have learned from my own experience that praying is often
the most difficult thing to do. I don't hold myself up a master
of prayer. In fact, I admit that I have often said these words
coldly: "God, have mercy on me." I prayed that way because I
was worried about my own unworthiness. Yet ultimately the Holy
Spirit convinced me, "No matter how you feel, you must pray!"
God wants us to pray, and he wants to hear our prayers—not
because we are worthy, but because he is merciful.

CONSIDERING OTHERS

❦

You, my brothers, were called to be free. But do not use your freedom
to indulge the sinful nature; rather, serve one another in love.
Galatians 5:13

Because there are two different types of people, two different offenses occur. On one side, the weak are offended; on the other side, the strong are offended. Paul is trying to keep them both in the middle and avoid both offenses.

The weak are offended when something is done that they don't understand and can't distinguish from evil. Romans 14 deals with this situation at length. For example, when the weak saw that others were eating foods forbidden by the law as unclean, they did not dare eat these foods because they were inhibited by their consciences. Yet they could not disapprove of what the others did. Here Paul became a Jew with the Jews, a weak person with the weak to serve them through love so that they would become strong in Christ.

On the other hand, the strong are offended when they become annoyed by the weak and grow impatient with their slowness and clumsiness. Without consideration for others, they overuse their freedom in Christ, resulting in weak people becoming offended. It would be better for them to keep all the laws before offending one person. This is what it means to live by the Spirit. What good does it do to use the Spirit of freedom against the Spirit of love?

But you may insist, "We are free to do this." Certainly. But you must put the weakness of your brother or sister ahead of your own freedom. It doesn't hurt you if you don't exercise your freedom. Yet it hurts them if they are offended by your freedom. Don't forget that the task of love is thinking of what's best for others. Rather than finding out how much freedom you can exercise, find out how much service you can give to your brother or sister.

COME TO CHRIST

All that the Father gives me will come to me,
and whoever comes to me I will never drive away.
John 6:37

If a servant was obedient and had earned the approval of his master, it would be normal for his master to want him to stay. The master wouldn't be showing any special virtue by doing this. But if a master threw a good servant out of his house, that would be to the disgrace of the master, not the servant. On the other hand, if the servant was disobedient and yet the master kept him in the house, then that would be to the master's credit. So even if you fall and sin, Christ won't push you away. A mother would never want to get rid of a child because the child was dirty, sick, or injured. Although young children often misbehave, no father would disinherit them or throw them out of the house for their bad behavior. The father would merely scold them, "If you want to be my child, then you'd better stop doing what's wrong. I will overlook it this time."

The Lord takes the same approach. He's saying, "I see that you don't believe. If you are to have faith, I know that my Father must give it to you. If he gives you faith, then you will certainly be able to believe. Yet you want to be my master. You want me to be your student. That's not going to work. This shows that the Father hasn't called you. But others will come who will accept my message. These people may be weak and clumsy Christians. But if they only believe, I will never drive them away."

GOD'S COMMANDS ARE NECESSARY

※❧◇

Then the LORD rained down burning sulfur on Sodom and
Gomorrah—from the LORD out of the heavens. Thus he overthrew
those cities and the entire plain, including all those living
in the cities—and also the vegetation in the land.
Genesis 19:24–25

The story of Sodom and Gomorrah shows God's fierce anger being poured out on sinful people. Reflecting and meditating on this story is an unsettling experience. That's why I am deeply moved whenever I read or speak about it. Even though I am often furious at wicked people who refuse to change their ways, the terrible suffering and agony that took place at Sodom upsets me. I also feel the mental anguish that Abraham suffered when he interceded with God. Though the wicked people of Sodom refused to change, Abraham sincerely hoped that disaster wouldn't fall on them.

Today, some people want to de-emphasize God's commands. They think that people should be treated only with love and tolerance and shouldn't be frightened by examples of God's anger. Paul says quite the opposite. In the letter to the Corinthians, he tells many stories about God's anger against sinners. Then he states, "Now these things occurred as examples to keep us from setting our hearts on evil things as they did" (1 Corinthians 10:6).

Arrogant and stubborn people despise the Word of God and laugh at well-intentioned words of caution. They feel so good about themselves that whenever anyone tells them about the extent of God's mercy and grace, it only leaves them worse off than they were before. This is what happens when people try to get rid of God's commands. We must guard against this false teaching. It's not enough for these people to bring destruction on themselves. They intend to drag us down with them. Like the people of Sodom, they don't realize that their sins will soon be punished.

September 5

HAVING A PURE HEART

Blessed are the pure in heart, for they will see God.
Matthew 5:8

Some dreamers claim that in order to have a pure heart, people have to hide in a corner, enter a monastery or convent, or seek the solitude of the desert. They claim people shouldn't think worldly thoughts or spend any time on secular matters. Instead, all their thoughts should be about heaven. These dreamers deceive both themselves and others with their mistaken notions. They lead people astray and do a lot of damage. They consider secular leaders and institutions to be evil. Yet these are the very things that ensure a law-abiding and orderly society. These leaders and institutions keep the world running and are established by God himself.

Scripture talks about having pure thoughts and a pure heart in a way that is consistent with being a spouse, loving and caring for your family, and doing everything a parent does. In fact, God insists that we fulfill these responsibilities. Whatever God commands can't be impure. In fact, it's this very purity that allows us to see God.

When a judge carries out his responsibilities and imposes a sentence, he isn't acting on his own. He is carrying out God's laws and commands. If he's a Christian, he is performing a good, pure, and holy function. But a person in this position couldn't do anything if their heart wasn't pure. Even dirty and unpleasant work, such as shoveling manure or washing diapers, is pure and holy work if it comes from a pure heart.

THE GENUINE GOSPEL

Praise be to the God and Father of our Lord Jesus Christ!
In his great mercy he has given us new birth into a living hope
through the resurrection of Jesus Christ from the dead.
1 Peter 1:3

The book of 1 Peter is a wonderful letter and a model for us. Peter begins by explaining who Christ is and what we have received through him. He says that God has given us a new birth to a living hope through Christ's resurrection. Likewise, the Father out of pure mercy has given us everything, apart from our merit. These are genuinely evangelical words that must be preached.

May God help us. How little of this message we find in other books! Even among the best, such as those written by Jerome and Augustine, we find hardly anything. Therefore, we must preach about Jesus Christ, that he died and rose from the dead and why he died and was resurrected. We must preach so that the people will believe in him and through faith be saved.

This is what it means to preach the true gospel. Any preaching that is different than this is not the gospel, no matter who preaches it.

A BROKEN AND CONTRITE HEART

*The sacrifices of God are a broken spirit; a broken and contrite heart,
O God, you will not despise.*
Psalm 51:17

David talks about "a broken and contrite heart." In other words, this is a sincerely humble heart that is almost dying out of despair. David is saying that God doesn't hate a broken and contrite heart, but rather accepts it with joy. The message we proclaim brings life and God's approval to us because it strengthens us and fights against sin and death. In fact, the gospel demonstrates its power when we are sinful and weak. It's a message of joy that can be experienced only when sorrow and distress are present.

But we want to have the message of life and joy without any sorrow or death. What fine theologians we think we are! We must learn that as Christians we have to live with death all around us, with regret and a trembling conscience—between the teeth of the devil and hell. In spite of all this, we must hang on to the message of God's grace. Then in all circumstances, we can say, "Lord, you want only the best for me."

In this psalm, we read that God finds no sacrifice more pleasing than a broken heart. The tax collector exemplified this attitude when he said, "God, have mercy on me, a sinner" (Luke 18:13). The tax collector offered the Lord the most desirable sacrifice, a broken heart that trusts in God's mercy. This is a comforting way to think about God. God's true nature is to love people who are troubled, have mercy on those who are brokenhearted, forgive those who have fallen, and refresh those who are exhausted. This psalm calls us to trust in God's mercy and goodness alone. It encourages us to believe that God is on our side even when we feel abandoned and distressed.

STAY WHERE YOU ARE

❧

Nevertheless, each one should retain the place in life that the Lord
assigned to him and to which God has called him.
This is the rule I lay down in all the churches.
1 Corinthians 7:17

Christians have freedom. Faith and the Christian life aren't restricted to any particular station or position in life. But they are above, in, and throughout all positions in life. Therefore, it's not necessary for you to accept or give up any position in life to receive salvation. Stay in whatever place the gospel finds you. You can remain there and be saved. It's not necessary for you to give up your marriage and run from your non-Christian spouse for the sake of faith or salvation. On the other hand, it's not necessary for you to become married for the sake of faith or salvation. If you are married, whether it be to a Christian or non-Christian, whether to a good or evil person, you are neither saved nor condemned because of that. If you are unmarried, you also are not saved or condemned because of being single. It is all free—free!

As a result, if you are a Christian and remain one, you will be saved, and if you remain a non-Christian, you will be condemned. "This is the rule I lay down in all the churches" means "This is the rule I teach all Christians to whom I preach. For I do not teach them to leave their positions in life and stir up unrest, but to remain where they are and live in peace." So you see that Paul doesn't call any position in life a blessed one except this one: being a Christian. The others he frees up so that in and of themselves they neither save nor condemn us. But all positions in life—no matter how well kept—can be blessed through faith or cursed through lack of faith.

CLIP THE WINGS OF WISDOM

᷈༔᷈

"Stop grumbling among yourselves," Jesus answered.
"No one can come to me unless the Father who sent me draws him,
and I will raise him up at the last day."
John 6:43–44

When Jesus said, "Stop grumbling among yourselves," he wanted to curb human wisdom or reason. We also should clip the wings of human reason when it comes to Christian doctrine. God's Word isn't the kind of teaching you can grasp with reason. It doesn't reach the human heart that way. The more educated and the more sharpened the reasoning ability of people, the less they understand. Christian teaching doesn't appeal to reason. That's why our reason complains about it: "I don't want to take my salvation out of my own hands and throw away all my good works in order to achieve eternal life. I don't want to place my hands and set my feet on someone outside of myself, someone who was so silly and foolish as to let himself be crucified. How am I supposed to believe that Jesus is my Savior?" Reason cannot grasp this. We must take every thought captive so that it's obedient to Christ (2 Corinthians 10:5).

Jesus is saying, "Stop complaining that I claim to be the bread of heaven. You want to understand this on your own. You want to be smarter than I am when you ask, 'Don't we know his mother and father?' But when I tell you how the Father has drawn you to me, it can't be understood by your reason. When you hear about how the Father draws you, reason draws you in a different direction. Those who want to understand these words must close their eyes, shut the gates of reason, and let themselves become like a blind person." This is what God wants. Whoever refuses to be led by God, but instead wants to be led by reason, will be irritated by the message of Jesus and will continually complain about it.

PRAYER CHANGES US

*Do not be like them, for your Father knows
what you need before you ask him.*
Matthew 6:8

You might wonder, "Why does God insist that we pray to him and tell him our problems? Why doesn't he take care of us without our having to ask? He already knows what we need better than we do." God continually showers his gifts on the whole world every day. He gives us sunshine, rain, good harvests, money, healthy bodies, and so on. But we often neither ask God for these gifts nor thank him for them. If God already knows that we can't live without light or food for any length of time, then why does he want us to ask for these necessities?

Obviously, he doesn't command us to pray in order to inform him of our needs. God gives us his gifts freely and abundantly. He wants us to recognize that he is willing and able to give us even more. When we pray, we're not telling God anything he doesn't already know. Rather, we are the ones gaining knowledge and insight. Asking God to supply our needs keeps us from becoming like the unbelieving skeptics, who don't acknowledge God and don't thank him for his many gifts.

All of this teaches us to acknowledge God's generosity even more. Because we continue to search for him and keep on knocking at his door, he showers us with more and more blessings. Everything we have is a gift from God. When we pray, we should express our gratitude by saying, "Lord, I know that I can't create a single slice of my daily bread. You are the only one who can supply all of my needs. I have no way to protect myself from disasters. You know what I need ahead of time, so I'm convinced that you will take care of me."

MORE THAN COMMON SENSE

[Abraham] said to Ephron in their hearing,
"Listen to me, if you will. I will pay the price of the field.
Accept it from me so I can bury my dead there."
Genesis 23:13

Ephron, a landowner in Hebron, tried to talk Abraham into accepting a piece of land as a gift, free of charge. Ephron was saying, "Something this trivial shouldn't come between us. You are a prince of God, and I am rich. Even if you paid me ten pounds of silver for the land, that money wouldn't matter to me." This was a great show of respect for Abraham, a prophet and teacher. But Abraham used good sense and refused the offer. He preferred to own the land and purchase it at a fair price.

Abraham could have said, "I know that you are generous, devout, and kind. Yet I've known people in other places who taught me a hard lesson about how unpredictable people can be. So I've learned to be cautious. In Egypt and Gerar, the people treated me with respect and dignity at first, but in the end, they threw me out. I helped the people of Sodom, but all they showed me was ingratitude and abuse. If I accept this field as a gift, then your descendants may forget your unselfish gift to me after you're gone. They may decide to take back the land by force, exhume Sarah's body, and take it away. We are foreigners in a strange country. To prevent something like that from happening, I prefer to purchase this piece of land. Then your descendants will have no right to demand that the property be returned."

Even in purely secular matters, godly people should treat others with respect. As God's people live in the world, they should conduct their business carefully. Like Abraham, they should use common sense, be courteous, and show respect in their dealings with each other and with everyone else.

TRUSTING GOD FOR DAILY NEEDS

*Therefore I tell you, do not worry about your life, what you will eat
or drink; or about your body, what you will wear. Is not life more
important than food, and the body more important than clothes?*
Matthew 6:25

We can't seem to let go of our anxieties and worries as long as we live. Yet God gives us everything we need hour by hour, without needing any assistance from us. So why do we keep on having foolish fears and anxieties about trivial little needs, as though God can't or won't supply us with food and shelter? We should hang our heads in shame when people point out this foolishness to us. Yet foolish is the only way to describe those rich, well-fed people who are always worried about having a full pantry. They have plenty of food on hand to serve nourishing meals, but they never share a meal with anyone or invite dinner guests. They have empty beds but never ask anyone to spend the night.

Accordingly, Christ is plainly telling us what foolish people we are. It should be enough to make us want to spit on ourselves in utter disgust. Still, we continue to grope along in our blindness, even though it's obvious that we're incapable of providing for our basic needs without God. This alone should be enough to make us Christians and to keep this thought in mind: "Undoubtedly, I never held in my own hands even one fleeting moment of my life. If I must trust God for my very life and limb, why should I worry about how I'm going to find nourishment from day to day?" Not trusting God for our daily needs is like having a wealthy father who is willing to lavish thousands of dollars on us, yet not being able to trust him for money in an emergency.

SUFFERING FOR DOING GOOD

Who is going to harm you if you are eager to do good?
But even if you should suffer for what is right, you are blessed.
"Do not fear what they fear; do not be frightened."
1 Peter 3:13–14

Peter doesn't want you to say that the person who harmed you was doing right. For there is a much different judgment between me and God and between me and you. For example, I can have anger, hatred, and evil desire in my heart and not hurt you. You remain unharmed and have nothing against me. But before God, I am guilty. If he punishes me, he does what is right, for I have certainly earned it. If he doesn't punish me, then he shows mercy to me. He is right either way. But it doesn't follow from this that the person persecuting me is also doing right. For I have not wronged that person in the same way that I have wronged God.

In Ezekiel 29:19–20, God speaks about King Nebuchadnezzar. It's as if God were saying, "Don't you know that he has been my servant and has served me? Now I must give him a reward. I have not yet paid him. I will give him the land of Egypt as his reward." Nebuchadnezzar had no right to the land, but God had the right to punish others through him. In order that these evil scoundrels won't eat their bread free of charge, God has them serve him by persecuting his people. Human reason, then, steps in and thinks that people like this must be doing well. But God is only paying them in return for their work of punishing and persecuting devout Christians. But if you endure the punishment and bless God by saying, "You are right, Lord!" you will do well. Then God will cast those people into hell and punish them for doing wrong. But he will mercifully receive you and give you eternal salvation. So let God do what he will. He will certainly repay in the end.

CALL ON THE LORD

In my anguish I cried to the LORD, and he answered by setting me free.
Psalm 118:5

You must learn to call on the Lord. Don't sit all alone or lie on the couch, shaking your head and letting your thoughts torture you. Don't worry about how to get out of your situation or brood about your terrible life, how miserable you feel, and what a bad person you are. Instead, say, "Get a grip on yourself, you lazy bum! Fall on your knees, and raise your hands and eyes toward heaven. Read a psalm. Say the Lord's Prayer, and tearfully tell God what you need." This passage teaches us to call on him. Similarly, David said, "I pour out my complaint before him; before him I tell my trouble" (Psalm 142:2). God wants you to tell him your troubles. He doesn't want you to keep them to yourself. He doesn't want you to struggle with them all alone and torture yourself. Doing this will only multiply your troubles.

God knows you will be too weak to overcome your troubles by yourself. He wants you to grow strong in him. Then he will be the one who receives the glory. Out of difficult experiences emerge true Christians. Without troubles, people talk a lot about faith and the Spirit but don't really know what these things are or what they're saying.

You must never doubt that God knows your troubles and hears your prayers. You must not pray haphazardly or pray as if you're shouting into the wind. This mocks prayer and tests God. In this case, it would be better not to pray at all. You must learn to appreciate the part of the passage that says, "He answered by setting me free." The psalmist acknowledged that the Lord heard him and released him from his troubles.

THE GOSPEL FROM GOD

Jesus answered, "My teaching is not my own.
It comes from him who sent me."
John 7:16

Christ answered his adversaries carefully. He showed that he understood them and realized they were accusing and slandering him. They thought his teaching came from the devil. So Jesus answered them, "My teaching is not my own. It comes from him who sent me." Does that make sense? If Jesus' words were not his own, why did he preach, promote, and embrace them so strongly? Why did he refuse to accept the honor of his own words? Why didn't he say, "This is *my* teaching"?

Christians often say, "This is my sermon, my baptism, my Christ, my God." Or we might say, "my gospel." Yet none of these are ours, for we didn't create them. They didn't originate in us. They aren't our works. Yet, at the same time, they are ours because God gives them to us. In the same way, we might say, "my child," "my husband," or "my wife." Yet none of those people are truly ours, for we didn't create them. They are the work of another, and they are presented and given to us. We didn't pour them into a mold or carve them out of wood. They were given to us as gifts. Christ says the same about his teaching.

This is why I insist that this gospel is mine. It's different than the teaching of other preachers. This is my teaching—in other words, Luther's teaching. At the same time, I'm saying, "It's not my teaching. It's not my work, but God's gift." I didn't create it in my head. It didn't grow in my garden. I didn't give birth to it. Rather, it's God's gift. So both are true. The gospel is mine, yet it's not mine, because it's God's.

GOD RESCUES US FROM SATAN

The angel of the LORD encamps around those who fear him,
and he delivers them.
Psalm 34:7

This is one of the most remarkable passages in the Psalms. We can claim it as our own. But you might say, "I don't see or feel God's angels around me. Actually, I feel like I am under the power of the devil and am being led to hell." My answer would be, "Don't let yourself think that way! If you had been handed over to the devil, he wouldn't let you live one hour without plunging you into a life of crime. As a matter of fact, he probably wouldn't even give you time to do anything wrong, but would kill you right away. You are still alive because of the protection of the holy angels. The time will come when you have to leave this earth, and with God's permission, you may be subjected to Satan's anger. But God, in his mercy and grace, will strengthen you through his Word."

When you are handed over to Satan, it will only be for a very short time. This isn't to condemn you but to test you, to bring about salvation and endless blessings. Christ said, "Unless a kernel of wheat falls to the ground and dies, it remains only a single seed. But if it dies, it produces many seeds" (John 12:24). In the same way, Christ was handed over to murderers, but only for a short time and to bring about salvation. So when you feel Satan bothering and tempting you, pray and thank God that you won't fail but that you are only going through a trial in order to be purified. Jeremiah comforts us by saying, "Yet this I call to mind and therefore I have hope: Because of the LORD's great love we are not consumed, for his compassions never fail" (Lamentations 3:21–22).

KEEP YOUR EYES ON CHRIST

I have been crucified with Christ and I no longer live,
but Christ lives in me.
Galatians 2:20

The righteousness Paul is speaking about here is external and comes from Christ living in us. It's not internal, and it doesn't come from ourselves. So if we are concerned about Christian righteousness, we must completely set aside the self.

If I focus on myself, then I become concerned about works and become subject to the law—whether I intend to or not. Instead, Christ and my conscience must become one so that I see nothing else except the crucified and risen Christ. If I ignore Christ and look only at myself, then I am ruined. Soon I begin thinking, "Christ is in heaven; I am on earth. How can I come to him? I will try to live a holy life and do what the law requires so that I will find eternal life." If I consider myself—my condition and what I should be doing—then I will always lose sight of Christ. He alone is my righteousness and my life. If I lose him, no one else will be able to help me. Despair and condemnation will certainly follow.

Unfortunately, this happens all the time. When facing temptation or death, it's natural for us to ignore Christ and look at our own lives. If we aren't strengthened through faith during those times, we will perish. So during these struggles of conscience, we must learn to let go of ourselves. We must forget about the law and works. They only drive us to look at ourselves. Instead, we must turn our eyes directly toward the bronze snake, Christ, the one nailed to the cross (John 3:14). We must fix our gaze upon him.

BECOMING GOD'S CHILDREN

He came to that which was his own, but his own did not receive him.
Yet to all who received him, to those who believed in his name,
he gave the right to become children of God.
John 1:11–12

To everyone who believes in Christ, God offers the privilege of becoming his children. Yet this greatest of all offers is despised, ridiculed, and laughed at by the blind and condemned people of this world. In addition, God's offer is abused and even regarded as blasphemy. Although those who confess his name and trust his words are children of God, they're executed as though they were children of the devil, blasphemers, and revolutionaries. The religious leaders did the same to Christ, God's only Son. They accused him of stirring up trouble among the people, of keeping the people from paying taxes to the emperor (Luke 23:2), and of claiming to be the Son of God (John 19:7).

Sometimes the devil attacks devout Christians so fiercely with his flaming arrows (Ephesians 6:16) that they forget about the endless glory they have as God's children. They begin thinking the opposite and wonder if God has forgotten about them, abandoned them, and thrown them so far away that he can't see them anymore.

Our faith is still very weak and cold. If our faith were as strong and steady as it should be, we would practically die from sheer joy. But we praise God because we know that even those who have only a little faith are also children of God. That's why Christ said, "Do not be afraid, little flock" (Luke 12:32). So we always need to pray with the apostles, "Increase our faith!" (Luke 17:5), and pray with the man in the book of Mark who cried out, "I do believe; help me overcome my unbelief!" (Mark 9:24).

THE CROSS OF CHRIST

May I never boast except in the cross of our Lord Jesus Christ,
through which the world has been crucified to me, and I to the world.
Galatians 6:14

The cross of Christ doesn't refer just to the wood that Christ carried on his shoulders and on which he was nailed. It also signifies all the troubles of the faithful people whose suffering is Christ's suffering. Paul talks about Christians enduring these sufferings in 2 Corinthians 1:5. In Colossians 1:24, he says, "Now I rejoice in what was suffered for you, and I fill up in my flesh what is still lacking in regard to Christ's afflictions, for the sake of his body, which is the church." Therefore, the cross of Christ generally refers to all the afflictions that the church suffers for the sake of Christ.

Christ himself testifies to this in Acts 9:4 when he says, "Saul, Saul, why do you persecute me?" Saul didn't attack Christ. He persecuted his followers. But whoever touches them touches the apple of [God's] eye (Zechariah 2:8). We know by experience that the head is more sensitive than other parts of the body. For if a toe or another tiny part of the body is injured, the head recognizes the feeling, and the face shows it. The nose wrinkles, the eyes squint, and so on. Similarly, Christ, our head, makes our afflictions his own and suffers when we, his body, suffer.

It's helpful to remember this so that we don't despair when our opponents persecute, excommunicate, and kill us, or when heretics hate us with such deep hostility. We should remember Paul's example and pride ourselves in the cross. We have taken up this cross, not because of our own sins, but for the sake of Christ.

WHY WE DON'T PRAY

Or if he asks for a fish, will give him a snake? If you, then, though you are evil, know how to give good gifts to your children, how much more will your Father in heaven give good gifts to those who ask him!
Matthew 7:10–11

Our own urgent needs should be enough to make us pray. But as if that were not enough, Jesus uses a beautiful illustration from family life to coax us to pray. Even a problem child wouldn't receive a snake instead of a fish from his parents. With this illustration, Jesus is saying, "Your human nature is corrupt. You aren't nearly as good as God, but you still give your children good gifts. Because God, your heavenly Father, is perfect, won't he also give you good things if you ask him?" If we take this illustration to heart, we will want to pray.

Yet when we understand what God says in his Word, begin to live according to it, and teach it to others, we'll face many temptations and frequent opposition. Our sinful nature is an enemy of prayer. It quickly becomes bored, careless, and indifferent to what God says and the good life he gives us. For this reason, we will never have as much wisdom, knowledge of God's Word, faith, love, or patience as we should. Every day our sinful nature hangs around our necks and drags us away from prayer. The world is also an enemy of prayer. It's so envious that we have faith and God's precious Word that it refuses to put up with any of it, no matter how weak we may be. The world condemns us, tries to take away what we have, and gives us no peace.

These are the two enemies of prayer: our sinful nature and the world. On the inside, they try to decrease our desire to pray, and on the outside, they try to chase us away from prayer. All we can do is continue crying out to God. We should pray for strength and better understanding of his Word.

PARTICIPATING IN THE DIVINE NATURE

Through these he has given us his very great and precious promises,
so that through them you may participate in the divine nature
and escape the corruption in the world caused by evil desires.
2 Peter 1:4

Peter says that through the power of faith we participate in the divine nature and have fellowship with the divine nature. What a verse! We can't find another one like this in either the New or Old Testament. Yet unbelievers consider this a small matter.

But what is the divine nature anyway? It's eternal truth, justice, wisdom, eternal life, peace, joy, happiness, and whatever else can be called good. Those who share in the divine nature receive all of this so that they live eternally and have eternal peace, pleasure, and joy. They are pure and clean, and they have power over the devil, sin, and death. Peter is saying, "Just as one cannot take eternal life and truth from God, no one can take it from you." If anyone does something to you, they also do it to God. If anyone oppresses a Christian, they also oppress God. The way Peter uses the little phrase "divine nature" means all of this.

It's truly wonderful when a person believes. However, Peter didn't mean for all these instructions to be a foundation for faith. Instead, he is underscoring what great, rich possessions we receive as a result of faith. This is why Peter adds that we will have all of this if we demonstrate our faith by fleeing evil desires.

PRAYING THE PSALMS

꘏❦꘏

Be filled with the Spirit. Speak to one another with psalms, hymns
and spiritual songs. Sing and make music in your heart to the Lord.
Ephesians 5:18–19

Consider what the most respected church fathers, especially
Athanasius and Augustine, taught about using psalms. They said
we should adapt and adjust our minds so that we are in tune with
the psalms. We must sing the psalms with the help of the Holy
Spirit. They are like a school for the attitudes of the heart.

For example, when you read in Psalm 1, "Blessed is the man
who does not walk in the counsel of the wicked," you must actually reject the advice that wicked people give you. When you read,
"But his delight is in the law of the LORD," you shouldn't take it
easy and pat yourself on the back as if you are a person who already
loves the Lord's teachings. For as long as you live, you will need to
think of yourself as a person who desperately needs to love God's
teachings even more. When you read, "Whatever he does pros-
pers," you should wish this for yourself and feel sorry for those
who find themselves in trouble.

Don't think that you are being asked to do the impossible. All
you need to do is try, and I know you will be glad you did. First,
practice on one psalm or even one verse of a psalm. You will be
successful as soon as you have learned how to make just one verse
come alive and live in your heart—even if it takes a day or a whole
week. However, after you begin, everything else will follow naturally, and you will find a rich treasure of insight and love. Just be
careful you don't let weariness and discouragement prevent you
from getting started.

SPIRITUAL THIRST

*On the last and greatest day of the Feast, Jesus stood and said in
a loud voice, "If anyone is thirsty, let him come to me and drink."*
John 7:37

This message of Jesus was eagerly received by the sad hearts of
ordinary people, especially the ones who were devout. They honored Christ as a prophet and as the Messiah. But the rest of the
people didn't regard Jesus' words very highly. That's why Jesus
chose words that would speak to the heart. He chose words that
would reach those who needed to hear them. They are comforting, friendly, and precious words. They refresh, comfort, and
strengthen the thirsty. Christ phrased his message this way
because his Word, unless it's preached to the thirsty, is usually
despised rather than accepted.

Those who are thirsty have a comforting preacher in Christ
himself. He shows them where they can quench their thirst—in
him, the Lord Christ. But first we must ask, "What kind of thirst is
this?" Only then will we understand what Christ means by drinking and how we can quench our thirst. This thirst is not a physical
thirst that can be satisfied by drinking beer and wine. Rather, it's a
spiritual thirst—a thirst of the soul. It's the desire of a sad, miserable,
frightened, and battered conscience. It's the desire of a despairing
and terrified heart that wants to know how it stands before God.
The thirsty are the timid and fainthearted people who feel their sinfulness and the weaknesses of their spirit, soul, and body. They study
God's warnings. They fear the Lord God and take note of his law,
anger, judgment, death, and other punishments. This fear is true
thirst. Naturally, those with fears, temptations, and needs are very
thirsty because of their anxiety. Their tongues become dry. They
become feverish, and their fears dehydrate them. This fear is what
creates spiritual thirst.

LIGHT FOR A DARK WORLD

Your word is a lamp to my feet and a light for my path.
Psalm 119:105

God considers human reason, wisdom, morality, and even sunlight, for that matter, to be dark and hazy compared to his Word. God's Word is a flame that shines in the darkness. Through teaching, preaching, and the sacraments, its glow spreads. If we use this light, then God will no longer remain hidden from us.

When we're faced with disasters, when we're overwhelmed by darkness, when things seem so dark that we doubt that we are part of the church or pleasing to God, then we should learn to reach for the Bible. We shouldn't let people who fall away from the faith distract us. Instead, we should recognize that we live in a dark world. The only reason we can see at all is that the light of God's Word shines brightly (2 Peter 1:19).

Jesus said, "Whoever believes and is baptized will be saved" (Mark 16:16). The light of these words is shining in our hearts. Even if the sun was shining brightly, it couldn't reveal this truth. Human reason by itself can't grasp it. Wherever the Bible sheds its light, no real danger exists. Without the Bible, we wouldn't know or understand anything.

HONORING GOD

※◦◦✦◦◦※

Consider Abraham: "He believed God,
and it was credited to him as righteousness."
Galatians 3:6

With these words, "He believed God," Paul shows us that faith in God is the highest worship, the greatest allegiance, the ultimate obedience, and the most pleasing sacrifice. Whoever has a way with words should expand on this topic. That person will discover that faith is all-powerful. Its power is immeasurable and infinite. Faith gives God the greatest honor anyone can give him. Giving God honor is believing him, considering him truthful, wise, righteous, merciful, and all-powerful. In short, it's recognizing that he is the Creator and Giver of every good thing. Reason doesn't do this; only faith does.

Faith makes God real to us and real in us. Without faith, God's honor, glory, wisdom, righteousness, truth, and mercy cannot be in us. Where there is no faith, God has no majesty and divinity. God doesn't require anything more from us than to acknowledge his divinity and give him the glory and honor he deserves. We should think of him, not as an idol, but as God—the God who accepts us and hears us, who is merciful to us, and who stands by us. When we honor God, his divinity remains complete and intact—he has everything that a believing heart can give him. When we honor God in this way, we are showing the greatest wisdom, the highest justice, and the best worship, while offering the most pleasing sacrifice.

A PLEASURE TO OBEY

For the law was given through Moses;
grace and truth came through Jesus Christ.
John 1:17

John wanted to make a point about God's laws when he said, "The law was given through Moses; grace and truth came through Jesus Christ." It's as if he wanted to say: "The laws given through Moses are laws that lead to life, righteousness, and everything else that is good. But much more was attained through Christ. He came and filled our empty hands. He fulfilled the demands of God's laws. He brought God's grace and truth."

Christ enabled us to keep the first, second, and third commandments. In this way, we came to trust and have faith in God as our Father. We began to praise him with a cheerful heart and regard his name as holy.

Where did all this kindness come from? We certainly didn't do anything to deserve it. None of our good works performed in obedience to God's laws earned it. Instead, it came from being enlightened by the Holy Spirit, being renewed by the Word of God, and having faith in Christ. Through these, we have received a new spirit that makes God's Word and God's laws a pleasure to obey. Now we find joy in trusting God above everything else. We feel that we can do it. We have made a new beginning and have already learned the basics. The grace that Christ has given us through faith makes the first commandment a pleasure to obey.

TRUST GOD TO PROVIDE

The eyes of all look to you, and you give them their food at the proper time. You open your hand and satisfy the desires of every living thing.
Psalm 145:15–16

Look at the well-known religious orders, and you will immediately notice that all their physical needs are completely taken care of. They have a guaranteed income, food, clothing, shelter, and all kinds of extra things acquired by the work and care of others and given to them. Therefore, they don't risk any danger, nor would they want to. Rather than having confidence in the things that no one can see (Hebrews 11:1), which is a characteristic of faith, they have confidence in their possessions.

If you find a spouse and marry, the first challenge is how to provide for your family. This challenge continues as long as you live. So marriage by its nature teaches and moves you to look to God's hand to provide. It forces you to trust in his grace and to believe. For where there is no faith in marriage, there is a difficult, miserable existence, full of worry, anxiety, and hard work. In contrast, the less faith these famous religious orders have, the better they seem to have it. For their bellies are fed free of charge, and they don't have to see God's hands supply, nor do they have to wait for his goodness.

So tell me, which order could rightly be called the spiritual one? Is it not the one in which faith is necessary and has its own work to do? Is it not the one that has reason to trust in God daily, according to Psalm 145:15–16?

The order of marriage has a reason to trust in God. But religious orders don't have this and don't want it, for they were founded and endowed so that they wouldn't have to worry about their needs. By doing so, they have pushed faith out and plugged up all the holes for fear it will come back in.

VICTORY THROUGH DEATH

*Since the children have flesh and blood, he too shared in
their humanity so that by his death he might destroy
him who holds the power of death—that is, the devil.*
Hebrews 2:14

We must have the kind of Savior who can save us from the power
of this world's god (2 Corinthians 4:4) and this world's prince
(John 16:11), the devil. We must have a Savior who can save us
from the power of sin and death. Christ must be the true, eternal God, through whom all believers receive God's approval and
are saved. If Christ wasn't greater or better than Moses, Elijah,
Isaiah, or John the Baptist, then he wouldn't have been able to
reclaim us. Because he is God's Son, he was able to reclaim us and
free us from our sins when he shed his blood. If we believe this,
we can rub it in the devil's face whenever he tries to torment or
terrify us with our sins. This will quickly defeat the devil. He will
be forced to retreat and leave us alone.

Here's an illustration that can help us understand how Christ
defeated the devil by dying. The fishing hook, which is Christ's
divinity, was concealed by the earthworm, which is Christ's humanity. The devil swallowed both when Christ died and was buried.
But Christ's divinity ripped open the devil's stomach so that it
couldn't hold Christ anymore. The devil had to throw him up. The
devil ate something that proved to be fatal. This truth gives us
wonderful comfort. Just as the devil couldn't hold on to Christ in
death, so the devil can't hold on to us who believe in Christ.

HE GAVE HIS ONLY SON

For God so loved the world that he gave his one and only Son,
that whoever believes in him shall not perish but have eternal life.
John 3:16

Someone might ask: "How is it possible for the Son of man to save us and give us eternal life?" Another might ask: "How could God allow his only Son to be crucified?" Certainly it's reasonable to say that the Son of Man died on the cross, but to say that a man can give us eternal life doesn't make sense. It also doesn't seem reasonable that God would let his own Son die for the world. But we must remember that when we speak about Christ, we are not speaking about a mere human being, but one person with two natures—human and divine. All of the characteristics attributed to these two natures can be found in this one person, Jesus Christ. Therefore, we can say that the Son of Man created heaven and earth, and we can also say that the Son of God created heaven and earth. We shouldn't divide Christ into two separate natures, as the heretics do. They claim that it wasn't the Son of God, but only Mary's son, who suffered and died for us.

This passage, however, clearly states that God gave his Son for the world. When Christ was handed over to Pilate to be crucified and was led by Pilate to the judgment hall, Pilate took hold of the hand of not only a human being, but also God. That's why Paul said that if the people of Jerusalem had known, they wouldn't have crucified the Lord of glory—the one all creation adores (1 Corinthians 2:8). Therefore, it was not only the Son of Man, but also God's Son who was conceived by Mary, suffered and died, was buried, descended into hell, and was raised again from the dead.

SEEING OUR LORD

After that, we who are still alive and are left will be caught up together
with them in the clouds to meet the Lord in the air.
And so we will be with the Lord forever.
1 Thessalonians 4:17

We will all be taken up to the Lord together at the same time, both those who previously died and those who live until Christ's coming. In one moment, all will hover together and see each other again. Although we who are still living will have our eyes wide open, we will not see the Lord Christ before those who have died. It would make more sense that we, who are still living, should be the first to see the Lord, because the dead have long since decayed and, to our thinking, are no more.

But Christ has determined that the dead will rise with us at the same moment and will have beautiful eyes that see as well as we do. God will do for Christians what he did for Christ. He pulled Christ out from the closed and sealed grave in an instant, so quickly that in one moment he was both in and out. So in the last moment, God will bring together both. He will bring us, who are still alive and have our five senses, together with those who are dead, decayed, pulverized, and scattered all over the world. We will all, at the same time, be drawn to heaven and soar in the clouds. We will be lighter than the birds and much more beautiful than the sun.

WE ARE GOD'S CHILDREN

*How great is the love the Father has lavished on us, that we
should be called children of God!... Dear friends, now we are
children of God, and what we will be has not yet been made known.*
1 John 3:1–2

John wants to protect against faintheartedness by giving each of us
this reassurance—God loves you. He repeats this and wants to
deeply impress it on our hearts. He also reassures us that we are
called children of God. It's difficult to recognize that we are children of God because we are still in these bodies and we experience
troubles from the world and from ourselves. We don't yet feel like
children of God because we are still in these bodies. But we shouldn't
let that lead us astray, because "what we will be has not yet been
made known."

John tells us about the hidden Son of God. Previously, Christ
revealed himself in the shadows, but he didn't reveal himself completely. And God could not conceal himself any more than he does
now. Nevertheless, God doesn't withdraw himself from us. But the
world, the sinful nature, and the devil obscure our vision so that
we don't see God. The world is one layer, the sinful nature the second, and the devil the third. We must break through all these layers with faith, which comes from the Word of God. This is how
we are children of God—not by physically seeing God, but by
believing in God.

Faith in the Word promises great things to us about what we
will become. Yet as long as we are in the world, our sinful nature
entices us and the devil seduces us. It isn't yet clear to us what our
future happiness will be, nor will it become clear. "No eye has seen,
no ear has heard, no mind has conceived what God has prepared
for those who love him" (1 Corinthians 2:9).

CONTENTMENT COMES FROM GOD

To the man who pleases him, God gives wisdom, knowledge and
happiness, but to the sinner he gives the task of gathering and
storing up wealth to hand it over to the one who pleases God.
Ecclesiastes 2:26

Whenever someone is able to feel content with what they have, it's a gift from God. God gives those who please him contentment without having to strive for it. God sees only two kinds of people: those who are faithful and those who are sinners. Besides the gifts he gives to all people, God gives wisdom and discretion to the faithful. On top of that, he adds joy. The faithful are content with what they have and are not tormented by the same kind of thoughts and desires sinners have. They go about their business with joy and peace.

On the other hand, sinners are always troubled. They are preoccupied with gathering and storing up wealth, but they're never satisfied. Even if they've been given wisdom and skill, so many difficulties are mixed in with these gifts that they feel more like punishment. Sinners don't enjoy their work, whether it's farming or building—even though others enjoy doing these things and find happiness in them. What sinners produce cannot be used in the right way by anyone except those who have God's approval. So whatever sinners accumulate belongs to those who have God's approval. The faithful know how to use God's gifts with joy and thanksgiving, even when they have very little.

But sinners don't even use what they have, in spite of all the trouble they go through to accumulate their possessions. In the end, faithful people truly own the whole world because they enjoy it with happiness and contentment. Even when they possess a lot, sinners have nothing. That's how pointless their lives are.

CHRIST DIDN'T COME TO JUDGE

You judge by human standards; I pass judgment on no one.
John 8:15

Christ doesn't want to judge. He wants to help. So don't picture Christ as a judge for whom you must do this or that to be reconciled. No, he is the Light of the World. He judges no one. Whoever follows him will no longer walk in darkness. Christ says, "If you feel your sin and admit it, and if you're terrified by it, then hold tightly to me, follow me, and believe in me. Think of me as the Light. Then you won't have to be afraid of being brought to court and being convicted. I have come to save the world. However, those who reject my help will bring judgment on themselves because they don't want to be saved."

Christ's words are similar to what a physician would say to a patient: "I haven't come to poison you. I want to help you. If you follow my advice, you won't need to worry. If you refuse my advice and call me a scoundrel, if you hate me and reject my medicine, then you are willfully sentencing yourself to death. Then it's your own fault. Certainly I am not putting you to death. No, I'll have to let you to die because you despise and reject my medicine."

We're in the same situation. Christ will certainly keep his promise to us: "I pass judgment on no one. So don't judge yourselves. You aren't condemned in my eyes, for I am the Light that illumines the way to eternal life and salvation."

BAD EXAMPLES GIVE US HOPE

*About three months later Judah was told, "Your daughter-in-law
Tamar is guilty of prostitution, and as a result she is now pregnant."
Judah said, "Bring her out and have her burned to death!"*
Genesis 38:24

God's people often fall into sin. Their examples show us God's endless grace and mercy. He saves, not only those people who are faithful and moral like Abraham, Isaac, and Jacob, but also those who are immoral like Judah, Tamar, Reuben, Simeon, and Levi. Therefore, none of us should be self-righteous about our own morality or wisdom. On the other hand, none of us should give up because of our sins. Scripture praises the examples of Abraham, Isaac, and Jacob. At the same time, it describes the worst kinds of sinners. We see the virtues of the godliest people and the sins of the most wicked people—yet they all come from the same family.

These bad examples teach us about repentance, faith, and forgiveness for sins. None of us should brag about how good we are, but those who have fallen into sin shouldn't give up either. The Bible records the mistakes, weaknesses, and horrible sins of God's people. This is meant to uplift and comfort those who are depressed because of their sins. Sinners need to be told, "Don't give up. God wants you to trust him and believe in his promises. He can forgive you, make you holy, and bless you just like he blessed Judah, Tamar, and other sinners." God doesn't want us to depend on our own efforts or despair because of our sins. He wants us to trust entirely in his mercy and grace.

We would have no hope if Peter hadn't denied Christ; if the apostles hadn't taken offense at Christ; and if Moses, Aaron, and David hadn't fallen into sin. God wants to comfort sinners with these examples. It's as if he is saying to each of us, "If you have sinned, turn around. The door of grace is open to you."

CHRIST THE SUN

❧

Christ redeemed us from the curse of the law by becoming a curse for us,
for it is written: "Cursed is everyone who is hung on a tree."
Galatians 3:13

The gospel—the most loved and comforting doctrine of all—doesn't focus on our works or the works of the law. Rather, it shows us the incomprehensible, inexpressible mercy and love of God toward us, who are unworthy and lost people. The merciful Father saw that we were oppressed by the curse of the law and held under it. On our own and through our own efforts, we never could have freed ourselves. He sent his only Son into the world. He put all the sin of all the people on his Son and said, "You will be Peter, who denied me; Paul, who persecuted, blasphemed, and acted violently; David, who committed adultery; the sinner who ate the apple in Paradise; the thief on the cross. In summary, you will be the one who committed all the sins of all the people. Make sure you pay for these sins and make atonement for them."

At this point the law said, "I find Christ to be a sinner—the one who has taken the sins of all the people upon himself. I do not see sin on anyone else except him. Therefore, he must die on the cross." Then the law grabbed him and killed him.

Since this happened, the entire world has been cleansed and atoned of all sin and freed from death and all evil. If everyone in the whole world believed, God would see only purity and righteousness. This is because Christ would have taken away all sin and death. And even if there were any remnants of sin remaining, God wouldn't see them because of the brightness of Christ, the Sun.

THE LAMB OF GOD

The next day John saw Jesus coming toward him and said,
"Look, the Lamb of God, who takes away the sin of the world!"
John 1:29

God's laws tell us how we should live. They command us: "Never desire to take your neighbor's wife. Never murder. Never commit adultery. Give to the poor." It's good to follow God's laws in order to guard against outward sins. Before God, however, it won't work to try to get rid of sin by obeying God's laws. What does work is stated in this verse: "Look, the Lamb of God, who takes away the sin of the world!" Isaiah explains that "the LORD has laid on him the iniquity of us all" (Isaiah 53:6) and "for the transgression of my people he was stricken" (v. 8). Everything points to Christ.

As a Christian, you should hold tightly to these words and not let them be taken away from you. Then you will know that godless people and religious people who hope to satisfy God with their pilgrimages and good works are blind. Many boast of their good works and console themselves by thinking they will get a second chance to be saved. The Holy Scripture, in contrast, says that the sins of the world aren't laid on the world. John's sins weren't laid on John, and Peter's sins weren't laid on Peter, for no one can bear their own sins. Rather, the sins of the world were laid on Christ. He is the Lamb of God. He stepped forward to become a sinner for us, to become even sin itself, and to act as though he had committed the sins of the entire world from the beginning of its creation (2 Corinthians 5:21). The Lamb's mission, role, and function were to take away the sins of the world. The Lamb carried them all.

THE PROBLEM OF TEMPTATION

Now the serpent was more crafty than any of the wild animals
the LORD God had made. He said to the woman, "Did God really say,
'You must not eat from any tree in the garden'?"
Genesis 3:1

This passage raises a lot of questions. Some people become curious and ask, "Well, why did God permit Satan to lure Eve into sin? Why did Satan appear to Eve in the form of a serpent instead of some other animal?"

No one can explain why God permits things to happen. No one understands what he does or why he does it. So we should remember the lesson that Job learned: no one can summon God into court to account for what he does or allows to happen. We might as well argue with him about why the grass and trees aren't green all year long. It's enough for us to know that all these things are under God's power. He can do as he pleases. Idle curiosity causes guessing and questioning. Since we are merely clay in God's hands (Isaiah 64:8), we should avoid debating these matters. We can't sit in judgment over the all-knowing God. Instead, we should allow him to judge us.

The only satisfactory answer to these and similar questions should be that it pleased God for Adam to be tempted in order to test his ability to resist. That is how God still works today. After we have been baptized and brought into Christ's kingdom, God doesn't want us to become idle. Instead, he wants us to pay attention to his Word and make use of his gifts. So even today, he allows poor, weak people like us to be sifted and strained by the devil.

THE MERCY SEAT

For we must all appear before the judgment seat of Christ,
that each one may receive what is due him for the things done
while in the body, whether good or bad.
2 Corinthians 5:10

Scripture teaches us that God has set up two seats. One is the judgment seat for those who are proud and don't acknowledge or want to confess their sins. The other is the mercy seat for the poor, timid consciences who feel their sins and confess them, who despair of God's judgment, and who hope to find his grace.

In Romans 3:25, Paul says this mercy seat is Christ. God has given this seat to us as a place where we can find refuge, because we cannot withstand God's judgment on our own. I want to find my refuge there too, for I have done and am still doing too little. I keep sinning against God's law even after my justification and sanctification. My heart and conscience, no matter how pure they might appear to others, will count for nothing there. But they will be covered with a vaulted ceiling called mercy and forgiveness of sins. It will serve as a strong protection and defense for me. My heart and conscience will crawl under it and be safe.

For God has led his apostles to preach and proclaim that everyone who believes in his name will receive forgiveness of sins (Acts 10:43). Likewise, "Whoever believes and is baptized will be saved" (Mark 16:16). And Jesus says, "For God so loved the world that he gave his one and only Son, that whoever believes in him shall not perish but have eternal life" (John 3:16). Therefore, God himself has established this mercy seat. He is the one who directs us away from the judgment seat and toward the mercy seat.

ACCEPTING WHAT CAN'T BE CHANGED

*As a man comes, so he departs, and what does he gain,
since he toils for the wind? All his days he eats in darkness,
with great frustration, affliction and anger.*
Ecclesiastes 5:16–17

"Eating in darkness" is a Hebrew expression for "living in sadness." The phrase is derived from the way people look when they're feeling sad. When people's hearts are sad, their eyes almost look as though they are covered by a cloud. But when people's hearts are happy, their faces light up and shine. Light represents happiness, and darkness represents sadness. For example, we read in the Psalms, "The LORD is my light and my salvation" (27:1), and "Look on me and answer, O LORD my God. Give light to my eyes" (13:3). To eat in darkness, therefore, means to lead a harsh life of sadness.

The only cases that come before judges are bad ones. A judge who is unwise will torture himself and wear himself out with worry because he doesn't think he's making any difference. But someone who is wise will say, "I plan and do everything that I can. But what I can't change, I'll accept. I have to endure it. In the meantime, I'll commit everything to God. He alone knows how to make things better according to his will. He is the only one who can make my efforts succeed."

Therefore, just like a judge, our eyes and ears must get used to seeing and hearing bad things, even if this isn't what we want. We shouldn't think we'll see and hear only good things that please us. That's not what the world offers. So we should prepare ourselves for bad things, for we know that this is the way life goes. Those who don't want to have any trouble will find more things that trouble them than others will.

TRUE FREEDOM AND FALSE FREEDOM

꒰❦꒱

So if the Son sets you free, you will be free indeed.
John 8:36

There are two kinds of freedom. The first is a false freedom of false disciples. These people want freedom for satisfying their desires. They become Christians for that reason, just as the people in this passage became followers of Christ because they heard his followers were devout, good, patient, and gentle people, not thirsting for revenge. His followers freely gave to the poor and were generous. They also heard that his followers worshiped a merciful God, not an angry one. When they heard all of this, they liked the idea that believers would give to them and serve them. So they said, "I will gladly have others give to me, serve me, and forgive me. The Lord God will also forgive my sins and help me get to heaven." They were glad to be on the receiving end of all this.

However, people like this are scoundrels and don't want to leave their lives of sin and idolatry or give anything to anyone. They want to live lives of sexual immorality and self-gratification as they did before coming to Christ. Yet they still want to be considered Christians. These are false disciples who only want freedom for their physical desires. They praise the gospel and at first follow it earnestly. Soon after, they do what they want, following their evil lusts and desires. They become worse and more indecent than before. They are smugger, wilder, and greedier. They even steal more than others do.

The second type of freedom is the true freedom of genuine disciples. Those who stick to God's Word and endure, suffer, and tolerate what they must are the ones who will be set free. They will become stronger as time goes on.

GOD'S MYSTERIOUS WAYS

*As you do not know the path of the wind, or how the body
is formed in a mother's womb, so you cannot understand
the work of God, the Maker of all things.*
Ecclesiastes 11:5

God leads and directs his people in mysterious ways. In the Bible, we read, "Your path led through the sea, your way through the mighty waters, though your footprints were not seen" (Psalm 77:19). Christ himself told Peter, "You do not realize now what I am doing, but later you will understand" (John 13:7). Christ seems to be saying, "You want to see me and want me to do what seems good and right to you. But I will act in a way that will make you think I'm a fool rather than God. You will see my back, not my face. You won't understand what I'm doing or why I'm doing it. Then I'll be able to mold you and remold you the way I would like. My methods may appear as foolish to you as if they were from the devil himself."

We need to learn how God guides his people as they grow and develop. I too have often tried to dictate to our Lord God a certain way in which I expect him to run things. I have often said, "O Lord, would you please do it this way and make it come out that way?" But God did just the opposite, even though I said to myself, "This is a good suggestion that will bring honor to God and expand his kingdom." Undoubtedly, God must have laughed at my so-called wisdom and said, "All right, I know that you are an intelligent, educated person, but I never needed a Peter, a Luther, or anyone else to teach, inform, rule, or guide me. I am not a God who will allow himself to be taught or directed by others. Rather, I am the one who leads, rules, and teaches people."

THE SPIRIT IN US

*Do you not know that your body is a temple of the Holy Spirit, who is
in you, whom you have received from God? You are not your own.*
1 Corinthians 6:19

We shouldn't doubt that the Holy Spirit lives in us, but we should
certainly recognize that we are temples of the Holy Spirit, as Paul
says in 1 Corinthians 6:19. If someone feels a love for God's Word
and gladly hears, speaks, thinks, teaches, and writes about Christ,
you should know that this comes, not from a person's will or reason, but from the Holy Spirit. It's impossible for this to happen
without the Holy Spirit. On the other hand, where there is hatred
and contempt for the Word, we should know that the devil, the
ruler of this world, blinds the hearts of the people and holds them
captive so that the light of the gospel, the glory of Christ, can't
shine on them. We see this today in the masses who are not moved
by the Word but despise it as if it has nothing to do with them.

But those who have any kind of love and desire for the Word
should gratefully acknowledge that these attitudes are poured into
them by the Holy Spirit. For we are not born with these attitudes
and cannot acquire them through the law. This transformation
rests completely and absolutely in the hand of the Almighty. So
when we eagerly listen to preaching about Jesus Christ, the Son
of God—who for our sakes became a human being and subjected
himself to the law to save us—then God sends the Holy Spirit
into our hearts through this preaching. Therefore, it's very useful
for us to remember that we have the Holy Spirit.

TRUSTING CHRIST INSTEAD OF PEOPLE

But Jesus would not entrust himself to them, for he knew all men.
John 2:24

No one understands how difficult it was when I first realized that I had to believe and teach an idea that was contrary to the teachings of the church fathers. This was especially shocking to me when many outstanding, reasonable, and educated people shared their views. The church fathers include many holy people, such as Ambrose, Jerome, and Augustine. Despite that, my dear Lord and Savior Jesus Christ must be worth more to me than all the holy people on earth—yes, even more than all the angels in heaven. When I read Augustine's books and discovered that he also had been in error, I was greatly troubled. Whenever this happens, it's very difficult for me to calm my own heart and differ with people who are so greatly respected.

But I dare not accept something just because a respected person says it. A person can be holy and God-fearing and still be in error. That's why I don't want to rely on people. As this passage says, the Lord Christ didn't rely on people either. Furthermore, in the book of Matthew, Jesus earnestly warns us to beware of false prophets, who will come and not only claim to be Christians, but also "perform great signs and miracles to deceive even the elect—if that were possible" (24:24).

Rather than trusting the church fathers and their writings, we should crawl under the wings of our mother hen, the Lord Christ, and look to him alone. The heavenly Father said, "This is my Son, whom I love; with him I am well pleased. Listen to him!" (Matthew 17:5). God wants us to listen to Christ alone.

HIDING FROM GOD

~⸙~

[Adam] answered, "I heard you in the garden,
and I was afraid because I was naked; so I hid."
Genesis 3:10

We need to realize that hiding from God is the essence of sin. Unless God immediately sends help and calls back sinners, they will keep on trying to hide from God. And because sinners try to justify themselves with lies, they pile one sin on top of another. In the end they reach the point of open hypocrisy and deep despair. As a result, one sin leads to another, until the weight of their sin pulls them down into the pit. Ultimately, the sinners accuse God of causing the sin rather than placing the blame on themselves.

Adam should have said, "Lord, I've sinned!" But he didn't do this. Instead, he blamed God, saying in effect, "Lord, you sinned. I would have enjoyed a holy life in Paradise in spite of eating the apple if you hadn't said anything." Adam's thoughts and feelings were revealed when he implied that he wouldn't have hidden if God's voice hadn't frightened him. Even though all people are guilty of sin, they don't acknowledge it. Rather, they place the blame on their Creator. This only increases the burden of sin to infinite proportions unless God shows his mercy and comes to help.

Adam believed that his wicked and foolish thoughts were the highest wisdom. He was so overcome by his fear that he was barely aware of what he was saying or doing. As he tried to excuse himself, he actually condemned himself over and over and increased his burden of sin proportionately. At any rate, we must not think that these things happened to Adam alone. Every one of us does the same. Our human nature allows us to do nothing else, especially after we have committed a sin. We all prefer to put the blame on God rather than admit that we are sinners.

PRAYING FROM THE HEART

These people honor me with their lips, but their hearts are far from me.
They worship me in vain; their teachings are but rules taught by men.
Matthew 15:8–9

Everyone who feels burdened should pray the Lord's Prayer. Even those who don't know the meaning of the words may pray it from their hearts. That type of prayer is the best, because the heart is saying more than the lips.

On the other hand, other people may stand in church, turning the pages and counting the prayer beads—almost rattling. Meanwhile, their hearts are far from what their lips are praying. That is not prayer. For God describes these kinds of people through the prophet Isaiah: "These people come near to me with their mouth and honor me with their lips, but their hearts are far from me" (Isaiah 29:13). We also find some religious people who blabber the prayers for each day without any inner feeling. Then they say without shame, "Oh, I feel happy. I have now paid back our Lord." They think they have satisfied God through their prayers.

Although some might praise them for their efforts, God will say, "These people honor me with their lips, but their hearts are far from me." What's frightening is that these people rely on these kinds of prayers and never send up any other prayer to God. So those who appear to pray the least pray the most. And those who appear to pray the most pray the least.

GOOD AND BAD TIMES

When times are good, be happy; but when times are bad,
consider: God has made the one as well as the other.
Therefore, a man cannot discover anything about his future.
Ecclesiastes 7:14

When you are given a good day, here's what you should do: be happy. In other words, enjoy the present. Forget your troubles. Lay your plans aside. But keep your emotions in check. Let your wisdom come from God. Commit to him both your past and your future.

So be happy in the present, but do so in a way that you don't forget about the bad times. In other words, you should be ready for times of sorrow. Enjoy the present, but don't start thinking that life will always stay that way. Beware of becoming overconfident. Don't look forward exclusively to good things. You also need to be prepared for bad times. Always try to remain even-tempered and open to whatever happens. In contrast, foolish people cling to the joys of the moment. They become completely absorbed in them as if these good times were going to last forever. Then God uses bad times to remove their improper attitudes and arrogance.

So you should be happy in such a way that you don't immerse yourself in the present. You should always keep a part of your heart reserved for God, for he is the one who will help you get through the bad times. Then, when trouble comes, you will be less bothered, because you will have anticipated it.

JESUS IS THE WAY

*Thomas said to him, "Lord, we don't know
where you are going, so how can we know the way?"
Jesus answered, "I am the way and the truth and the life.
No one comes to the Father except through me."*
John 14:5–6

Thomas thought it was strange that Christ was saying, "You know the way to the place where I am going," when Jesus had said nothing about where he was going. Thomas was thinking in simple and concrete terms. He was envisioning a road that a person takes from one city to another or a path that a person walks on. The disciples were saying, "We don't know the way. We don't even know through which city gate you're planning to leave. How can we know the way?"

Christ replied to their worldly thoughts, "Here's what I mean: You know the way. In other words, you know the person who is the Way—me. For you see me and know that I am the Christ, your Lord and Savior. You are my disciples, for you have heard my message and have seen my miracles. Since you know me, you also know the way and everything else you need to know."

This is remarkable. All our teaching and faith should center and depend on Christ. Setting aside all of our wisdom and skill, we should know nothing except the crucified Christ (1 Corinthians 2:2). From God's perspective, the highest wisdom and knowledge above all other wisdom and knowledge is to truly know this person Christ. We come to God through Christ alone.

KEEP ON BELIEVING

Now the men were frightened when they were taken to his house.
They thought, "We were brought here because of the silver that
was put back into our sacks the first time. He wants to attack us
and overpower us and seize us as slaves and take our donkeys."
Genesis 43:18

Joseph's brothers didn't know what was going to happen to them. They certainly didn't expect this ruler of Egypt, who was actually their brother Joseph, to be kind and sympathetic to them. They didn't expect this man to make them rich and promote them to positions of honor. It wasn't time for them to recognize the wonderful things God was doing for them.

In the meantime, they were sleeping and snoring, paying no attention to God's promise. They thought they were going to be severely punished. Everything they thought, said, and did was happening as if they were in a dream. Later on, when Joseph told them, "I am your brother Joseph, the one you sold into Egypt!" (Genesis 45:4), they would wake up and see that everything they were so afraid of was nothing but a dream.

Often we too live as if we were sleepwalking. No one can tell we're asleep by looking at us. But we aren't awake. If we truly believe God's Word, a time will come when we will finally wake up and open our eyes. But when facing difficult situations, our hearts might not be able to be as strong and confident as God's Word requires. Then, at the very least, we should keep on believing in a weak sort of way, as Joseph's brothers did here. We shouldn't start complaining against God or grow tired of praying and calling out to him. In difficult times, we may not be able to believe God as strongly, praise him as wholeheartedly, and pray to him as sincerely as we do in good times. But at least we should believe and pray as much as we are able.

LOVING OUR NEIGHBORS

❧

The entire law is summed up in a single command:
"Love your neighbor as yourself."
Galatians 5:14

After having heard and accepted the true teaching about faith, the apostle Paul seriously admonishes Christians to practice genuine good works. This is because remnants of sin remain in those who are justified. These remnants resist faith and divert us from doing true good works. Human reason and the sinful nature resist the Spirit in believers and control unbelievers. Reason is naturally inclined toward hypocritical superstition. It wants to measure God according to its own thoughts rather than according to his Word. It does works of its own choosing more enthusiastically than the ones God commanded. That's why faithful teachers must teach and impress on people true love and true good works just as much as they teach faith.

No one should think they fully understand this command: "Love your neighbor." Certainly this command is very short and very easy as far as the words are concerned. But where are the teachers and learners who actually practice this in life? These words, "Serve one another humbly in love," and "Love your neighbor as yourself," are eternal words. No one can think about, urge, and practice them enough.

It's remarkable that believers will immediately have troubled consciences if they fail to do something trivial. But these same people feel nothing at all when they neglect love and when their hearts aren't sincere and affectionate toward their neighbor. Unfortunately, this happens every day. For they don't regard God's command to love as highly as their own superstitions.

SPIRITUAL AND PHYSICAL LIFE

Flesh gives birth to flesh, but the Spirit gives birth to spirit.
John 3:6

We can't feel the new birth or the spiritual life with our five senses. We can't see it. The spiritual life will endure, while the physical life will one day end. Our lives on earth will eventually become like dust, which is blown away and never seen or felt again. Then only the spiritual life will remain. We will be raised from the dead and will come alive once again.

We can't see or understand this spiritual birth. We must simply believe it. What is born of the Spirit is spiritual, and the primary benefit of this new birth is the forgiveness of sins and eternal life. Nevertheless, Christians still have an external existence. While they live here on earth, they are nurtured by a mother and father, eat and drink, wear clothes and shoes, have a house and garden, and own money and property. They view all of this as if they were guests who were traveling through this land to another city—their true destination. When they arrive there, they will no longer care about the places where they stayed along the way. During the journey, they were always thinking, "Today, I am a guest. Tomorrow, I will continue my trip." In the same way, a Christian also thinks, "Today, I am a guest on this earth. I eat and drink here. I live honorably and modestly in this life. But tomorrow, I'll proceed on my way to an eternal life in the kingdom of heaven, where I am a citizen." So Christians also journey through this life. When they come to the end of this life, they will let go of everything physical and enter a spiritual life that will never end.

NO BRAGGING ALLOWED

For who makes you different from anyone else?
What do you have that you did not receive? And if you did
receive it, why do you boast as though you did not?
1 Corinthians 4:7

God is loving and kind by nature. Therefore, he cannot keep himself from giving us abundant gifts. He gives us homes and families, healthy bodies, wisdom, skills and talents, and knowledge of the Scriptures. Unfortunately, we cannot keep ourselves from taking credit for these gifts and boasting about them. Without God's gifts, our lives would be miserable. But even with God's gifts, our lives end up being miserable because we are still experiencing the effects of original sin. The whole human race is thoroughly infected with original sin. Unbelievers don't understand the seriousness of it, so they act as if it doesn't matter.

We see this problem, not only in ourselves, but in others as well. We brag about our material possessions, even though these are rated as the least valuable of God's abundant gifts. Consequently, the wealthy, regardless of whether they are nobles, merchants, or farmers, consider other people to be mere pests. Even more serious abuses exist with the more important gifts, such as wisdom and justice. The fact that God gives his gifts to everyone results in the following predicament: God cannot tolerate boasting, and we cannot keep from doing it.

This was how the world sinned before the flood. Among Cain's descendants were some of the finest and most intelligent people in the world. But in God's eyes they were very evil because they had become filled with pride about the gifts God had given them. Then they despised God, who gave them their gifts in the first place. The world doesn't understand why this is wrong and therefore doesn't condemn this behavior. But God condemns it.

TERRIFIED BY PRAYER

This, then, is how you should pray:
"Our Father in heaven, hallowed be your name."
Matthew 6:9

The Lord's Prayer teaches you to recognize your great misery and corruption before God. In other words, if you think about what you are praying, you will soon notice you're blaspheming God. You will become terrified by your own prayer. For you certainly haven't kept God's name holy. And whoever isn't keeping God's name holy is dishonoring his name. Moreover, dishonoring God's name is a serious sin, and you would deserve the punishment of eternal fire if God were to judge you. Where, then, will you turn? Your own prayer punishes you and works against you. It accuses and deplores you. You're stuck, lying there. Who will help you?

After you have sincerely repented and are humbled by recognizing the miserable position you're in, then the comforting teaching will come and lift you up again. The Lord's Prayer teaches you not to despair but instead to ask for God's kindness and help. You must firmly believe that he will hear you, because he is the one who taught you to pray this way. The result of your prayer will be that God won't credit your sin to you or deal with you harshly. God approves only of those who seriously confess that they have dishonored his name and sincerely want it to be hallowed at all times. However, it isn't possible for people to be saved if they trust in their consciences and don't think they're dishonoring God's name, for these people are still too confident, secure, arrogant, and irreverent. They're not the kind of people Christ speaks about in Matthew: "Come to me, all you who are weary and burdened, and I will give you rest" (Matthew 11:28). They don't understand the Lord's Prayer and don't know what they are praying.

THE PROBLEM WITH PROSPERITY

Hear this word the LORD has spoken against you,
O people of Israel—against the whole family I brought up
out of Egypt: "You only have I chosen of all the families of the earth;
therefore I will punish you for all your sins."
Amos 3:1–2

In this book, the prophet Amos rebukes and warns the people of Israel to look inward and repent of their godlessness. By doing so, Israel could be aware of God's coming judgment. However, the message of Amos was widely ignored and scorned by the Israelites. The world generally hates God's Word as well as the messengers of the Word. But worse yet, Amos prophesied during Jeroboam's reign, when the kingdom of Israel was at its peak and everything was going well. Though godless, Jeroboam was a famous and brave king who won many military victories. Through these victories, "he was the one who restored the boundaries of Israel from Lebo Hamath to the Sea of the Arabah" (2 Kings 14:25). As a result, he became deluded by the prosperity of his kingdom.

When things are going well, godless people tend to become foolish and end up destroying themselves (Proverbs 1:32). They don't think they need God, and in their blindness, they continue to behave in an ungodly way. They keep on doing this until they face God's judgment and perish. The Word is proclaimed to them uselessly, which is what we see happening in the book of Amos. So Amos prophesied at an unfortunate time, but also at a very appropriate time.

We can learn a lot from this. When times are bad, we should remind ourselves of God's goodness and mercy. In good times, however, we should remember to fear God.

SHOW US THE FATHER

Jesus answered: "Don't you know me, Philip, even after I
have been among you such a long time? Anyone who has seen me
has seen the Father. How can you say, 'Show us the Father'?"
John 14:9

We should carefully guard against separating Christ and God. This is what Philip was doing here. He ignored Christ and looked for God in heaven. He was thinking, "I hear Christ talking to me. But how do I know what God in heaven thinks about me or has decided to do with me?" What else is this than unbelief and a secret denial of God? Christ had to correct Philip in order to tear him away from such a misconception. He said, "Philip, why are you trying to separate the Father from me? With your thoughts, you're climbing up into the clouds and leaving me here on earth talking uselessly. Don't you hear what I'm saying? Whoever sees me sees the Father too. Don't you believe that I am in the Father and the Father is in me?"

Those are loving yet serious words from the Lord, for he can't tolerate us fluttering around in uncertainty. Christ wants us firmly tied to him and his Word so that we don't search for God anywhere else except in him.

A devout hermit named Anthony noticed that some of the young and inexperienced monks wanted to be smart and figure out God's secrets and everything else besides. But Anthony warned his brothers that if they saw someone climbing heavenward and planting one foot in heaven, they should immediately pull that person down. For if he set his other foot in heaven too, he would come crashing down headfirst. These are appropriate words for those who like to speculate about lofty matters. Those people would like to drill a hole into heaven to peek in and see God himself and everything he is doing. In the meantime, they ignore Christ. We need to protect ourselves from ideas that go beyond God's Word and that separate Christ from God.

October 25

THE FAR-REACHING EFFECTS OF SIN

When Joseph's brothers saw that their father was dead,
they said, "What if Joseph holds a grudge against us and
pays us back for all the wrongs we did to him?"
Genesis 50:15

The Bible tells us how easy it was for Simeon, Levi, and Joseph's other brothers to sin. But it also tells us how difficult it was for them to be reconciled with Joseph again and be healed. This is the reason that many people who don't hear the message of God's kindness are driven to despair. Some even commit suicide by drowning or hanging themselves. They can't handle the power of sin they feel working inside them. When "sin is crouching at your door" (Genesis 4:7), people neglect it. Then it takes hold, and one offense leads to the next—each more outrageous than the last. When sin is stirred to life, the precious blood of God's Son is the costly medicine needed to remove it.

We need to stay away from sin if we can. But if we have fallen into sin, we must learn how to get up again and regain a firm faith. These very struggles show us what it means to really believe.

We need to realize that sin is a horrible evil. This doesn't seem to be true when we're committing sin. We enjoy it while we are doing it. But after God's laws make us aware of our sin, we realize that sin is hell itself and far more powerful than heaven or earth. After that, we can't understand God's grace without great effort. But a heart burdened by sin can say, "Even though I have committed many sins, 'God did not send his Son into the world to condemn the world, but to save the world through him'" (John 3:17). Without this comfort, we would have no remedy or defense against sin and its sting.

FIGHTING AGAINST SIN

※◦※

For the sinful nature desires what is contrary to the Spirit,
and the Spirit what is contrary to the sinful nature. They are
in conflict with each other, so that you do not do what you want.
Galatians 5:17

As a believer, you can be deeply comforted by Paul's teaching. You have both the sinful nature and the Spirit in the same body in such a way that the Spirit reigns and the sinful nature is subordinate. Righteousness rules, and sin serves. Not everyone is familiar with this teaching. If you think that believers must be completely flawless, and yet you feel deeply flawed, then you will be consumed by sorrow and will despair. Whoever recognizes and makes use of this teaching will discover that even the worst will work out for the best. For when your sinful nature entices you to sin, you will be motivated to seek forgiveness of sins through Christ. You will want to grasp the righteousness of faith, which you wouldn't normally regard or desire.

Christians should keep the wickedness of their sinful nature in mind so that they are encouraged and motivated to believe and call on Christ. At such an opportunity, Christians become skillful artists and wonderful creators. They can create joy from sorrow, comfort from fear, righteousness from sin, and life from death when they restrain their sinful nature in this way, make it their servant, and subject it to the Spirit.

If you are aware of the desires of the sinful nature, you shouldn't despair of your salvation. Though you will be aware of these desires, you must not give in to them. The more you grow in Christ, the more you will sense this conflict. Anger or sexual desire may still be stirred up in you, but you must not allow it to rule. Sin may arouse these desires, but you must not give in to them.

GOD WANTS YOUR HEART

*For God so loved the world that he gave his one and only Son,
that whoever believes in him shall not perish but have eternal life.*
John 3:16

To whom does God give his beloved Son? God gives him to the world—the lost multitude who never deserved it. They could only expect to remain lost and condemned without him. God gave his Son to the lost so that they might be saved. Then what should you do for this loving God in return? Nothing! Don't go on pilgrimages. Don't do this or that good work. Instead, simply believe in Christ alone. Then you will be able to get rid of your old nature and cling to him. Your faith, of course, should be the kind that produces good works.

You cannot take hold of this gift—the Son of God—with your hand. The Son of God cannot be contained in a jar. He is grasped only with the heart and by faith. When this gift comes into your heart, when you believe in Christ with your whole heart, then you won't be the same person. Even if you once were a thief, an adulterer, or a murderer, you will become a new person, for you have the Light in your heart.

What the Lord Christ wants first and foremost is your heart—a heart that believes in him alone. God wants your best, not your mouth or your hand, but your heart. He wants you to be righteous on the inside. When you believe in Christ, your heart becomes clean. Peter says that faith purifies the heart (Acts 15:9). That same faith doesn't permit you to be arrogant or proud. For when the heart is cleansed, the hands, eyes, feet, and all other members are also cleansed. You will act differently than before. Faith won't permit you to be a sinner, fornicator, or adulterer any longer. So your entire life will reflect what's in your heart.

RESIDENTS IN A FOREIGN LAND

The LORD had said to Abram, "Leave your country, your people and your father's household and go to the land I will show you."
Genesis 12:1

We ought to admire Abraham because he allowed God to reprimand him. Even though he was afraid of God's anger, he admitted that he had been worshiping idols and had not trusted God. Then he started a journey without knowing where he was going. Abraham left his familiar homeland to look for an unfamiliar foreign country. While faith convinced him that he would get there, outward appearances made this seem uncertain. As a matter of fact, according to the Bible, he never had a permanent place to live after that. Even David praises this lifestyle, using it as an example when he says, "For I dwell with you as an alien, a stranger, as all my fathers were" (Psalm 39:12).

Someone might say, "What? Wasn't David a king? Wasn't Abraham a very wealthy man, even though he moved from place to place?" Although all of this is true, David and Abraham didn't have much, because they treated their possessions as if they didn't belong to them. As Paul said, those who use the things of the world should do so "as if not engrossed in them" (1 Corinthians 7:31).

Faithful people have always lived this way. They take care of their home and family, participate in society and government, raise children, and have occupations in agriculture, commerce, and industry. All the while, they realize that they, like their ancestors, are temporary residents of a foreign land. This world is merely a hotel that they will have to leave soon. Because they know this, they don't allow themselves to become too attached to the things of this world. They take care of their physical needs with their left hand while raising their right hand toward their eternal home.

PRAYING WITH CONFIDENCE

So I say to you: Ask and it will be given to you; seek and you will find;
knock and the door will be opened to you.
Luke 11:9

A good prayer that is heard by God has two prerequisites. First, we must consider God's promise that he will hear us. By reminding him of his promise, we can dare to pray confidently. For if God hadn't asked us to pray and hadn't promised to hear us, then all people praying their requests together wouldn't be able to receive even the smallest item.

So no one receives anything from God because of the quality of the prayer, but only because of God's goodness. God anticipates all of our requests and desires. With his promise, he prompts us to pray and desire these things so that we will learn how much he cares for us. He cares for us so much that he is prepared to give us even more than we are ready to ask for or to receive. Because he is offering us so much, we can pray with confidence.

Second, we must not doubt what the true and faithful God promises to do. He promises to hear our prayers—yes, he even commands us to pray. He promises this so that we might firmly believe that our prayers will be answered. As Christ says, "Whatever you ask for in prayer, believe that you have received it, and it will be yours" (Mark 11:24; see also Matthew 21:22). Christ also says, "Ask and it will be given to you; seek and you will find; knock and the door will be opened to you. For everyone who asks receives; he who seeks finds; and to him who knocks, the door will be opened" (Luke 11:9–10). By trusting in these promises and obeying these commands, we can pray with confidence.

LETTING EVIL FLOW PAST

And I saw that all labor and all achievement spring from man's envy of his neighbor. This too is meaningless, a chasing after the wind.
Ecclesiastes 4:4

In this passage, the writer of Ecclesiastes is saying, "I saw people who were extremely capable at their jobs, but they didn't accomplish anything the way they wanted to, because it was not within their power. Their hostile neighbors hindered their efforts."

It's biblical and comforting to know that we shouldn't worry about all the problems in the world. Human concerns and trouble are everywhere. When I was a new preacher, I tried to solve everyone's problems. But people rightfully told me, "You're too inexperienced to reform rascals." The same advice could be given in any job situation. Every occupation has its own problems. Therefore, you should live in the present, enjoy what you have, and just let all the evil flow past you. This is how to defy the world.

In short, if you want to live peacefully, remember that much of what happens in this world will seem meaningless. Don't be sad when something bad happens in your life. Instead, enjoy the blessings you still have. If you have been officially given the responsibility for making something better, then do what you can and leave the rest up to God. But if you want to voluntarily take on more responsibility, trying to straighten out everything that is crooked, cure every evil, and throw the devil out of this world, then you'll only cause yourself a lot of pain and sorrow. It's like trying to stop the flow of a swift river. You can't control what people do in this world. Rather, the one who created all things is the one who controls them.

FINDING THE TRUE GOD

꧁ ꧂

Although they claimed to be wise, they became fools
and exchanged the glory of the immortal God for images made
to look like mortal man and birds and animals and reptiles.
Romans 1:22–23

Human reason can't quite identify God correctly. Reason knows that there is a God, but it can't figure out which god is the true God. This is exactly what happened to the Jewish leaders while Christ was on earth. John the Baptist plainly told them that Christ was present. They knew that Christ was living among them and walking among the people. But they couldn't tell which person it was. Hardly any of them could believe that Jesus of Nazareth was the Christ.

In a similar way, human reason plays "blindman's bluff" with God. Reason always makes foolish mistakes and keeps on missing the mark. It calls something god that isn't really God and can't quite identify the real God. If reason didn't have any awareness of God's existence, it wouldn't attempt to identify God. If reason knew exactly who God was, it wouldn't mistakenly identify something else as god. Reason just blurts out, calls something god, and gives divine honor to its own concept of god. By doing so, it misses the true God and instead finds the devil—or its own idea of god, which is ruled by the devil.

There's a big difference between knowing there is a God who exists and knowing who that God is. All of creation teaches us that there is a God. This is already written on all of our hearts. But only the Holy Spirit can teach us who that God is.

DRIED-UP BRANCHES

*If anyone does not remain in me, he is like a branch that is
thrown away and withers; such branches are picked up,
thrown into the fire and burned.*
John 15:6

When I was a monk, I read the mass daily. I weakened myself with
prayer and fasting so much that I couldn't have kept it up for
much longer. Yet all of my efforts couldn't help me in the smallest temptation. I could never say to God, "I have done all this.
Look at it, and be merciful to me." What did I achieve with all
this striving? Nothing. I merely tormented myself, ruined my
health, and wasted my time. Now I'm forced to listen to Christ's
judgment on my works. He says, "You did all this without me.
That's why it amounts to nothing. Your works don't belong in my
kingdom. They can't help you or anyone else obtain eternal life."

So in this passage, Christ has passed a terrifying judgment over
all works—no matter how great, glorious, and beautiful they might
appear. If these works are performed apart from Christ, they
amount to nothing. They may appear to be great in the eyes of the
world, for the world considers them excellent and precious. But in
Christ's kingdom and before God, they are truly nothing. They
don't grow out of him, nor do they remain in him. They won't pass
God's test. As Christ says, they will be tossed into the fire as if they
were rotten, withered branches—branches without any sap or
strength. So let others carve from these branches and see what they
can create apart from Christ. Let them try to fashion a new birth
from their good works. Let them try to create a tree from its fruit.
No matter what they do, all of their works will add up to a big zero.

BALANCING FEAR AND JOY

※⌒⌒

Serve the LORD with fear and rejoice with trembling.
Psalm 2:11

When I was a young man, I hated this verse because I didn't want to hear that I should fear God. I didn't realize that fear should always be combined with joy and hope. I didn't understand the difference between what we do and what Christ does for us. Everything we do is corrupt, just as all of creation is spoiled. So we shouldn't become overconfident. We need to be afraid of God's judgment. But what Christ does for us is holy and perfect, and we should cling to his mercy.

So we should fear God in a way that doesn't entirely exclude joy. It should be a genuine joy—a joy that can't be kept bottled up in our hearts. When we truly believe that we have been reconciled to God because of Christ, we will have a smile on our face, a twinkle in our eyes, and a song of praise on our lips. The Holy Spirit tells us to serve our heavenly King with inward and outward joy, combined with reverence. If we don't, we'll become overconfident. We'll start acting like animals and sink into lustful human pleasures. If we make sure we don't become overconfident, then God won't be offended by our happiness. In fact, he's offended by sadness and demands joy. That's why people who were in mourning were not allowed to bring God sacrifices, and why the offerings in Malachi were unacceptable to God (Malachi 2:13). We have to mix joy with fear and mix fear with hope.

This psalm warns us not to become either proud or despondent. Falling into despair is as offensive to God as being overconfident. God doesn't want us to be down in the dumps or high up in the clouds. He wants us to be somewhere in the middle.

AVOID ARROGANCE

Since we live by the Spirit, let us keep in step with the Spirit.
Let us not become conceited, provoking and envying each other.
Galatians 5:25–26

When we are praised, we should know that we are not the ones being praised, but Christ, to whom all praise and honor belong. The fact that we may teach in a godly way or live in a holy manner is not our gift, but God's. So we are not the ones being praised, but God in us. If we acknowledge this, we won't get out of line. We won't become proud because of this praise. For "what do you have that you did not receive?" (1 Corinthians 4:7). Instead, we will give God the glory. We also won't allow ourselves to give up our calling because of abuse, disgrace, and persecution. God covers our glory with shame by his special grace. He covers it with the world's bitter hatred, persecution, and blasphemy. Furthermore, we face contempt and ingratitude from our own followers—peasants, townspeople, and nobles. Though hidden and inward, their animosity toward and persecution of the gospel are more harmful than enemies who persecute openly. God allows this so that we don't become proud of our gifts. This millstone must be hung around our necks so that we will not be infected by the plague of honoring ourselves.

Certainly many of our own followers honor us because we are in official positions as preachers. But for every one who honors us, there are a hundred who hate, despise, and persecute us. The blasphemy and persecution from our opponents, combined with the contempt, ingratitude, and secret hatred from our own followers, delight us so much that we easily forget all about personal glory. As a result, we rejoice in the Lord and stay in line.

ASKING FOR FORGIVENESS

This is the verdict: Light has come into the world, but men loved darkness instead of light because their deeds were evil.
John 3:19

Suppose you're a homeowner and something in your home is damaged. You become angry about it but soon discover that "No One" did it. Even though nobody admits to it, the damage remains, and it bothers you. Every so often, a servant is caught in the act of damaging property but still denies doing it. If only the servant would confess, the master could easily forgive the servant.

The devil and death have brought "No One" into the world. People today are so bad, evil, and full of sin that they place their own guilt on other people's shoulders. If only they would admit their sin, they could be forgiven and would find that God is merciful. God wouldn't deny us anything if only we would crawl to his cross. But we don't do it, and in the process we pile seven other sins on top of one sin. Yes, we multiply our sins to no end and beyond all measure!

The devil does the same. He denies everything and makes many sins out of one sin. If a child were to say, "O Father, I have done wrong. Forgive me," she would be forgiven. But the child stubbornly says no and refuses to admit any wrongdoing. She adds a lie to the sin and to the damage she has already caused. Once again, more sins spring from the first sin. On the other hand, if she were to confess the sin and say, "I have done it," she would remain in the light and would be like an angel.

ESSENTIALS OF THE BIBLE

You know the commandments: "Do not commit adultery, do not murder, do not steal, do not give false testimony, honor your father and mother."
Luke 18:20

God has ordered matters so that a Christian who might not be able to read the Bible should still learn the Ten Commandments, the Apostles' Creed, and the Lord's Prayer. The essentials of Scripture and everything else a Christian needs to know are summed up in these three. They are written so briefly and clearly that no one has an excuse. No one should complain that it's too much or too difficult. In essence, people only have to know three things to be saved.

First, they must know what they should and shouldn't do. Second, when they see that they aren't able to do good or refrain from doing evil in their own strength, they must know where they can find the strength. Third, they must know where they should look for their strength. It's similar to being sick. To begin with, a sick person needs to know what his illness is and what he can and cannot do. After that, he needs to know where he can find the medicine that will make him well. Finally, he must want this medicine, obtain it, or have someone bring it to him.

So the Ten Commandments teach people to recognize their illness. They help them see what they cannot do or refrain from doing. They help them see themselves as sinners. Then the Apostles' Creed shows them where they can find the medicine—the grace—to help them become faithful so that they can keep the commandments. The Apostles' Creed points out that God and his mercy are offered in Christ. Finally, the Lord's Prayer teaches believers how to desire and obtain all this through orderly and humble prayer. In this way, they will receive the cure and be saved.

BELIEVERS WILL LIVE BY FAITH

See, he is puffed up; his desires are not upright—
but the righteous will live by his faith.
Habakkuk 2:4

Habakkuk wrote down the words from God on a tablet, which included this brilliant statement: "The righteous will live by his faith." This means that those who want to be righteous and live righteous lives must believe in God's promise. This truth can't be changed. As a result, ungodly people will die in their unbelief. So we must believe the writing on the tablet if we want to live now and forever. We must believe that Christ will come with his kingdom. But when things appear otherwise, when we are troubled in this world, we must not lose our way. God's Word holds things before us that are beyond our senses and higher than our understanding. We feel troubled because we look at our current condition. By faith, we need to get beyond these feelings. Even when surrounded by trouble, we must be confident that the kingdom will come and be established in a glorious way.

In this passage we see a clear example of how the prophets in the Old Testament preached and emphasized faith in Christ, just as much as we do in the New Testament. We see that Habakkuk was so bold that he condemned all other works. He attributed life exclusively to faith. Habakkuk states very plainly that unbelievers won't succeed on their own. Let them pray and work themselves to death. Their efforts are already judged. Their works won't be worth anything, won't achieve anything, and won't help them at all. Meanwhile, believers will live by faith.

FRIENDS OF GOD

I no longer call you servants, because a servant does not know his master's business. Instead, I have called you friends, for everything that I learned from my Father I have made known to you.
John 15:15

Christ stresses the word *friend* and highlights the difference between a servant and a friend in this passage. Jesus is saying, "I don't call you servants, as you were under the law before I came. For servants don't know what their master is thinking or wants to do. Servants don't share ownership in a master's properties but are given an hourly wage for their service. You aren't servants, as the false believers are. They serve me for personal gain, not from a heart of love. But you are my friends, for I have given to you everything that I have received from my Father."

Take note of whom Jesus calls his friends and why he calls them his friends. We can tell who his friends are by whether or not they receive good things from him. This is illustrated by the parable in Luke 10:30–37. A wounded man had fallen among murderers, and the Samaritan was the one who showed him mercy. The Samaritan treated the wounded man like a friend. We usually reverse it and call people "friends" who do good to us. However, Christ shows us how we become God's friends—it's by receiving good things from Christ. We can't give him anything, and we can't earn the right to be called his friends.

As Jesus says in the next verse, "You did not choose me" (John 15:16). Jesus initiated friendship with us by receiving us. He's the one who made friends out of his enemies. So we ought to thank God and admit that it's only because of his grace and goodness we are his friends.

LOVING AND HATING

I abhor the assembly of evildoers and refuse to sit with the wicked.
Psalm 26:5

We should have nothing to do with evildoers and wicked people. David said, "I have nothing but hatred for them" (Psalm 139:22). The author of Psalm 1 praises believers who avoid them: "Blessed is the man who does not walk in the counsel of the wicked or stand in the way of sinners or sit in the seat of mockers" (v. 1). If you spend too much time with false teachers, you will eventually share in their false doctrine, lies, and errors. If you play with tar, you're going to get dirty.

But doesn't our Lord Jesus Christ command us to love our enemies in Matthew 5:44? So why does David brag that he hates the mob of evildoers and won't sit with wicked people? Shouldn't a person do good things for them and by doing so make them feel guilty and ashamed? Yes, we should hate them, but only in regard to their false teachings. Otherwise, we must be ready to serve our enemies so that we might be able to convert some of them. We need to love them as people but hate what they teach. So we are forced to choose between hating them or hating God, who wants and commands us to cling to his Word alone. Our hatred is a sacred animosity that flows from love. So love is subject to faith, and faith must be in charge of love.

When the Word of God is at stake, love ends and hate begins. But if only personal things are at stake, such as our property, honor, or bodies, we should show respect and serve others. God gives us these gifts to help others. We can risk them in order to serve. However, we cannot risk God's Word, because it belongs to the Lord our God.

SEAL OF APPROVAL

*Do not work for food that spoils, but for food that endures
to eternal life, which the Son of Man will give you.
On him God the Father has placed his seal of approval.*
John 6:27

The words of Jesus in this passage seem foolish, crazy, and unintelligible to those who are clever and educated. The Jewish people must have thought of Christ as senseless, crazy, and foolish.

How did it look? How did it sound? This poor, simple man comes on the scene and tells intelligent people that he can give them food that will endure forever. He sounds like a charlatan in the marketplace who tells the crowd he is selling a cure-all that will prevent illness, gunshots, wounds, and even death. Everyone would laugh at his claim. Here Christ, a beggar, who doesn't own a square foot of land, is talking about giving away eternal food. If a great king had claimed this, the people might have considered it. But Christ is saying, "I can do what no one in the entire world can do. I will give you a new kind of food that will endure forever." Even I would have said, "Where did this fool come from? Have you ever heard a greater fool in your life? A beggar who doesn't have a penny will give us more than all the powerful rulers on the earth. He wants to give us eternal riches, and yet he doesn't own anything himself."

These words of Christ require faith. So this message is aimed only at believers. The world doesn't understand these words, for it doesn't know anything about this type of food. Christians, those who are familiar with God's Word and are convinced of its truth, know Christ through faith alone. They remain loyal to Christ. They believe he is the one on whom "God the Father has placed his seal of approval."

CONTENT IN YOUR CALLING

❧

Brothers, each man, as responsible to God,
should remain in the situation God called him to.
1 Corinthians 7:24

Everyone has a calling in life. Believers serve God when they wholeheartedly take care of these responsibilities. An official who governs well serves God. A mother who cares for her children, a father who goes to work, and a student who studies diligently are all servants of God.

Many overlook this God-pleasing lifestyle because they consider simple, day-to-day work insignificant. They look instead for other work that seems more difficult and end up becoming disobedient to God.

Doing what God requires is a sign of superior wisdom. God requires that believers work hard at their callings without worrying about what anyone else is doing. Yet few people do this. A poet who reflected on what people are like once said, "The farmer would like to be a shopkeeper, and the shopkeeper a farmer." As the saying goes, "The grass is always greener on the other side of the fence."

Few people are satisfied with their lives. The person in the pew wants to be a member of the clergy. The student wishes to be the teacher. The citizen wants to be mayor. Few people are content with their callings. However, there is no other way to serve God except simply living by faith, sticking to your calling, and maintaining a clear conscience.

EFFORTLESS PRAYER

And when you pray, do not keep on babbling like pagans,
for they think they will be heard because of their many words.
Matthew 6:7

Believers view prayer, not as hard work, but as a responsibility that's easy to fulfill. They pray in faith because they know God has promised to hear them. They pray from the heart, revealing their agony and needs. They pray with groans and sighs. As Paul says, "The Spirit himself intercedes for us with groans that words cannot express" (Romans 8:26). The Spirit knows that God is listening to him and that excessive rambling isn't necessary.

Elijah, Elisha, David, and others in the Old Testament used few words when they prayed and came straight to the point. The fathers in the early church said it well: "Nothing will be accomplished by long-winded prayers." In fact, the church fathers recommended short, whispered expressions of sorrow and prayers consisting of only a word or two. This kind of praying can be done anytime, even when reading, writing, or doing other tasks.

However, people who think of prayer as bothersome, difficult work will never find any joy or satisfaction in their prayer lives. Their only source of pleasure will be their continual rambling. If you try to pray, but you have no faith and you feel no sense of need, your heart won't be in it. And if your heart isn't in your prayers, but you still feel obligated to pray, then prayer becomes boring and difficult. This becomes obvious when you look at physical work. If a job is done reluctantly, it will be boring and annoying. But if your heart is in your work, you aren't even aware of the difficulty of your task. So those who have an inner joy when they pray aren't aware of the hard work and trouble involved. God doesn't want long, drawn-out prayers. Instead, he wants sincere prayers that flow out of a faithful heart.

SPIRITUAL POVERTY

*Listen, my dear brothers: Has not God chosen those
who are poor in the eyes of the world to be rich in faith
and to inherit the kingdom he promised those who love him?*
James 2:5

You may wonder, "What? Do all Christians have to live in complete poverty and not own anything? Do we have to get rid of all of our honor, prestige, and power? What are prosperous people, such as business owners and government officials, supposed to do? Should they sell all their possessions and give up their authority in order to buy heaven from the poor?" The answer is no. Scripture doesn't say that you can buy heaven from the poor. But it does say that you should be counted among the poor and also be spiritually poor. Jesus said, "Blessed are the poor in spirit, for theirs is the kingdom of heaven" (Matthew 5:3).

The little words *in spirit* show that self-imposed poverty won't bring God's blessing. It's not intrinsically evil to have money, own possessions and land, or employ workers. These are all gifts from God and the way God has ordered our society. No one is blessed simply because he is a beggar and owns nothing. Jesus was talking about being spiritually poor, or poor in spirit.

The world can't keep on going without money, respect for authority, land ownership, and servants. A lord or prince can't be poor and fulfill his responsibilities in life. In order to carry out his official duties, he must have the necessary resources. So the idea that we must live in poverty is incorrect. The world couldn't keep going if we were all beggars and owned nothing. We couldn't support our families and servants if we didn't have any money. To sum up, being financially poor isn't the answer. So be satisfied with whatever God gives you, whether it's poverty or prosperity. But be sure of this: each and every one of us must become spiritually poor in the sight of God.

CHRIST'S VICTORY

I have told you these things, so that in me you may have peace. In this world you will have trouble. But take heart! I have overcome the world.
John 16:33

We should learn to remind ourselves of Christ's victory. In Christ, we already have everything that we need. We live only to spread this message of victory to other people. With our words and example, we tell them about the victory that Christ secured for us and gave to us. Christ, our victor, accomplished everything. We don't need to add anything to it. We don't need to wipe away our own sins or try to conquer death and the devil. Everything has already been done for us. We're not fighting the real battle. We're only suffering now in order to share in Christ's victory. All of our suffering combined, even all the suffering and blood of the martyrs and saints, wouldn't give us the victory. It's not accomplished by what we do. Some people claim that we ought to be able to conquer sin, death, and hell on our own. By saying this, they insult Christ. But our struggles and fighting come way too late. The battle must have been won already if we are to have any comfort and peace. Christ says, "I have already won. Accept my victory. Sing about it and glorify it. Take comfort in it."

We know from the past that when believers were severely tested, the Holy Spirit reminded them of Christ's victory and strengthened so that they could endure everything. They could even face martyrdom, relying on Christ's victory. May God help us also to hold on to Christ's victory during our troubles and when we're dying. Even though we don't understand these words of Christ completely, we can still believe in them in times of trouble and reassure ourselves: "My Lord and Savior spoke these words to my heart. In Christ I have a victor over the world, death, and the devil. It doesn't matter how small and weak I am. Amen."

DANGEROUS PRAISE

O Lord, open my lips, and my mouth will declare your praise.
Psalm 51:15

By asking the Lord to open his lips, David showed how difficult it is to offer thanks to God. This is something God demands of us (Psalm 50:14). Talking about the Lord and thanking him publicly require an extreme amount of courage and strength, because the devil is constantly trying to stop us from doing this. If we could see all of Satan's traps, we would know why David prayed for the Spirit's strength and asked the Lord himself to open David's lips. He wanted to tell the devil, the world, kings, princes, and everyone about the Lord.

Many things can keep our lips shut: the fear of danger, the hope of gaining something, or even the advice of friends. The devil uses these ways to stop us from offering thanks to God, as I have often experienced in my life. And yet, at important times, when God's honor was threatened, God stood by me and opened my mouth in spite of the obstacles. The Spirit urges us on—just as Peter says, "We cannot help speaking about what we have seen and heard" (Acts 4:20). The Spirit prays to God for us with many groans (Romans 8:26). Then the Lord opens our lips to announce his praise.

Whenever Scripture talks about praising God publicly, it's talking about something extremely dangerous. This is because announcing his praise is nothing other than opposing the devil, the world, our own sinful nature, and everything evil. For how can you praise God without first declaring that the world is guilty and condemned? All who condemn the world are asking to be hated and put themselves in a very dangerous situation.

HOLDING HIGH THE CROSS

*May I never boast except in the cross of our Lord Jesus Christ, through
which the world has been crucified to me, and I to the world.*
Galatians 6:14

Paul is saying here, "I am foolish, a sinner, and weak. I boast in my
suffering. I brag that I am without the law, without works, without the righteousness that comes from the law, and finally, without
anything except Christ. I want it to be this way. I am happy that I
am viewed as unwise, evil, and guilty of all crimes." As Paul says to
the Corinthians, "Therefore I will boast all the more gladly about
my weaknesses, so that Christ's power may rest on me" (2 Corinthians 12:9). For the cross of Christ has condemned everything
that the world calls good, including wisdom and righteousness. As
Scripture says, "I will destroy the wisdom of the wise; the intelli-
gence of the intelligent I will frustrate" (1 Corinthians 1:19). Christ
says, "Blessed are you when people insult you, persecute you and
falsely say all kinds of evil against you because of me" (Matthew
5:11). So this means not only being crucified with Christ and shar-
ing in his cross and suffering, but also boasting about it and going
along joyfully with the apostles, who were considered worthy of
suffering disgrace for speaking about Jesus (Acts 5:41).

But some seek honor, riches, and pleasure for the name of Jesus
and flee contempt, poverty, and suffering. Do they boast about the
cross of Christ? No. Rather, they glory in the world while using the
name of Christ for appearances. They end up making a mockery
of it.

DIFFICULT TO UNDERSTAND

*They said, "Is this not Jesus, the son of Joseph, whose father and mother
we know? How can he now say, 'I came down from heaven?'"*
John 6:42

This passage shows how the Israelites complained about what Jesus
taught. They thought it was ridiculous, foolish, and offensive for
him to claim that he came down from heaven and could give eternal life. After all, they knew his father, Joseph, and his mother,
Mary. They complained because they thought either he was telling
an outrageous lie or he was a complete fool. Why would he try to
convince them that he had come down from heaven when his parents lived near Capernaum?

John writes this as a warning to everyone. When it comes to
God's Word and how God deals with us, we shouldn't worry
whether or not it makes sense. If you want to be a Christian and
understand the teachings of the Christian faith, you shouldn't judge
the Christian doctrines with your mind to find out whether or not
they sound correct. Instead, you should immediately say, "I'm not
asking how it all makes sense. All I need to know is whether it is
God's Word or not. If God said it, then that decides it." Often I
have warned you not to argue about lofty, spiritual matters or try
to figure them out. For as soon as you try to make sense of them
and put them in terms you can understand, you slip and fall.

Origen and other church fathers had that experience. They
made the mistake of reaching too high. They tried to combine
reason and worldly righteousness with the doctrines of the Christian faith. These teachings transcend our reason.

HANDLING SECULAR MATTERS

*So Abraham brought sheep and cattle and gave them to Abimelech,
and the two men made a treaty. . . . So that place was called Beersheba,
because the two men swore an oath there.*
Genesis 21:27–31

Abraham made a binding agreement with King Abimelech. This
incident shouldn't be passed off as purely secular and superficial.
Instead, we should carefully note what Abraham did here, because
it can bring us comfort. Some people think Christians shouldn't
get involved in public matters. But this story goes against that
mistaken notion. God didn't establish the church to get rid of the
family and government. He wants the church to support them.
That's why Abraham, the father of the promise and king of all
earthly kings, doesn't refuse to take an oath and enter into a binding secular agreement with this king.

No one should use Christianity as an excuse for not wanting
to have a job or hold public office, as certain religious people do.
They're only trying to avoid serving others. But by avoiding this,
they're ignoring God's command to love him and to love other
people. In the end, they will receive what they deserve for their
hypocritical behavior.

We should carefully consider God's laws and Abraham's example. Abraham didn't concern himself only with religious matters.
He was a prophet of God, but he also dealt with matters relating
to the government and his own household. So we need rulers in
the world, as well as in the church. The church doesn't have the
right to do away with the family structure or the government.
Rather, the church should affirm and support these institutions.

FORGIVE AND YOU WILL BE FORGIVEN

※◦◦◦

For if you forgive men when they sin against you,
your heavenly Father will also forgive you. But if you do not
forgive men their sins, your Father will not forgive your sins.
Matthew 6:14–15

Some people wonder why Christ would attach such a condition to this part of the Lord's Prayer: "If you forgive men when they sin against you, your heavenly Father will also forgive you." He didn't attach similar conditions to other parts of the prayer. He could've said, "Give us today our daily bread, as we give it to our children." Or "Lead us not into temptation, and we won't tempt anyone else either." Or "Deliver us from the evil one, just as we try to help others."

None of the parts of this prayer has a condition tacked on to it except this one. We may be left with the impression that we earn forgiveness for our sins by forgiving others. What does this mean for the doctrine that forgiveness of sins comes only through Christ and is received through faith?

Jesus phrases the prayer so that God's forgiveness is linked to our own willingness to forgive others in order to make mutual love a Christian duty. We should always forgive others. After faith in Christ, loving and forgiving others should be our primary concern. We shouldn't cause other people pain. Instead, we should remember to forgive others even when they have caused us suffering, as we often experience in this life. If we are unwilling to forgive, we can be certain that we won't be forgiven ourselves. If we are full of resentment and hostility, that prayer will be spoiled and all of the requests in that prayer will be rejected. We must establish a strong and durable bond of love with other Christians that will keep us united. When we come before God in prayer, we shouldn't be divided into various splinter groups. Instead, we should be guided by love, tolerate differences of opinion, and preserve unity.

CHRIST'S MISSION ON EARTH

Therefore, prepare your minds for action; be self-controlled; set your hope fully on the grace to be given you when Jesus Christ is revealed.
1 Peter 1:13

The gospel tells us who Christ is. Through it, we learn that he is our Savior. He delivers us from sin and death, helps us out of all misfortune, reconciles us to the Father, makes us godly, and saves us apart from our own works. Anyone who doesn't acknowledge Christ in this way will fail. For even if you already know that he is God's Son, that he died, rose again, and sits at the right hand of the Father, you still haven't known Christ in the right way. This knowledge doesn't help you. You also must know and believe that he has done all of this for your sake—in order to help you. Some have contemplated only Christ's pain and suffering and mistakenly think he is now sitting in heaven with nothing to do, enjoying himself. As a result, faith cannot come alive, and their hearts remain barren.

We should not think the Lord Christ belongs to himself alone. We must preach that he also belongs to us. Otherwise, why would it have been necessary for him to come to earth and shed his blood? As Jesus said, "God did not send his Son into the world to condemn the world, but to save the world through him" (John 3:17). So Jesus must have accomplished what the Father sent him to do. God sent to earth, not only Christ's divine nature, but also his human nature. As soon as he was baptized, he began what he had been sent to the world to accomplish. God sent him to proclaim the truth and win us over so that all who believe in him would be saved.

DEATH'S STING

The sting of death is sin, and the power of sin is the law. But thanks be to God! He gives us the victory through our Lord Jesus Christ.
1 Corinthians 15:56–57

This is a beautiful passage for Christians. It shows us how, through Christ's victory, we can get rid of death's sting. It shows us how we can get rid of the power of the law, which drives that sting into us and kills us. Ultimately, the sting will be completely removed from us. Paul closes with an appropriate song, which we also can sing: "But thanks be to God! He gives us the victory." With this song, we can continually celebrate Easter, praising God for this victory. We didn't win this victory or achieve it in battle, for it's too great and lofty. But this victory was given to us out of God's grace. He had mercy on our misery, and he knew no one else could help us. So he sent his Son into battle. Christ secured the victory. He defeated the enemies—sin, death, and hell. He gave us this victory so that we can call it our own, just as if we had won it.

Now we must take it seriously and not live in contradiction to God, as do those who presume to conquer sin and death by themselves. Also, we don't want to be found ungrateful, as apathetic Christians often are; we should rather hold this victory in our hearts with firm faith and strengthen ourselves with it. We should keep this message of Christ's victory in mind and sing about it as we travel along joyfully until that day when we experience this victory in our own bodies.

THE SOURCE OF LIFE

*Jesus said to them, "I tell you the truth, unless you eat the flesh
of the Son of Man and drink his blood, you have no life in you."*
John 6:53

No matter what anyone says, this passage is clear. If Jesus had
phrased this in the affirmative, "Whoever eats my flesh has life,"
then somebody could have challenged it by saying, "Those who
don't eat it will also be saved." Some scoundrels also say, "Your
teaching is correct, but ours is also correct. The Lord didn't mean
to exclude other ways." They create many ways to receive eternal
life, including praying to the saints, worshiping the Virgin Mary,
or living in a monastery. But none of these ways can achieve eternal life. Christ excludes all other ways. They are all unacceptable.

Take a look at this from another angle. If I were to say, "Wittenberg beer quenches thirst. Annaberg beer also quenches thirst,"
then I don't exclude other beers. But it would be very different if
I were to say, "If you don't drink Wittenberg beer, no other beer
will quench your thirst." In the same way, Christ doesn't speak in
the affirmative here. He excludes everything else when he says,
"Unless you eat the flesh of the Son of Man and drink his blood,
you have no life in you." If we despise his flesh, nothing else will
prove helpful. I may call on Saint Mary or Saint Peter, but they
cannot help me. It's out of the question. In a word, all other ways
are rejected.

Life, grace, and salvation come to us by faith alone and not
by good works. They become ours by believing and by eating and
drinking the body and blood of Christ.

DOING WHAT YOU CAN

❧

[Rebekah] sent for her younger son Jacob and said to him, "Your brother
Esau is consoling himself with the thought of killing you. Now then,
my son, do what I say: Flee at once to my brother Laban in Haran."
Genesis 27:42–43

Rebekah shows her wisdom in sending Jacob away to avoid Esau's anger. She didn't test God by saying, "The one who blessed you will also care for you," and let it go at that. To be sure, whatever God wants will indeed happen, but he uses people and things to accomplish what he wants. Rebekah believed that the worship of God and the blessing entrusted to Jacob would be protected. So she made use of what God had provided to find a way for Jacob to avoid danger.

Those who assume God will take care of everything and don't think it's important to make use of what's available should carefully note this example. These kinds of people sometimes don't take any action, because they believe that if something is meant to happen, then it will happen with or without their help. They even put themselves in unnecessary danger, expecting God to protect them because of his promises.

But these kinds of thoughts are sinful, because God wants you to use what you have available and make the best of your opportunities. He wants to accomplish his will through you. For example, he gave you a father and mother, even though he could have created you and fed you without them. This means that in your everyday life, you have the responsibility to work. You plow, plant, and harvest, but God is the one who provides the outcome.

If you stopped giving a baby milk, reasoning that the baby could live without food if the baby were meant to live, then you would be fooling yourself and sinning. God has given mothers breasts to nurse their babies. He could easily feed children without milk if he chose to. But God wants you to use the resources he has provided.

OUR CHILDREN WILL BE BLESSED

❧

Praise the LORD. Blessed is the man who fears the LORD,
who finds great delight in his commands. His children will be mighty
in the land; the generation of the upright will be blessed.
Psalm 112:1–2

Why will the descendants of God-fearing people become mighty in the land? They will become mighty because they have God's blessing. God will bless their children and grandchildren. Even if they don't have a penny right now, they will get what they need at the right time. Even if the whole world is hungry, they will have enough. In another psalm we read, "In days of famine they will enjoy plenty" (Psalm 37:19). David said, "I have never seen the righteous forsaken or their children begging bread" (v. 25). Even when times get bad, the descendants of a God-fearing person will always have what they need.

Which situation would you prefer? Do you want to have a lot of money and property but be so greedy that you never use the cash, constantly look for more money, hoard what you have, and never find happiness? Or would you rather have no money but be so happy and peaceful that you trust in God and never doubt that he will provide for you?

Greedy people have the feeling that they can't use what they have. A man who has ten thousand dollars might say, "I have to keep this for my children, but what will I use to buy food?" He acts like a poor person because he doesn't want to use what he has. Christians, on the other hand, don't hoard things this way. They store up their treasures with God in heaven (Matthew 6:20; Luke 12:33–34). Christians say, "Dear Lord, I know that you have so much that you'll never run out of anything. So I will never be in need. I want you to be my cabinet and pantry. You are my treasure. When I have you, I have enough."

THE SOURCE OF BLESSING

[Abram] recovered all the goods and brought back his relative Lot and his possessions, together with the women and the other people.
Genesis 14:16

Lot and his people were captured and carried off by enemies, but Abram rescued them. After suffering this great defeat, Lot had his land and possessions restored to him through Abram's efforts. This was far more than he had hoped. Similarly, people in the world today receive good things because Christians are living faithfully on the earth. So we should be encouraged and comforted when we see God's blessings. It proves that the church is still present on earth and that God's people, though small in number, haven't disappeared completely. It's for the sake of Christians that God shows his grace to everyone in the world.

Unbelievers do just the opposite. They think they are responsible for the blessings they receive, attributing all good things to their own wisdom and efforts. In their misplaced self-confidence, they indulge in their pleasures, getting drunk and gorging themselves as arrogantly as did the people of Sodom. In the end, they will receive the punishment they deserve, while God's people will remain securely in his care.

Furthermore, this passage makes us aware that devout Christians will always suffer in this world. Their lives are filled with problems, but it's precisely these problems that help them to become holier and more righteous. In all things, even problems and troubles, "God works for the good of those who love him, who have been called" (Romans 8:28). Suffering kills the sinful nature, strengthens faith, and allows the gifts of the Holy Spirit to multiply.

PHYSICAL AND SPIRITUAL BLESSINGS

By faith Abraham, even though he was past age—
and Sarah herself was barren—was enabled to become a father
because he considered him faithful who had made the promise.
Hebrews 11:11

The Bible clearly shows that promises of physical blessings also include spiritual blessings. We weren't created for an existence like that of cattle and donkeys. Instead, we were created for eternity. When God gives us a promise, he doesn't limit himself to our physical needs. He isn't concerned only about our stomachs. He also wants to keep our souls from being destroyed and wants to give us eternal life.

Consequently, promises concerning external and physical matters are like the shell of a nut. But the real essence, or inner kernel, is Christ and eternal life. God, who makes the promises, isn't speaking to donkeys and cattle. As Paul points out, "Is it about oxen that God is concerned?" (1 Corinthians 9:9). Rather, he's concerned about intelligent human beings created in his image to live with him for eternity.

Clearly the promises of physical blessings are like the nuts and apples we use to get the attention of our children. God gets our attention with physical blessings so that we will learn to appreciate eternal blessings. This is how God encourages us to expect eternal life. God's purpose in giving us food and water isn't merely that we eat and drink without thinking, as horses and donkeys do. Rather, he gives us physical blessings so that we will realize that he is loving and kind. This will help us to believe he will take care of all our needs. Even if God gave us only a piece of straw, he would want us to acknowledge him as the eternal God whose kindness is overflowing. If we still believe in him, we will have eternal life. Even though Abraham didn't see all of these promises fulfilled in his own lifetime, he still believed God. That's why he was given eternal life.

SHOVING ASIDE GOD'S GRACE

*I do not set aside the grace of God, for if righteousness could be
gained through the law, Christ died for nothing!*
Galatians 2:21

Wanting to be justified by our own works through the law is so
wrong that the apostle Paul calls this throwing away God's grace.
It shows not only ingratitude—which is extremely bad in itself—
but also contempt, because we should eagerly seek God's grace.
Instead, we shove aside his grace, which we receive free of charge.
This is a serious error. Consider Paul's argument: "If righteousness
could be gained through the law, Christ died for nothing!" Paul
confidently declares that either Christ's death was pointless, which
is the highest blasphemy against God, or Christ's death was essential, and through the law we can have nothing but sin.

Some teachers categorize various kinds of righteousness using
distinctions they have made up in their heads. If these teachers try
to bring these ideas to theology, they should be kept far away from
the Holy Scriptures. For these people say one kind is moral righteousness, another is righteousness of faith, and they describe others I don't even know about. Let civil government have its kind of
righteousness, the philosophers have theirs, and each person have
their own. But we must understand righteousness the way the Bible
explains it. The apostle clearly says that there is no other righteousness than through faith in Jesus Christ. All other works, even those
according to the holiest laws of God, do not offer righteousness.
Not only that, but they are actually sins.

Our sins are so great and so far away from righteousness that
it was necessary for the Son of God to die so that righteousness
could be given to us. When discussing theology, don't call anything righteousness that is apart from faith in Christ.

GOD'S PROMISES ARE CERTAIN

Abram believed the LORD, and he credited it to him as righteousness.
Genesis 15:6

We must recognize that God's promises and commands are distinctly different. God's promises require faith. God's commands demand action. God's promises are absolute and will certainly happen because God himself carries them out. On the other hand, his commands are never fully obeyed. People don't live up to God's standards because they are pathetic sinners. Fortunately, our righteousness doesn't depend on our efforts to obey his commands. We can never live up to God's standards. Instead, our righteousness depends on his promise, which is firmly established and cannot be changed. The promise will certainly happen when we believe it. Therefore, it's undeniably true that faith alone justifies because faith alone accepts the promise.

Our own efforts to obey God's commands don't earn us God's approval. Still, we must teach God's commands and try to obey them in order to become aware of how desperate our situation is. We need to realize just how much we need God's mercy and goodwill. We didn't make this theology up, and it didn't grow inside our heads, as our opponents keep yelling and screaming. Paul teaches it by quoting Moses, who says that Abraham believed God and that God credited it to him as righteousness. In other words, Abraham was justified because he believed the promise.

All of God's promises are based on Christ. If we didn't have Christ as our mediator, God would have nothing to do with us. There's only one difference between Abraham's faith and ours. Abraham believed in the promised Christ who was still to come. We believe in the Christ who has already come. We all are saved because of this same faith.

GOD IS OUR REFUGE

A prayer of Moses the man of God.
LORD, you have been our dwelling place throughout all generations.
Psalm 90:1

Moses begins this psalm with comforting words for people who fear death. They have learned to trust in God's mercy because of this fear. They are glad they have life. They recognize they're sinners and don't ignore their sins or laugh them off. They are teachable and willing to be comforted. When I was a monk, I often had to set down the Bible when I came to this psalm. I didn't understand the harsh language in the later verses. Back then, I didn't understand that this psalm wasn't meant for those who are already frightened by their sins. Moses is primarily preaching to the indifferent and arrogant masses of humanity who aren't concerned about God's anger, their impending deaths, or their own misfortune.

Look at the title of this psalm, and you will see it's called a prayer. The most important requirement of a true, sincere prayer is that we firmly believe that we have eternal life and that God is merciful. It's only because God is merciful that we can be sure the Lord will protect us from eternal death. If this weren't true, why would Moses call God our dwelling place? Therefore, these words assure us that God is able to give us eternal life.

Although Moses was aware of his sin and God's anger, he dared to say, "Lord, even though you are rightfully angry with us because of our sins, you have never abandoned us. You have always preserved your faithful people on earth in spite of our sins. You have continued to be a dwelling place and safe harbor for those who, through you, confidently expect eternal life." The most important requirement of prayer is firmly holding on to God and believing that he is merciful and compassionate—someone who wants to help us.

PRAYING SINCERELY

And when you pray, do not be like the hypocrites,
for they love to pray standing in the synagogues and on the street
corners to be seen by men. . . . But when you pray, go into your room,
close the door and pray to your Father, who is unseen.
Matthew 6:5–6

In this passage, Jesus emphasizes that our prayers must be sincere. Christ teaches us the right way to pray so that our prayers won't be hypocritical. Instead of standing on street corners reciting long prayers, it would be more appropriate if we would pray at home in private. Most of all, Christ wants to make it clear that we need to get rid of improper motives. We shouldn't pray in order to be recognized or to gain something from others.

This doesn't mean that we should never pray in public. Christians aren't restricted to certain places where they may or may not pray. Locations, like street corners, marketplaces, outdoor areas, and churches, are certainly not off-limits for prayer. We can pray anywhere. But we shouldn't show off when we pray or use prayer to gain admiration or profit. Christ doesn't denounce blowing trumpets or ringing bells to attract attention for good causes. But he does rule out impure motives in prayer when he says emphatically, "to be seen by men."

Going into a private room and locking the door aren't required when we pray. However, we might want to be alone to pour out our wants and needs to God with words and gestures that we wouldn't feel comfortable having others see. Although we can pray in our hearts without saying anything aloud, words and gestures help kindle the spirit. So our entire lives should be devoted to God—spreading his Word and praising his kingdom. Whatever we do must be grounded in sincere prayer.

GOD USES WEAK PEOPLE

When the men of that place asked him about his wife,
he said, "She is my sister," because he was afraid to say,
"She is my wife." He thought, "The men of this place might
kill me on account of Rebekah, because she is beautiful."
Genesis 26:7

The theologians argue about whether Isaac was sinning when he lied and said that Rebekah was his sister. In his weakness, he thought, "I'll say she's my sister, or else they might kill me." That almost sounds like, "Go ahead. Take my wife and disgrace her, as long as I don't get hurt. If I say she's my wife, you'll only feel like you can't have her unless you kill me first." Isn't that a foolish, silly, and unworthy attitude for such an important man? Shouldn't he just have said, "She's my wife. I don't care whether you kill me or not"? But the passage says that Isaac was afraid. What a shame that someone as important as he was should be so afraid of death!

This story was written to comfort God's people. It shows how merciful and kind God really is. Even though we are sinful and weak, the Lord will be patient with our weaknesses, as long as we stay away from those who deny, hate, or curse God. I don't want to excuse our ancestors in the faith, as some people do. It's comforting to hear that even good people in the Bible slipped and did wrong. I don't hold up their actions as if they were good. Similarly, I don't excuse Peter for denying Jesus. I don't excuse the apostles for deserting Jesus or for any other foolish thing they did.

Among Jesus' little flock, there are some poor, miserable, and weak souls. Jesus is the king of the weak as well as the strong. He hates arrogant people and opposes the stubborn. He punishes hypocrites and people who are overconfident. But he doesn't want to discourage or crush those who are scared, sad, or worried. He doesn't want to snuff out the smoldering wick (Isaiah 42:3).

COMMANDED TO PRAY

*In that day you will no longer ask me anything. I tell you
the truth, my Father will give you whatever you ask in my name.
Until now you have not asked for anything in my name.*
John 16:23–24

In this passage, Christ shows us how to defend against the obstacles thrown at us by the devil and our sinful nature. These threaten to tear us away from prayer. Christ tells us, "My Father will give you whatever you ask in my name." First, Christ commands us to pray. Then he admonishes us for not asking. He repeats his command and drives it home to show that he's serious. He demands prayer as true worship and as the real work of Christians.

Study what Christ commands in this passage and put it into practice. Don't consider prayer something you do voluntarily, as if it wouldn't be a sin if you neglected to pray. Don't act as if it's enough for others to pray. Now you know that Christ earnestly commands prayer. If you don't pray, you risk the greatest disgrace and the highest penalty. Christ's command here is similar to the commandment that prohibits worshiping any other gods and blaspheming God's name. Those who never pray should know that they aren't Christians and don't belong in God's kingdom. Now don't you think that God has good reason to be angry with idolaters, murderers, thieves, blasphemers, and others who despise his Word? Don't you think he's right to punish these sins? Why, then, aren't you afraid of God's anger when you disrespect his command and confidently act as if you aren't obligated to pray?

So this passage should serve as a strong encouragement to pray diligently. Prayer is our comfort, strength, and salvation. It's our first line of defense against all of our enemies.

GOD WAITS FOR THE RIGHT TIME

*So Pharaoh sent for Joseph, and he was quickly brought
from the dungeon. When he had shaved and changed his clothes,
he came before Pharaoh.*
Genesis 41:14

Abraham, Isaac, Jacob, and Joseph were humble people. They waited patiently for God's help. God was with Joseph in prison. The Lord knew the exact time he wanted to free Joseph. Joseph had no idea how he was going to become free, but he sat in the dark and didn't worry about it. He put himself totally in God's hands.

Joseph had exceptional faith, and God came and rescued him in a miraculous way: "They bruised his feet with shackles, his neck was put in irons, till what he foretold came to pass, till the word of the LORD proved him true. The king sent and released him, the ruler of peoples set him free" (Psalm 105:18–20). Oh, what a wonderful freedom that was! While in prison, Joseph would have loved to have someone intercede for him. Whether his defender was his father, the chief cupbearer, or his former master, he would have jumped at the opportunity. He even would have accepted help from his master's wife if she felt sorry for her sin. But God chose none of these methods. God wanted the king to proclaim Joseph's freedom. This made it a public and spectacular event, especially since Joseph was elevated to a position second only to the king.

We must learn to trust the Lord and wait for him, just as Joseph did. His faith enabled him to wait patiently for a long time, even though he had no idea when he would be released. Joseph's example should encourage us to resolve, "I know my sinful nature is going to complain, but I will try to restrain it." Biblical examples, like Joseph's, set the hearts of faithful people on fire and inspire them to faith, hope, and love.

LOVE YOUR NEIGHBOR

The second is this: "Love your neighbor as yourself."
There is no commandment greater than these.
Mark 12:31

When you're wondering whom you should show love to, there's no living creature better than your neighbor to show love to. Your neighbors are not devils, lions, bears, or wolves. They are not made of stone or wood, but they are living beings who are much like you. Nothing living on the earth is more lovable, kind, useful, good, comforting, or necessary. They were even created for friendly conversation and for social life. Nothing in the whole world is worthier of our love than our neighbors.

But it's the remarkable craft of the devil that he not only severely darkens our hearts and tears this superior object of our love from our hearts, but also persuades our hearts of the opposite opinion so that we think our neighbors are more deserving of bitter hatred than of love. This is easy for the devil to do. He simply nags us: "See, this person has such and such a fault. They abused you. They hurt you." Then this object of love quickly becomes contemptible to us so that we no longer recognize our neighbors as those who should be loved but rather as enemies worthy of intense hatred. In this way, Satan can amazingly change the love in our hearts so that, instead of loving our neighbors, we become capable of demeaning, hating, and persecuting them. Then all that remains of this commandment, "Love your neighbor as yourself," are the bare and empty letters and syllables.

THE WORD MAKES US CLEAN

You are already clean because of the word I have spoken to you.
John 15:3

In this passage, Christ is offering us a remedy for the poison of arrogance, which is overestimating your own holiness. Jesus says this so none of us will think that our own suffering, apart from Christ, can attain forgiveness of sins or make us fruitful branches in the sight of God. Here's what usually happens: Someone does many good works and endures much suffering. That person becomes aware of producing fruit. In other words, they are aware of achieving something through preaching or some other method. Then that sweet poison begins to make the person think, "Oh, I have now done something that will make God notice me and be merciful to me." In this way, little wild branches begin growing alongside the true branches. These wild branches steal the sap and energy from the true branches so that they don't flourish. That is why the Gardener must be alert. He has to restrain such arrogance and presumption by constant application of the Word.

Christ is saying here, "You aren't clean because of what you do, what you suffer, or the fruit you produce. You wouldn't have done any of these things if you hadn't already been pruned and been made into good and true branches. Only God's Word can make you clean." It must be present at all times. The Father sends various kinds of suffering, danger, anxiety, need, and temptation to you so that you may hang on to God's Word tightly and so that it may work powerfully in you. In this way, he humbles you and teaches you that you can't make yourself clean. Your suffering doesn't make you clean before God. Yet it drives you to reach for God's Word and hold on to it more tightly and firmly. This is how God exercises your faith.

NO FEAR OF DEATH

Abraham lived a hundred and seventy-five years.
Then Abraham breathed his last and died at a good old age,
an old man and full of years; and he was gathered to his people.
Genesis 25:7–8

This passage teaches us that the death of one of God's people is a dignified event and precious in God's sight. These departing souls don't suffer in the same way unbelievers do. Instead, they pass away calmly.

The world hates God's people, looks down on them, and rejects them. Although their deaths appear to be sad, depressing events to the world, in reality, believers give up this life as if they were slipping into a restful, gentle sleep. When they lie down to die, death descends on their minds and bodies like a liberating slumber. The trials of life have taught them to be humble and peaceful. Death doesn't terrify them. They're able to say, "My Lord and my God, I am ready to die if that's what seems best to you." But unbelievers are full of panic and anxiety at even the thought of their impending deaths.

This should be a lesson to us. It should encourage us to surrender to God when he calls us out of this miserable existence. We should freely declare, "I don't wish to live a moment longer than what you intend for me. Lord Jesus, you may come for me whenever you want." Abraham, the man of God, died at a very old age, having lived a full and satisfying life. But where did Abraham go? Moses tells us, "He was gathered to his people." Do people still exist after this life? This passage makes it sound as though Abraham migrated from one group of people to another, from one place to another. This passage is outstanding evidence of the resurrection and eternal life.

INVISIBLE GUARDIANS

*The angel of the LORD encamps around those who fear him,
and he delivers them.*
Psalm 34:7

No Christians should think that they are alone when they are dying. Instead, they should know that many eyes are on them. First, if a person believes God's words and clings to the sacraments, they know that God himself and Christ are present. Second, angels, saints, and all Christians also are looking on.

If Christians can picture this and not doubt it, then they can die with confidence. Whoever doubts this must not understand the sacrament of the body of Christ in which Communion, help, love, comfort, and support in times of need are pointed out, promised, and pledged. For if you believe in the signs and words of God, then God keeps an eye on you. As the Lord says in the Psalms, "I will counsel you and watch over you" (Psalm 32:8). If God looks upon you, then all of the angels, saints, and other beings will look in the same direction. And if you remain in faith, they all hold you with their hands. When your soul leaves your body, they will be there to receive it. You will not perish.

This is confirmed by the story of Elisha and his servant when enemies surrounded them. Elisha said, "Those who are with us are more than those who are with them." The servant could see no one else, but "then the LORD opened the servant's eyes, and he looked and saw the hills full of horses and chariots of fire all around Elisha" (2 Kings 6:16–17). Similarly, those who trust God also are surrounded, even though they can't see it. The words of Psalm 34:7 fit well here: "The angel of the LORD encamps around those who fear him, and he delivers them."

LIVING IN HOPE

*May the God of hope fill you with all joy and peace as you trust in him,
so that you may overflow with hope by the power of the Holy Spirit.*
Romans 15:13

The only reason we are living on earth is to help other people. Otherwise, it would be best if God choked us and let us die as soon as we were baptized and began to believe. But he allows us to live here so that we will bring other people to faith, just as he has done for us. Meanwhile, because we are still on earth, we must live with a confident hope. Although we know that we possess God's treasures through faith—for faith gives us the new birth, our standing as children of God, and the inheritance that comes with it—we don't see them yet. They are still in the future, like something put off to the side, hidden from our eyes.

Peter calls this a living hope (1 Peter 1:3). We have God's treasures, but they are still concealed. They can be grasped only with the heart and through faith. John writes about this in his letter: "Now we are children of God, and what we will be has not yet been made known. But we know that when he appears, we shall be like him, for we shall see him as he is" (1 John 3:2). For this life and the future life are separate and cannot coexist with each other. We can't eat, drink, sleep, wake up, and go through the other activities of this life and also be in heaven at the same time. We can't enter eternal life without dying and having this life pass away. So while we are here, and until that day God wants us to see the treasures we possess, we must keep on living in hope.

WE WILL BE REWARDED

*Blessed are you when people insult you, persecute you and
falsely say all kinds of evil against you because of me. Rejoice
and be glad, because great is your reward in heaven.*
Matthew 5:11–12

If it's impossible to receive God's grace except through faith in
Christ, why does the Bible include so many passages about God
rewarding people for the good things they've done? These passages are intended to comfort Christians. When you become a
Christian, you will find forgiveness both for past sins and for the
ones you commit every day. But you'll have to work hard and suffer a lot as a result of your faith and baptism. Jesus makes it clear
that the devil, the world, and your sinful nature will attack you
from every direction and make you feel hemmed in on all sides.

If you were left in this predicament without anything to
comfort you, you would give up in despair and say, "Who wants
to be a Christian, or speak about Christ, or do good works? Look
at what happens to Christians. The world walks all over them,
slanders and humiliates them. It plays all kinds of cruel tricks on
them. In the end, they lose their honor, property, and lives. Christ
calls them helpless, sorrowful, hungry, meek, afflicted, and persecuted! Is that all he can say? Will this last forever and never
change?"

At that point, Christ strengthens and comforts us by saying,
"You are children of God. He is going to take care of you. Even
though you have to suffer in the world now for being children of
God, don't let that suffering frighten you. Don't let what you
experience tire you out or wear you down. Every one of you must
continue to do your duty. This is painful, but it won't do you any
real harm. The kingdom of heaven is yours, and you will be richly
rewarded."

EVERYDAY MIRACLES

❧

Great are the works of the LORD; they are pondered
by all who delight in them.
Psalm 111:2

The works of the Lord are great. But in this passage, the psalmist points out that only a few devout people notice what God has done. Most people don't praise God or thank him. They never say, "Great are the works of the Lord." Though they are completely surrounded by his gifts, they have gotten used to them. They take advantage of what God has given them, rooting around in God's gifts like a hog in a bag of feed. They say, "What's so special about the fact that the sun shines, fire gives warmth, the ocean provides fish, the earth yields grain, cows have calves, women give birth to children, and hens lay eggs? These things happen every day!"

Is something insignificant just because it happens every day? If the sun wouldn't shine for ten days, suddenly it would be a great thing when it began shining again. If fire existed only in one place on the earth, I think it would be more precious than gold or silver. If there were only one well in the world, I would imagine that a drop of water would be worth more than a thousand dollars.

God showers people with rich and wonderful blessings. But how ungrateful and blind people are! They don't recognize these blessings as amazing miracles from God, so they don't admire them, give thanks for them, or act happy about them. However, if a clown can walk on a tightrope or train monkeys, people are ready to admire and praise him for it. The psalmist points out that the Lord's works are great, but these works are appreciated only in the eyes of God's faithful followers.

BELIEVING IN THE TRIUNE GOD

*In the beginning was the Word, and the Word
was with God, and the Word was God.*
John 1:1

The following illustration is overly simplistic, but it makes the birth of the Son of God a little easier to understand. As a human son receives his body and his very being from his father, so the Son of God, born of the Father, receives his divine essence and nature from the eternal Father. But this or any other illustration can never adequately describe how the divine majesty can be given to another, as when the Father gives his entire divine essence to the Son. A human father can't give his entire being to his son. This is where the comparison breaks down.

However, as far as the divine being is concerned, all of God's divine essence and nature passes into the Son. Yet the Son, who remains in the divine being together with the Father, is one God together with the Father. Likewise, the Holy Spirit has the same divine nature and majesty as the Father and the Son.

You must simply believe this. No matter how clever, sharp, or intelligent a person may be, the human mind will never be able to fully comprehend it. If human wisdom were able to grasp this, then God wouldn't have needed to reveal it from heaven or announce it through Holy Scripture. So you should say, "Even though I can't completely comprehend it, I believe and confess that there is one eternal God, who is also three distinct persons. Holy Scripture is God's Word and says that this is the way it is. I will live by what it says."

THE WORD IS GOD

*In the beginning was the Word, and the Word was with God,
and the Word was God. He was with God in the beginning.
Through him all things were made; without him
nothing was made that has been made.*
John 1:1–3

John wrote about the majesty and divine nature of our dear Lord and Savior Jesus Christ in a profound way. John said that Christ, in his divine essence, is the Word of the eternal Father. If the Word existed from the beginning before anything was created, then it must follow that this Word is God. We can easily draw this conclusion: whatever had its existence before the creation of the world must be God, because only the Creator can exist separate from creation. Everything that exists is either Creator or creation— either God or creature. Through John, the Holy Spirit stated that "in the beginning was the Word" and "without him nothing was made that has been made." For this reason, we can never think of the Word as something created. The Word is eternal. No one can deny or disprove the conclusion that this Word is God.

This passage establishes that Christ is God. On the basis of this fact, we believe and know with certainty that Mary gave birth to our Lord and Savior and that he is true and natural God, born in eternity by the Father. This is why he can't be considered an angel. Instead, he is the Lord and Creator of angels and of all other creatures. As Paul states, "For by him all things were created: things in heaven and on earth, visible and invisible" (Colossians 1:16).

Now, we know that Holy Scripture is God's Word and will last forever (1 Peter 1:25). Scripture clearly states that the Word existed in the beginning before anything was created and that the Word made everything. So it follows that believers can't hold any other opinion or come to any other conclusion: The Word was not created or made, but already existed from eternity.

CREATOR OF THE UNIVERSE

He was with God in the beginning.
Through him all things were made;
without him nothing was made that has been made.
John 1:2–3

This passage is a clear, concise statement about Christ's divinity. John included all creatures when he said that everything was made by the Word. Whoever uses the term *everything* hasn't left anything out. In other words, John was asserting that the Word existed before all creatures and that the Word was a coworker with the Father. He was an equal creator of everything along with the Father.

Everything that exists has been made through the Word. The Word is the Creator of all creatures. There is no difference between the Word and the Father regarding the divine essence. The Word is the true God because he shares the divine essence with God the Father. The Word was with God in the beginning. He demonstrated this when he created the universe. He made heaven and earth, angels, and all creatures. Christ declared, "My Father is always at his work to this very day, and I, too, am working" (John 5:17). So this passage clearly asserts that he is the coequal Creator: "Through him all things were made; without him nothing was made that has been made" (John 1:3). "He is the image of the invisible God, the firstborn over all creation. For by him all things were created: things in heaven and on earth, visible and invisible" (Colossians 1:15–16). "He has spoken to us by his Son, whom he appointed heir of all things, and through whom he made the universe" (Hebrews 1:2).

This passage affirms that the Father created everything through his Son. This keeps us from having doubts about who the Son is. We can know and believe that our dear Lord and Savior, born of the Virgin Mary, is also the real, true, natural God and Creator together with the Father and the Holy Spirit.

GOD BECAME A MAN

❦

The Word became flesh and made his dwelling among us.
We have seen his glory, the glory of the One and Only,
who came from the Father, full of grace and truth.
John 1:14

"The Word became flesh." We can never fully grasp this teaching concerning our salvation and eternal life using human reason. Nevertheless, we must believe it, and we must cling tightly to what Scripture says about it. The Bible says that Christ, our Lord, is true and natural God and true and natural man. The Bible says that in his divine essence and nature, Christ is coequal with the Father. The heretics have cast doubts on both the divine nature and the human nature of Christ. During the lifetime of the apostles, some heretics claimed that Christ was not God. Centuries later, others claimed that Christ was not human. Some of our contemporaries teach similar things. They claim that because he was conceived solely by the Holy Spirit, Christ could not have been a human being like we are. He could not have had the same kind of body that we do. They insist that because he was a man from heaven, his body must have been from heaven too.

That's why I urgently warn believers to beware of religious splinter groups. If Christ isn't true and natural God, born in eternity of the Father, and if he isn't the Creator of all creatures, then we are doomed. What good are Christ's suffering and death to us if he was only a human like you and me? If he were just a human, he couldn't have overpowered the devil, death, or sin. He would have been too weak for them and never would have been able to help us. We must have a Savior who is true God and Lord over sin, death, hell, and the devil. Christ is eternal in nature, lacks nothing in his being, and is perfect in every way.

GOD IS ABLE AND WILLING

And Mary said: "My soul glorifies the Lord and my spirit rejoices in God my Savior, for he has been mindful of the humble state of his servant. From now on all generations will call me blessed."
Luke 1:46–48

Mary praised God for his power, knowledge, and desire to perform many amazing and great works. This song of praise strengthens our faith, comforts those who are humble, and terrifies all the powerful people on earth. She didn't sing it for herself alone. She wanted all of us to sing this song with her.

The great works God has done won't comfort you unless you believe that God is capable of doing them. More important, you must believe that God is willing to do them. However, believing that he is willing to do them for others but not for you is inadequate too. If you only believe this much, you will put yourself beyond the reach of what God wants to do for you. This is what people who don't fear God do, as well as what people who have weak faith do. Those with weak faith have lost hope in God and, because of their hardships, have fallen into despair.

Believing that God is willing to help other people but unwilling to help you shows that your faith is dead. It's like believing in a fairy tale. You shouldn't waver or have any doubts about God's intentions toward you. You must train yourself to firmly believe that he is able to do great things for you and that he is willing to do them. This kind of faith is alive and real. It will spread throughout every aspect of your life and transform you. If you are powerful, it will make you afraid. If you are humble, it will give you comfort. The more powerful you are, the more afraid you will be. The humbler you are, the more comfort you will receive.

LOVING GOD FOR WHO HE IS

And Mary said: "My soul glorifies the Lord and my spirit rejoices in God my Savior, for he has been mindful of the humble state of his servant. From now on all generations will call me blessed."
Luke 1:46–48

Mary had total confidence that God was her Savior, even though she couldn't tell that this was true by seeing or feeling it. Mary was able to fully trust God because the Lord had placed this faith inside of her.

Mary put things in the right order in this verse. First, she called God her Lord. Next, she called him her Savior. Then she proclaimed what God had done. By doing this, she teaches us to love and praise God for who he is. She shows us the right place to start. We shouldn't begin our prayers by selfishly asking what God can do for us. Mary's example teaches us to love and praise God for no other reason than his goodness. We should find joy and pleasure in who he is. This is an exalted, pure, and tender way of loving and praising God. It shows us Mary's extraordinary and tender spirit.

By contrast, some people are only parasites, always expecting to get things from God. They don't love or praise God because he is good. They're only concerned about how good God is to them, how much they feel his goodness, and how many good things they receive from him. The moment he hides his face and withdraws his goodness, leaving them in misery without anything, they stop loving and praising him. They no longer love and praise the goodness that they now can't see or feel. By doing this, they prove that they don't find joy in God, their Savior. They don't love or praise the goodness when it's hidden in God. They find much more joy in their salvation than in their Savior, in the gift than in the Giver, and in the creature than in the Creator.

TRUE HUMILITY

And Mary said: "My soul glorifies the Lord and my spirit rejoices in God my Savior, for he has been mindful of the humble state of his servant. From now on all generations will call me blessed."
Luke 1:46–48

A good deal of pride lurks behind the outward show of humility we see in the world today. People put themselves down but don't want others to look down on them. They decline honors, but they really want more honors to follow them. They appear to avoid prominence, but they still want to be praised and don't want to deal with unimportant matters.

Yet in this passage, Mary says little about herself except that she is a servant. She was content to remain in her lowly position the rest of her life. She never gave any thought to her own glory or honor. She wasn't even aware of her own humility. Humility is so fragile and sensitive that it's not capable of looking at itself. Only God can look at it, as we read in Psalm 113:5–9.

If we were able to look at our own humility, we would conclude that we deserve to be saved because we know that God saves humble people. That's why God reserves the right to look at humility for himself. He hides it from us by making us look at unimportant things and by keeping us busy with them so that we forget to look at ourselves. That's the reason we have to endure so much suffering, death, and all the other kinds of hardships here on earth. Pain and difficulties force us to get rid of the envy within us.

By using the word *humble*, Mary shows us that she served God with the attitude of a despised, unimportant, lowly servant. She had no idea that her humility was so highly regarded by God.

WHAT THE ALMIGHTY HAS DONE

For he has been mindful of the humble state of his servant.
From now on all generations will call me blessed, for the
Mighty One has done great things for me—holy is his name.
Luke 1:48–49

What's the proper way to speak about Mary? If you think about the words in this passage, they will teach you to say, "Blessed virgin, mother of God, you were unimportant and ignored by people. However, because God is kind, he looked favorably on you and performed great things in you. You didn't deserve any of those things, and you never could have earned them. Nevertheless, God's rich and unlimited grace rested on you. You were blessed the first moment you found such a God, and you will be blessed forever."

To show Mary the proper respect, you must always think of her in relation to God—standing far beneath him. Mary said that God looked favorably on her for being a humble servant. Don't think about all the honors people have heaped on Mary. These people don't see that they are drowning out Mary's own words in this passage. Their eloquent words make the mother of God sound like a liar and diminish God's grace. To the degree that they say she earned or deserved what God did for her, they lower the value of God's grace and make the truths in this passage more difficult to understand.

You should marvel at God's unlimited grace. He generously and tenderly cared for, embraced, and blessed such a despised, insignificant person as Mary. If you think about her in this light, you will be inspired to love and praise God for his abundant grace. You will be encouraged to look for everything that is good from him alone. From what happened to Mary, you can learn that God doesn't reject humble, poor, insignificant people. He tenderly cares for them. This will strengthen your faith, love, and hope.

CHRIST'S BIRTH AND HIS KINGDOM

*In those days Caesar Augustus issued a decree that a census
should be taken of the entire Roman world. (This was the first
census that took place while Quirinius was governor of Syria.)*
Luke 2:1–2

It's interesting that Luke makes a point of saying this census was the very first one. A new census was conducted from time to time, but taxes were demanded every year. The religious leaders challenged Christ about these taxes in Matthew 22:17. When Christ was arrested, they even falsely accused him of telling people not to pay taxes to the Romans. The Israelites paid their taxes unwillingly and hated the taxation and laws of the Roman emperor. They claimed that because they were God's people, they ought to be free from the emperor. They argued over whether they should have to pay tribute money at all. But they had to pay it anyway because they couldn't defend themselves by force. They wanted to pull Christ into the middle of this dispute and hand him over to the Roman authorities. So this census was nothing more than a common duty in all lands. Every year, a tribute was due from every person.

Notice how Luke chooses his words precisely. The birth of Christ occurred during the reign of Caesar Augustus and while Quirinius was governor of Syria—the Roman district that included Israel at that time. The fact that Christ was born during the first census shows that his kingdom wasn't political and his reign wasn't over secular rulers. Instead, he subjected himself and his parents to these rulers.

If Christ had wanted to show that he wouldn't be subject to others, he could have been born before this census. The timing of Christ's birth, which was by God's design and intention, shows us that he didn't want to reign in the world.

LYING IN A MANGER

She gave birth to her firstborn, a son. She wrapped him in cloths and placed him in a manger, because there was no room for them in the inn.
Luke 2:7

All of us should use the gospel to evaluate ourselves. How near or far are we from Christ? How are we doing in faith and love? Many become inflamed with dreamy devotion when they hear about how impoverished Christ was when he was born. They grow furious at the people of Bethlehem and criticize their blindness and ingratitude. They think that if they had been there, they would have served the Lord and his mother. They wouldn't have allowed them to be so miserable. But these people don't even notice their own neighbors who are nearby and need their help. They ignore them and leave them as they are. Who on earth doesn't have miserable, sick, blundering, or sinful people around them? Why don't they show their love to these people? Why don't they do for their neighbors what Christ did for them?

Don't deceive yourself by thinking you would have treated Christ well when you don't presently do anything for your neighbor. If you had been at Bethlehem, you would have paid just as little attention to him as everyone else did. You only want to serve him because you know who he is. Let's say that he were to come, lie in the manger, and let you know that he is the one you now know so much about. Of course you would want to do something to help. But before that, you wouldn't have done anything.

Similarly, if you could see your neighbors now as they will be in the future, and if they were lying in front of you, then you certainly would take care of them. But because you only see them for what they are now, you ignore them. You fail to recognize Christ in your neighbors.

THE GLORY OF THE LORD

*An angel of the Lord appeared to them, and the glory of the Lord
shone around them, and they were terrified.*
Luke 2:9

First of all, the event described in this passage wasn't merely one
person telling another some good news. An angel came from
heaven and announced the birth of Christ to the shepherds. No
human being knew anything about it. Second, notice that Christ
was born at midnight. This shows that the world was dark at his
coming and human reason on its own can't recognize Christ.
Heaven must reveal it. Third, the bright light, which surrounded
the shepherds, shows that something completely different from
the light of reason is needed.

Luke says, "The glory of the Lord shone around them." He
calls the light that shone the glory of the Lord. Why? He does this
to emphasize the mystery and show us the nature of the gospel. It
is a heavenly light that teaches Christ alone.

This light from heaven shines around us through the apostles
and their followers who now preach the gospel. The angel in this
story is like all of the preachers of the gospel, and the shepherds are
like all listeners. Accordingly, the gospel comes from heaven and
doesn't tolerate any other teaching added to it, for human teaching
is earthly light and human glory. It lifts up human glory and praise
and makes people arrogantly rely on their own efforts. But the
gospel teaches everyone to trust in Christ. So rely completely on
God's grace and goodness. Glorify Christ and be bold in him.

CHRIST IS BORN FOR YOU

✦

But the angel said to them, "Do not be afraid. I bring you good news of great joy that will be for all the people. Today in the town of David a Savior has been born to you; he is Christ the Lord."
Luke 2:10–11

No matter where you're reading in the Bible, faith is the first mystery you should recognize. Faith is not believing that the story you're reading is true as written. That does nothing for anyone. Even unbelievers can believe that this Bible story about Jesus' birth is true. Faith is not a natural work apart from God's grace, as the Scripture clearly teaches. Rather, the right kind of faith, the kind that flows from grace and that God's Word demands, is firmly believing that Christ was born for you. His birth is yours and occurred for your benefit.

For the gospel teaches that Christ was born for our benefit and that everything he did and suffered was for us. As the angel says here, "I bring you good news of great joy that will be for all the people. Today in the town of David a Savior has been born to you." With these words, you can clearly see that he was born for all of us.

The angel doesn't say, "A Savior was born," but rather "A Savior has been born to you." In the same way, he doesn't say, "I have good news," but rather "I bring you good news." For you! "I bring you good news of great joy that will be for all the people." This joy is for everyone who has this kind of faith.

JOYFUL NEWS

❧

But the angel said to them, "Do not be afraid. I bring you good news
of great joy that will be for all the people. Today in the town of David
a Savior has been born to you; he is Christ the Lord."
Luke 2:10–11

The angel here is making an announcement. He doesn't say, "I
would like to preach to you," but simply "I bring you good
news." In other words, he is saying, "I am an evangelist; my words
are the gospel." So the gospel is a good, joyful message, which
will become the main message of the New Testament. What is
the gospel? Listen to the angel. He says, "I bring you good news
of great joy that will be for all the people." The gospel speaks of
a great joy. Where do we find it? Listen again: "Today in the town
of David a Savior has been born to you; he is Christ the Lord."

So the gospel is a joyful message about Christ our Savior.
Whoever preaches correctly preaches the gospel and nothing but
joy. How can our hearts have a greater joy than knowing that Christ
has been given to us to be our own? The angel doesn't merely say,
"Christ has been born," but also indicates that his birth is for us
by saying, "Christ has been born to you."

So the nature of the gospel is revealed, not just by teaching
the story and life of Christ, but also by personalizing it and offering it to all who believe. What would it help me if Christ were
born a thousand times, and the news of his birth was sung to me
every day with wonderful music, if I didn't understand that his
death was for me and that I should make it my own? No matter
how badly it's preached, my heart hears the gospel with joy. It
penetrates all the way through and sounds wonderful. If there
were something else to preach, then both the evangelical angel
and the angelic evangelist would have mentioned it.

GOD HONORS THE LOWLY

Suddenly a great company of the heavenly host appeared with the angel,
praising God and saying, "Glory to God in the highest, and on earth
peace to men on whom his favor rests."
Luke 2:13–14

While Christ's birth goes unnoticed on earth, it's being highly honored in heaven—a thousand times more highly. Suppose a single angel came from heaven and praised you and what you have done. Isn't it true you would prefer this to all of the world's praise and honor? You would wonder if you could endure the humility and contempt that it would require to deserve it. What kind of honor is this that all the angels in heaven can't contain themselves for joy? They burst forth and let the poor shepherds in the fields hear them preaching, praising, singing, and pouring out their joy beyond measure. How could all the joy and honor of those in Bethlehem—even of all the kings of the earth—compare to this joy and honor?

Notice how lavishly God honors those who are despised by the world. Here you see that God's eyes are turned toward the low places, for God sits above the angels and looks down to the depths. The angels were sent, not to princes or powerful people, but rather to uneducated shepherds, the lowliest people on earth. Didn't they want to speak to the high priests, the highly educated men in Jerusalem, who had much to say about God and angels? No, the ones worthy of receiving such great honor from heaven were the poor shepherds, who were considered nobodies by the world.

God completely ignores what is high. Still, we race around madly to reach useless heights on earth in order to be honored in heaven. But God's eyes are turned only to the depths. So all we end up doing is stepping out of God's line of sight.

FAITH OF THE SHEPHERDS

When the angels had left them and gone into heaven, the shepherds said to one another, "Let's go to Bethlehem and see this thing that has happened, which the Lord has told us about."
Luke 2:15

If these shepherds hadn't believed the angels, they wouldn't have gone to Bethlehem. Neither would they have done any of what is recorded in Luke. But when unbelievers say, "Yes, I would certainly believe the message if an angel from heaven announced it to me," they don't know what they are saying. For whoever doesn't receive the Word on its own account will never receive it no matter who preaches it—even if all the angels come and preach it to them. Moreover, those who believe the message on account of the one preaching it aren't believing the Word. Neither do they believe in God through the Word. Instead, they believe in the preacher. As a result, their faith doesn't endure.

But those who believe the Word overlook the one who is preaching it. They don't honor the Word because of the person. On the contrary, they honor the person because of the Word. They never place the person higher than the Word. If the preacher is ruined, falls from faith, or begins preaching a different message, the believers would rather let go of the preacher than give up the Word. They would stick with the Word regardless of the person involved or the situation.

This is the true difference between genuine and human faith. Human faith is always attached to the person. It believes, trusts, and honors the Word because of the one who speaks it. On the other hand, genuine faith clings to the Word, which is God himself. Genuine faith believes, trusts, and honors the Word because of what it is, not who said it. Faith so strongly senses that the Word is true that no one can tear it away—not even the same preacher who first brought it.

JOSEPH AND MARY

❧

The child's father and mother marveled at what was said about him.
Luke 2:33

What are the amazing words that were said? Who said them about Jesus? Of course the amazing words were Simeon's. He took the baby Jesus in his arms and said, "Sovereign Lord, as you have promised, you now dismiss your servant in peace. For my eyes have seen your salvation, which you have prepared in the sight of all people, a light for revelation to the Gentiles and for glory to your people Israel" (Luke 2:29–32). Mary and Joseph were amazed that the baby was going to be a light to the whole world, a Savior to all people, and the glory of Israel. They also were amazed that Simeon himself thought so much of the child that he would gladly die after seeing him.

Now, it was remarkable for such a great man to praise this child in a public and holy place, for Jesus was only a poor, unimportant baby. His mother was poor and humble, and his father Joseph wasn't wealthy. How could such a child be looked upon as the Savior of all people, the Light to the nations, and the glory of Israel? Today, now that we know the entire story, it doesn't seem so amazing. But back then, no one knew anything about it, and it sounded very strange. The poor child was so very different from the great and mighty person whom Simeon spoke about. But Joseph and Mary believed him anyway, and that is why they were amazed. If they hadn't believed, they would have disregarded Simeon's words. What he said would have seemed false and useless rather than amazing. So the simple fact that Joseph and Mary were amazed shows us their great faith.

ANNA'S EXAMPLE

*[Anna] never left the temple but worshiped night
and day, fasting and praying.*
Luke 2:37

Someone might say about this passage, "In Anna's story, we see Scripture praising good works, such as fasting, praying, and going to the temple. Doesn't this keep us from rejecting good works?" Here's our answer: Who rejected good works? We only reject the false works that appear to be good works. Fasting, praying, and going to church are good works if they are done in the right spirit.

But the problem begins when blind fools jump into Scripture, clomp around in it with boots and spurs, and only look at the works and outward example of people in the Bible. They want to learn about being holy and so immediately try to follow their example. This only leads to people becoming hypocrites, because they forget that the Scriptures speak much more about the person than their works. For example, the Bible praises Abel's sacrifice, but it praises the kind of person he was even more. These hypocrites, however, skip right over the person and only take note of what they do. All they grasp is the works—they miss the faith. They eat the husk and throw out the grain. As the prophet Hosea says, "They turn to other gods and love the sacred raisin cakes" (Hosea 3:1).

If you wish to fast and pray as holy Anna did, that's fine. But see to it that you first follow the example of her as a person and then afterward follow the example of her works.

THE FAITH OF THE WISE MEN

After they had heard the king, they went on their way, and the star they had seen in the east went ahead of them until it stopped over the place where the child was. When they saw the star, they were overjoyed.
Matthew 2:9–10

The wise men struggled to continue believing the words of the prophets when they were led to such an inappropriate setting for a royal birth. God comforted and strengthened them with the star. It was closer to them now than it was at the beginning. It guided them. When they started out, it was far away from them, and they didn't know where they would find the king.

Christians experience something similar when they successfully endure trials. Near the end, God feels close to them. He becomes so clearly recognizable that they not only forget about their affliction, but also desire more of it so that they can become stronger. They are no longer bothered by the circumstances of Christ's life. They know by experience that anyone who wants to find Christ must realize that it will seem as if they are only finding disgrace. The wise men would have felt ashamed if they had slipped and said what they were probably thinking in their hearts: "Oh my, what have we here! I can't wait to take another journey and look for new kings!" They felt like they were being led down a blind alley.

Our foolish nature often feels this way when trying to follow God's words. Since the wise men were overjoyed when they saw the star, we can infer that they faced these doubts and were deeply depressed. Their joy indicates that their hearts had been greatly disturbed. They struggled with their doubts, and there was certainly enough reason for doubt in this situation. So Christ really means it when he says, "Blessed is the man who does not fall away on account of me" (Matthew 11:6).

USING WHAT GOD HAS PROVIDED

And having been warned in a dream not to go back to Herod, they
returned to their country by another route.
Matthew 2:12

Why does God warn the wise men not to return to Herod? Even if Herod had found out, God easily could have protected Jesus from him and the entire world. The reason God did it this way is so we would learn not to test God. We should never look down on what we can conveniently accomplish with the help of what God has created.

Certainly you should believe in God and say, "I will trust God. Everything will turn out all right." You should trust him as much as if you didn't want to work and were saying, "I will trust God. What is supposed to grow will grow anyway." But if this is all you do, what's the use of all that God has created? According to Genesis 1, God created everything in the world and established how human beings should use and work with all of it. He's not going to revoke that created order or make a special one just for you.

So in areas where God's Word gives you no command, you should continue to make use of your strength, your possessions, your friends, and everything else that God has given you. You should remain in the created order God established in Genesis 1, for he didn't give it to you for nothing. He will not make wine into water or turn stones into bread just for you. Rather, you should accept everything God has provided and use it just as he created it to be used, unless God's Word tells you to do otherwise.

NUMBERING OUR DAYS

Teach us to number our days aright, that we may gain a heart of wisdom.
Psalm 90:12

Until I realized how seriously and urgently Moses prayed in this passage, I didn't understand that we should ask God to teach us to number our days. I thought everyone was just as afraid of death as I was. However, out of ten thousand people, only ten might believe that numbering their days is important. The rest of the masses of people live as if God doesn't exist and death doesn't occur.

But this isn't the worst part. Some people who are about to die imagine that they'll go on living. Others, overwhelmed by misery, still dream of happiness. Still others, who are in extreme danger, foolishly think they're totally secure. Their delusion is the saddest part of all.

So Moses appropriately teaches us to pray that we might number our days. We aren't supposed to ask God exactly how much time we have left. Rather, we must pray that we may become aware of how miserable and short our lives are. Death and God's eternal anger threaten us every second.

Occasionally we'll find people who really are concerned about the shortness of life. They are preoccupied with thoughts of their impending death, even though they didn't pray for this knowledge. But most people aren't aware that their days are numbered. They live as if the present moment will last forever. So for most of us, praying the way Moses suggests in this passage is indispensable.

THE BEGINNING, MIDDLE, AND END

*By faith we understand that the universe was formed at God's command,
so that what is seen was not made out of what was visible.*
Hebrews 11:3

No creature can assist in its own creation or sustain itself. Similarly, we didn't create ourselves, and we can't keep ourselves alive for a single moment by our own strength. God alone is responsible for our growth and development. Without him, we would have died a long time ago. If our Creator, who continues to work, and his coworker, Christ, were to stop their work, everything would break down in an instant. This truth inspires us to confess, "I believe in God the Father Almighty, Maker of heaven and earth." If God hadn't been sustaining us all along, we would have died long ago—even in infancy or at birth.

The writer of Hebrews also teaches us about how God creates and sustains us: "By faith we understand that the universe was formed at God's command, so that what is seen was not made out of what was visible." In other words, the author of Hebrews is saying that through Christ, the Father continually makes the invisible become visible. He makes what is nonexistent come into existence. A hundred years ago none of us could be seen. People who will be born ten or twenty years from now can't be seen either. They haven't been born and don't exist yet. But when they are born, they will become visible and real.

Christ is the one who creates something visible from the invisible. Through him, heaven and earth were created out of nothing. Christ the Lord was present when everything was created. He wasn't merely a spectator, but was equal to the Creator. He was the Father's coworker. He will continue to rule and will sustain everything until the end of the world. He is the beginning, the middle, and the end for everything and everyone.

INDEX TO OTHER EDITIONS

❧

These readings were selected from Luther's sermons, lectures, and commentaries from many volumes of Luther's writings. To locate each reading in its original context, use the following chart. The American Edition is in English, and the Saint Louis Edition is in German. Within each column the first number refers to the volume and the second to the page number.

Date	American Edition (English) volume:page	Saint Louis Edition (German) volume:column
Jan 1	22:275	7:1849
Jan 2	5:157	2:320
Jan 3	43:24	3:160
Jan 4	26:136	9:186
Jan 5	42:88	14:1416
Jan 6	42:13	11:581
Jan 7	42:12	11:580
Jan 8	52:95	11:212
Jan 9	30:35	9:994
Jan 10	26:380	9:500
Jan 11	24:193	8:483
Jan 12	42:22	7:757
Jan 13	24:12	8:271
Jan 14	52:29	11:142
Jan 15	30:263	9:1447
Jan 16	30:126	9:1091
Jan 17	28:177	8:1229
Jan 18	26:356	9:470
Jan 19	24:48	8:315
Jan 20	12:318	5:493
Jan 21	4:364	2:64

Date	American Edition (English) volume:page	Saint Louis Edition (German) volume:column
Jan 22	30:108	9:1072
Jan 23	30:235	9:1416
Jan 24	12:328	5:507
Jan 25	26:232	9:308
Jan 26	42:76	7:817
Jan 27	30:142	9:1108
Jan 28	6:360	2:1091
Jan 29	23:23	7:2213
Jan 30	53:66	10:231
Jan 31	7:126	2:1318
Feb 1	21:235	7:609
Feb 2	24:249	8:548
Feb 3	26:114	9:158
Feb 4	23:28	7:2219
Feb 5	4:93	1:1484
Feb 6	9:74	3:1430
Feb 7	30:322	9:1515
Feb 8	6:158	2:817
Feb 9	27:355	8:1595
Feb 10	5:232	2:414
Feb 11	23:42	7:2235
Feb 12	30:269	9:1453
Feb 13	7:130	2:1324
Feb 14	27:166	8:1369
Feb 15	51:267	9:891
Feb 16	1:137	1:167
Feb 17	24:385	8:702
Feb 18	42:45	7:782
Feb 19	24:142	8:426
Feb 20	4:21	1:1392
Feb 21	24:264	8:567
Feb 22	6:148	2:805

Date	American Edition (English) volume:page	Saint Louis Edition (German) volume:column
Feb 23	27:73	9:687
Feb 24	51:348	12:1977
Feb 25	27:57	9:669
Feb 26	30:232	9:1412
Feb 27	28:104	8:1143
Feb 28	42:21	7:756
Mar 1	12:274	5:437
Mar 2	5:56	2:193
Mar 3	22:382	7:1977
Mar 4	6:360	2:1090
Mar 5	24:119	8:398
Mar 6	28:124	8:1167
Mar 7	12:188	5:298
Mar 8	6:133	2:785
Mar 9	42:19	7:753
Mar 10	3:311	1:1296
Mar 11	24:251	8:551
Mar 12	15:25	5:1397
Mar 13	2:103	1:556
Mar 14	24:202	8:494
Mar 15	26:341	9:452
Mar 16	4:296	1:1739
Mar 17	52:79	11:194
Mar 18	30:94	9:1056
Mar 19	4:122	1:1522
Mar 20	21:189	7:556
Mar 21	30:140	9:1106
Mar 22	4:181	1:1596
Mar 23	43:235	20:2211
Mar 24	6:401	2:1150
Mar 25	7:219	2:1443
Mar 26	27:78	9:694

Date	American Edition (English) volume:page	Saint Louis Edition (German) volume:column
Mar 27	6:405	2:1156
Mar 28	30:84	9:1047
Mar 29	30:3	9:958
Mar 30	22:143	7:1696
Mar 31	3:203	1:1163
Apr 1	7:219	2:1442
Apr 2	42:130	10:1836
Apr 3	30:109	9:1073
Apr 4	6:111	2:756
Apr 5	28:114	8:1155
Apr 6	4:334	2:21
Apr 7	27:140	9:765
Apr 8	7:221	2:1446
Apr 9	27:96	9:715
Apr 10	5:274	2:467
Apr 11	24:272	8:576
Apr 12	7:319	2:1577
Apr 13	3:275	1:1251
Apr 14	8:192	2:1905
Apr 15	24:103	8:380
Apr 16	4:190	1:1607
Apr 17	21:173	7:534
Apr 18	30:34	9:993
Apr 19	14:36	5:1170
Apr 20	23:190	7:2407
Apr 21	5:183	2:353
Apr 22	26:115	9:159
Apr 23	22:49	7:1588
Apr 24	4:334	2:22
Apr 25	21:213	7:584
Apr 26	30:122	9:1088
Apr 27	14:111	5:1305

Date	American Edition (English) volume:page	Saint Louis Edition (German) volume:column
Apr 28	23:240	8:45
Apr 29	6:104	2:747
Apr 30	22:322	7:1904
May 1	26:175	9:236
May 2	22:105	7:1662
May 3	42:46	7:784
May 4	21:334	7:1417
May 5	30:248	9:1430
May 6	15:40	5:1415
May 7	23:316	8:131
May 8	6:354	2:1083
May 9	26:255	9:337
May 10	22:155	7:1709
May 11	1:80	1:97
May 12	51:198	12:1329
May 13	15:74	5:1452
May 14	23:392	8:220
May 15	7:96	2:1280
May 16	26:351	9:464
May 17	22:197	7:1758
May 18	1:163	1:199
May 19	52:48	11:161
May 20	7:211	2:1432
May 21	27:48	9:658
May 22	22:282	7:1857
May 23	1:348	1:424
May 24	42:27	7:762
May 25	18:97	6:1440
May 26	24:52	8:319
May 27	8:202	2:1917
May 28	27:72	9:686
May 29	22:491	7:2103

Date	American Edition (English) volume:page	Saint Louis Edition (German) volume:column
May 30	5:140	2:298
May 31	24:23	8:284
Jun 1	2:117	1:573
Jun 2	42:76	7:816
Jun 3	18:363	14:1655
Jun 4	24:227	8:523
Jun 5	9:92	3:1447
Jun 6	27:85	9:703
Jun 7	22:379	7:1972
Jun 8	2:328	1:832
Jun 9	42:159	10:1901
Jun 10	19:73	14:879
Jun 11	24:241	8:539
Jun 12	12:178	5:291
Jun 13	27:230	8:1445
Jun 14	23:9	7:2197
Jun 15	3:55	1:983
Jun 16	43:199	10:1401
Jun 17	20:219	14:1841
Jun 18	24:377	8:693
Jun 19	12:366	5:559
Jun 20	27:391	8:1637
Jun 21	23:74	7:2273
Jun 22	3:288	1:1268
Jun 23	21:37	7:385
Jun 24	30:14	9:971
Jun 25	12:410	5:617
Jun 26	42:34	7:769
Jun 27	26:264	9:349
Jun 28	21:145	7:507
Jun 29	6:92	2:730
Jun 30	22:355	7:1944

Date	American Edition (English) volume:page	Saint Louis Edition (German) volume:column
Jul 1	21:113	7:472
Jul 2	22:411	7:2011
Jul 3	15:117	5:1502
Jul 4	30:80	9:1042
Jul 5	23:105	7:2309
Jul 6	28:44	8:1071
Jul 7	23:96	7:2298
Jul 8	5:121	2:275
Jul 9	21:192	7:560
Jul 10	30:68	9:1029
Jul 11	14:47	5:1180
Jul 12	23:218	8:19
Jul 13	6:42	2:662
Jul 14	26:133	9:183
Jul 15	22:64	7:1604
Jul 16	21:232	7:605
Jul 17	24:89	8:363
Jul 18	30:158	9:1353
Jul 19	15:8	5:1378
Jul 20	23:295	8:109
Jul 21	6:310	2:1018
Jul 22	26:235	9:311
Jul 23	22:145	7:1699
Jul 24	15:50	5:1426
Jul 25	23:345	8:165
Jul 26	7:65	2:1238
Jul 27	26:314	9:416
Jul 28	22:168	7:1724
Jul 29	1:146	1:179
Jul 30	51:284	9:909
Jul 31	30:278	9:1464
Aug 1	15:100	5:1483

Date	American Edition (English) volume:page	Saint Louis Edition (German) volume:column
Aug 2	23:409	8:240
Aug 3	7:174	2:1381
Aug 4	27:27	9:631
Aug 5	22:278	7:1852
Aug 6	1:257	1:314
Aug 7	42:25	7:759
Aug 8	15:292	3:1908
Aug 9	24:37	8:301
Aug 10	8:4	2:1657
Aug 11	27:56	9:668
Aug 12	22:339	7:1923
Aug 13	2:105	1:558
Aug 14	42:41	7:777
Aug 15	18:262	14:1239
Aug 16	24:115	8:393
Aug 17	9:74	3:1431
Aug 18	27:80	9:697
Aug 19	22:376	7:1969
Aug 20	2:266	1:756
Aug 21	42:125	10:1823
Aug 22	19:63	14:868
Aug 23	24:231	8:528
Aug 24	12:169	5:280
Aug 25	27:112	9:733
Aug 26	23:5	7:2192
Aug 27	3:52	1:980
Aug 28	43:193	10:1394
Aug 29	20:164	14:1779
Aug 30	27:76	9:691
Aug 31	20:212	14:1834
Sep 1	24:260	8:562
Sep 2	12:314	5:488

Date	American Edition (English) volume:page	Saint Louis Edition (German) volume:column
Sep 3	27:382	8:1628
Sep 4	23:48	7:2242
Sep 5	3:239	1:1206
Sep 6	21:32	7:380
Sep 7	30:9	9:966
Sep 8	12:405	5:611
Sep 9	28:39	8:1066
Sep 10	23:90	7:2292
Sep 11	21:144	7:506
Sep 12	4:215	1:1637
Sep 13	21:195	7:563
Sep 14	30:104	9:1067
Sep 15	14:60	5:1195
Sep 16	23:224	8:26
Sep 17	6:94	2:733
Sep 18	26:166	9:224
Sep 19	22:89	7:1633
Sep 20	27:134	9:758
Sep 21	21:230	7:603
Sep 22	30:154	9:1349
Sep 23	14:310	4:251
Sep 24	23:267	8:77
Sep 25	6:148	2:805
Sep 26	26:226	9:301
Sep 27	22:143	7:1697
Sep 28	28:18	8:1041
Sep 29	22:24	7:1559
Sep 30	22:350	7:1938
Oct 1	51:252	12:2095
Oct 2	30:267	9:1451
Oct 3	15:47	5:1424
Oct 4	23:337	8:155

Date	American Edition (English) volume:page	Saint Louis Edition (German) volume:column
Oct 5	7:10	2:1168
Oct 6	26:280	9:372
Oct 7	22:167	7:1723
Oct 8	1:144	1:176
Oct 9	51:278	9:902
Oct 10	15:91	5:1473
Oct 11	23:401	8:230
Oct 12	7:103	2:1289
Oct 13	26:376	9:495
Oct 14	22:256	7:1826
Oct 15	1:175	1:214
Oct 16	42:23	7:758
Oct 17	15:120	5:1505
Oct 18	24:32	8:294
Oct 19	7:319	2:1578
Oct 20	27:54	9:664
Oct 21	22:290	7:1866
Oct 22	2:5	1:440
Oct 23	42:35	7:770
Oct 24	18:128	6:1686
Oct 25	24:64	8:334
Oct 26	8:325	2:2078
Oct 27	27:74	9:689
Oct 28	22:374	7:1966
Oct 29	2:252	1:738
Oct 30	42:87	14:1414
Oct 31	15:64	5:1442
Nov 1	19:54	14:859
Nov 2	24:229	8:525
Nov 3	12:80	5:172
Nov 4	27:102	9:722
Nov 5	22:319	7:1994

Date	American Edition (English) volume:page	Saint Louis Edition (German) volume:column
Nov 6	43:13	3:150
Nov 7	19:197	14:1464
Nov 8	24:256	8:558
Nov 9	12:193	5:304
Nov 10	23:13	7:2202
Nov 11	3:128	1:1071
Nov 12	21:143	7:505
Nov 13	21:12	7:357
Nov 14	24:421	8:743
Nov 15	12:393	5:595
Nov 16	27:404	8:1653
Nov 17	23:78	7:2278
Nov 18	4:88	1:1477
Nov 19	21:148	7:511
Nov 20	30:29	9:988
Nov 21	28:212	8:1272
Nov 22	23:136	7:2346
Nov 23	5:173	2:340
Nov 24	13:399	5:1107
Nov 25	2:378	1:894
Nov 26	3:149	1:1097
Nov 27	27:240	8:1457
Nov 28	3:26	1:949
Nov 29	13:86	5:744
Nov 30	21:139	7:500
Dec 1	5:25	2:150
Dec 2	24:389	8:706
Dec 3	7:133	2:1327
Dec 4	27:57	9:670
Dec 5	24:210	8:503
Dec 6	4:309	1:1754
Dec 7	42:112	10:1998

Date	American Edition (English) volume:page	Saint Louis Edition (German) volume:column
Dec 8	30:11	9:968
Dec 9	21:290	7:672
Dec 10	13:366	5:1074
Dec 11	22:6	7:1540
Dec 12	22:14	7:1549
Dec 13	22:19	7:1555
Dec 14	22:21	7:1556
Dec 15	21:306	7:1384
Dec 16	21:309	7:1388
Dec 17	21:316	7:1397
Dec 18	21:322	7:1402
Dec 19	52:7	11:118
Dec 20	52:26	11:138
Dec 21	52:18	11:130
Dec 22	52:14	11:126
Dec 23	52:20	11:132
Dec 24	52:13	11:125
Dec 25	52:32	11:144
Dec 26	52:102	11:234
Dec 27	52:122	11:256
Dec 28	52:196	11:334
Dec 29	52:198	11:337
Dec 30	13:128	5:786
Dec 31	22:28	7:1564

SUBJECT INDEX

We want to hear from you. Please send your comments about this book to us in care of zreview@zondervan.com. Thank you.

ZONDERVAN™

GRAND RAPIDS, MICHIGAN 49530 USA

WWW.ZONDERVAN.COM